Contents

Teachers' greatest challenges tend to be fitting in special instruction during an already busy day, having appropriate materials and organizing them quickly, and maintaining structure and concentration when interruptions and distractions are frequent.

Houghton Mifflin Reading's materials for reaching all learners are a time-saving system of instruction for meeting those challenges. With this group of handbooks you can turn your attention to specific needs in your classroom—to advanced children, children who are struggling below level, or children who are learning English—while other children work independently. The Challenge, Extra Support, and English Language Learners handbooks are each tied to the core instruction in *Houghton Mifflin Reading*. For independent work, the *Classroom Management Handbook* provides meaningful activities related to literature selections and to core skills.

As a group, the handbooks for reaching all learners:

- help you manage your classroom and organize your time effectively

- provide excellent, additional instruction

- give you the resources you need to help *all* children achieve grade-level expectations

Extra Support Handbook Overview

The *Extra Support Handbook* provides support to enable lower-performing children to achieve grade-level expectations and to participate effectively in the instruction and reading opportunities in *Houghton Mifflin Reading*. Lessons in the handbook coincide with the daily skill instruction in your *Houghton Mifflin Reading* Teacher's Edition, providing critical support for children prior to core instruction. Handbook lessons are specifically designed for children needing extra support:

Your goal is to advance these children to greater proficiency and ultimately to on-level reading independence.

- Lessons are presented in a five-day plan for preteaching and reteaching key skills and previewing core literature.

- Lessons focus on essential decoding and comprehension skills.

- Instruction is explicit and systematic, with concepts presented in easy, step-by-step order.

- Learning is scaffolded through teacher modeling, visual examples, and interactive guided practice.

- Lessons include regular checks to monitor children's understanding.

- The Practice/Apply step provides meaningful independent practice.

The *Extra Support Handbook* is one of several options in *Houghton Mifflin Reading* for providing extra support for children. Your Teacher's Edition provides suggestions for each anthology selection and includes a Resources section for support at the theme level. However, the *Extra Support Handbook* targets key skills in greater depth and gives students familiarity with skills before they participate in the core lesson—an important tool for building fluency and confidence.

Identifying Children Who Need Extra Support

Children who will benefit from Extra Support instruction include those who struggle to read on-level literature or who are in a Title 1 or similar program. These children may have difficulty with decoding or comprehension or both. They may be able to decode simple words but need help learning to decode longer words. Some may lack fluency, being unable to read rapidly and accurately and simultaneously grasp the meaning of the text.

Evaluating Children's Needs At the start of the year, and periodically throughout the year, you can evaluate children's instructional needs using the diagnostic assessments included in *Houghton Mifflin Reading*. These instruments include the Baseline Group Test, Leveled Reading Passages, Phonics Decoding Screening Test, and others. More information on diagnostic assessment can be found in the *Teacher's Assessment Handbook*. In general, children who need extra support will likely fall into one of the following groups:

- **Benchmark Group** These children's difficulties tend to be temporary or intermittent. In general, they are meeting their learning goals and are not performing far below grade-level expectations. You can determine specific difficulties using the Monitoring Student Progress boxes in the Teacher's Edition. Often, the Reteaching Lessons in the Resources section of the Teacher's Edition will provide the support these childen need. In some cases, these children may need the more ongoing support provided by the lessons in this handbook.

- **Strategic Group** Diagnostic assessment will show that these children's proficiencies are consistently below level, and this will be confirmed by your ongoing observations. These children need the regular, structured preteaching and reteaching support provided in this handbook. They should be evaluated regularly to make sure that they are progressing toward meeting grade-level expectations.

- **Intensive Group** These children are likely to be reading far below expectations. Diagnostic testing may reveal significant lack of decoding or comprehension skills. These children should receive intensive intervention or an individualized education plan. In the meantime, they can benefit from the lessons included in this handbook.

Frequent, positive feedback supports children's belief that they can do well. Make sure children who are struggling have opportunities for success.

Houghton Mifflin Reading includes a variety of assessments to help you determine the cause of reading difficulties, and the degree of severity, and to develop various grouping plans for instructing children at risk. At the beginning of the year, you'll use diagnostic tools to identify your children's skill proficiencies. Assessment tools in the Teacher's Edition and the *Teacher's Assessment Handbook* include:

- Diagnostic Checks
- Selection Tests
- Reading Fluency Tests
- Observation Checklists
- Selection Comprehension Charts
- Reading-Writing Workshops

Once you have diagnostics underway, the *Classroom Management Handbook* provides guidance for managing groups for differentiated instruction.

Lesson Structure

The number of Extra Support lessons are related to the frequency of word identification and comprehension lessons in the core program. Preteaching prepares students for whole-class instruction; reteaching after core instruction provides more practice. Further, each daily lesson includes a literature focus in the form of guided previews or through revisiting selections or ancillary literature. Lessons are not intended as substitutes for core instruction, but are in addition to it.

The handbook provides multiple ways of explaining a concept, flexibility in pacing, levels of complexity, and frequent checks of children's understanding.

Five-day Instructional Plan

	DAY 1	DAY 2	DAY 3	DAY 4	DAY 5
	Preteach Phonics skill(s)	**Preteach** Comprehension skill	**Reteach** High-Frequency Words	**Reteach** Phonics skill	**Reteach** Comprehension skill
Th. 1–4	**Preview** Phonics Library, first selection	**Preview** Get Set Anthology selection	**Preview** Main Anthology selection	**Review** Main Anthology selection	**Revisit** Anthology and Phonics Library selections
Th. 5–10	**Preview** Phonics Library, first selection	**Preview** Anthology selection	**Review** Phonics Library, second selection	**Review** Anthology selection	**Revisit** Anthology and Phonics Library selections

A consistent pattern of preteaching, reteaching, and revisiting skills is built into instruction day to day, and week to week. Consistency, repetition, and predictability help children progress more quickly. Skill focus instruction is modeled step-by-step for students. Appropriate examples are used to help them comprehend the skill. Student understanding is monitored carefully with reminders to check that every student comprehends.

An application of the skill is presented and modeled, using the Teaching Master. This master introduces the skill in an interactive, visual way. The teacher guides students through the process, and then students practice and apply the skill on their own.

Teacher support for each selection includes:

Skill focus

- Easily scanned objectives and materials
- Guided instruction
- Visual examples
- Guided practice using the Teaching Master
- Support for the Practice Master
- Teaching Master and Practice Master facsimile reference

Literature focus

- Literature citation
- Support for preview and review

See the Walkthrough on the following pages for more information.

To the Teacher

This walkthrough will familiarize you with the five-day instructional plans for Extra Support. Each plan is based on a week in this level of *Houghton Mifflin Reading*. Days 1 and 3 are presented here for Week 1 of Theme 6, *Animal Adventures*, and show the basic features of a typical lesson.

Objectives/Materials

Skill Focus objectives are listed each day. Most of the materials are provided at the back of the handbook; literature needed for the Literature Focus is listed.

Additional Resources

The Get Set for Reading CD-ROM builds background and summarizes the Anthology selection. Children can log on to the Education Place site for activities. The theme Audio CD helps with listening and comprehension skills. The Lexia Phonics CD-ROM provides phonics intervention.

Guided Practice

After teaching the skill, this section allows you to gradually turn the responsibility for practice to the students and to give immediate feedback. When two skill lessons are taught on Day 1, the guided practice and Teaching Master are provided for the first skill, while the practice/apply and Practice Master are provided for the second skill. (See Practice/Apply description on the facing page.)

Instruction Labels

Preteach or Reteach labels note when to use the lesson in relation to core instruction. The type of Skill Focus lesson is shown and a suggested amount of time to spend on it.

**THEME 6: Animal Adventures
WEEK 1**

Day 1

PRETEACH

SKILL FOCUS: PHONICS   10–15 MINUTES

Long *o* (CV, CVCe) and Long *u* (CVCe)

Objectives
- associate the /ō/ sound with the letters *o* and *o-e*
- associate the /yōō/ sound with the letters *u-e*
- blend and read long *o* and long *u* words

Materials
- Teaching Master ES6-1

Technology

Get Set for Reading CD-ROM
The Sleeping Pig

Education Place
www.eduplace.com
The Sleeping Pig

Audio CD
The Sleeping Pig
Audio CD for **Animal Adventures**

Lexia Phonics CD-ROM
Primary Intervention

Teach

Recite and repeat the chant shown, having children join in.

> **CHANT**
> A cute little doe
> Was eating a rose.
> She had a huge bump
> On the side of her nose.

Say *doe*, stretching the long *o* sound. Identify the sound as the long *o* vowel sound. If necessary, explain that a doe is a female deer. Have children repeat *doe* several times. Repeat with *rose*. Print *rose* on the board. Underline the *o* and *e* and explain that together, these two letters make the long *o* sound. Repeat the process with the long *u* words *cute* and *huge*.

Blend

Print *no* on the board and use Blending Routine 1 to model how to blend the sounds, stretching each sound and then saying the word. Blend and say the word with children, before asking them to blend it on their own. Point out that *no* has the consonant-vowel pattern. Repeat the process with the words *note*, *broke*, and *rope*. Point out that these words have the *o*-consonant-*e* pattern.

Follow a similar procedure with the word *mule*, pointing out that it has the *u*-consonant-*e* pattern. Repeat with the words *rule*, *fume*, and *tube*.

Guided Practice

Display or **distribute** Teaching Master ES6-1 and discuss the illustrations with children. Tell them to use what they know about long *o* and long *u* vowel sounds as they read the sentences with you. Point to words from the sentences randomly, and have children read them.

Check that children are blending the words correctly.

174   THEME 6: Animal Adventures

Blackline Masters

The Teaching Master and Practice Master are shown for reference. See the following pages for descriptions of the masters.

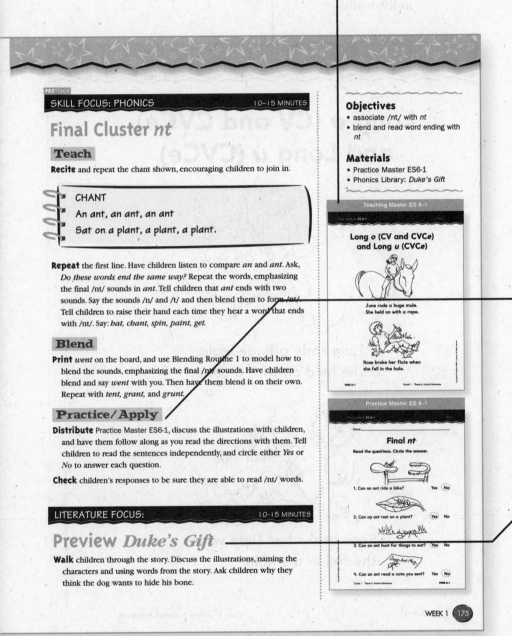

PRETEACH

SKILL FOCUS: PHONICS — 10–15 MINUTES

Final Cluster *nt*

Teach

Recite and repeat the chant shown, encouraging children to join in.

> **CHANT**
> An ant, an ant, an ant
> Sat on a plant, a plant, a plant.

Repeat the first line. Have children listen to compare *an* and *ant*. Ask, *Do these words end the same way?* Repeat the words, emphasizing the final /nt/ sounds in *ant*. Tell children that *ant* ends with two sounds. Say the sounds /n/ and /t/ and then blend them to form /nt/. Tell children to raise their hand each time they hear a word that ends with /nt/. Say: *bat, chant, spin, paint, get*.

Blend

Print *went* on the board, and use Blending Routine 1 to model how to blend the sounds, emphasizing the final /nt/ sounds. Have children blend and say *went* with you. Then have them blend it on their own. Repeat with *tent, grant,* and *grunt*.

Practice/Apply

Distribute Practice Master ES6-1, discuss the illustrations with children, and have them follow along as you read the directions with them. Tell children to read the sentences independently, and circle either *Yes* or *No* to answer each question.

Check children's responses to be sure they are able to read /nt/ words.

LITERATURE FOCUS: — 10–15 MINUTES

Preview *Duke's Gift*

Walk children through the story. Discuss the illustrations, naming the characters and using words from the story. Ask children why they think the dog wants to hide his bone.

Objectives
- associate /nt/ with *nt*
- blend and read word ending with *nt*

Materials
- Practice Master ES6-1
- Phonics Library: *Duke's Gift*

Teaching Master ES 6-1

Long *o* (CV and CVCe) and Long *u* (CVCe)

June rode a huge mule.
She held on with a rope.

Rose broke her flute when she fell in the hole.

Practice Master ES 6-1

Name ____

Final *nt*

Read the questions. Circle the answer.

1. Can an ant ride a bike?   Yes   No
2. Can an ant rest on a plant?   Yes   No
3. Can an ant hunt for things to eat?   Yes   No
4. Can an ant read a note you sent?   Yes   No

WEEK 1 175

Practice/Apply

Students use the Practice Master to work on the skill independently. When a single skill is taught on Day 1, the Practice Master provides an additional opportunity beyond the Teaching Master to teach and assess the skill. When two skill lessons are taught on Day 1, the Practice Master provides the only application of the second skill.

Literature Preview

The Phonics Library selection walk-through is targeted at the day's reading in the core program, and follows the previewing suggestions in the Teacher's Edition.

Blackline Masters

Shown here are the Teaching Master and Practice Master for Day 1 of Week 1 of Theme 6, *Animal Adventures*.

Teaching Master

The Teaching Master is used as a verbal guide to model the process and practice expected of children for applying the skill. Teaching Masters can be held up or displayed for guiding students through the activity, or they can be copied and distributed so that children can follow along individually.

Skill Title

To familiarize children with the academic language for the skills they are learning, the skill title is shown on both the Teaching and Practice masters.

Long *o* (CV and CVC*e*) and Long *u* (CVC*e*)

June rode a huge mule.
She held on with a rope.

Rose broke her flute when she fell in the hole.

TMES 6–1   Grade 1   Theme 6: Animal Adventures

Practice Master

Children practice the skill with a brief activity to check mastery. As children explain their answers, you have the opportunity to make corrections immediately and give positive feedback.

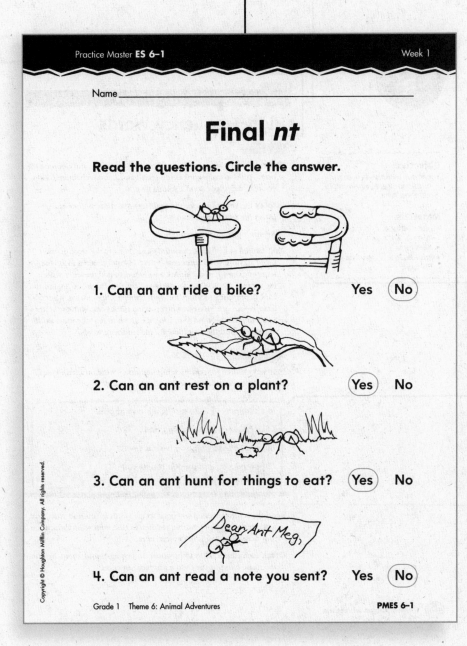

Practice Master **ES 6–1**   Week 1

Name _____

Final *nt*

Read the questions. Circle the answer.

1. Can an ant ride a bike?   Yes   (No)

2. Can an ant rest on a plant?   (Yes)   No

3. Can an ant hunt for things to eat?   (Yes)   No

4. Can an ant read a note you sent?   Yes   (No)

Grade 1   Theme 6: Animal Adventures   **PMES 6–1**

Skill Focus: Reteach

Day 3 lessons reteach high-frequency words. Notice the Reteach label and the skill title, along with the suggested amount of time for instruction.

3-Step Approach

Reteach lessons rely on a **Teach/Practice/Apply** lesson approach, using multiple examples for reinforcement.

Directive Verbs

For ease of use, the beginning verb of each paragraph is boldfaced.

Visual Support

Chalkboards and notebook art help organize instruction. They also promote visual learning and involvement for children.

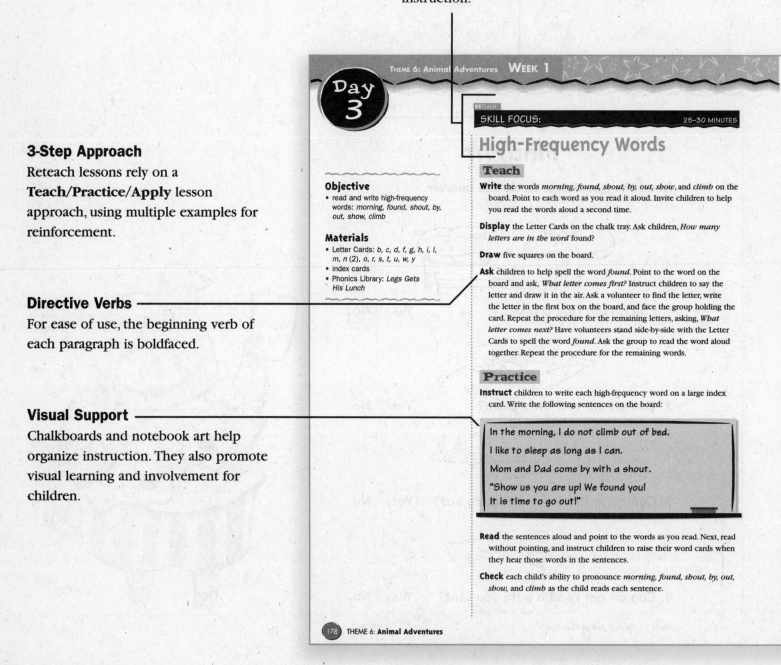

THEME 6: Animal Adventures **WEEK 1**

Day 3

RETEACH
SKILL FOCUS: 25–30 MINUTES

High-Frequency Words

Objective
• read and write high-frequency words: *morning, found, shout, by, out, show, climb*

Materials
• Letter Cards: *b, c, d, f, g, h, i, l, m, n (2), o, r, s, t, u, w, y*
• index cards
• Phonics Library: *Legs Gets His Lunch*

Teach

Write the words *morning, found, shout, by, out, show,* and *climb* on the board. Point to each word as you read it aloud. Invite children to help you read the words aloud a second time.

Display the Letter Cards on the chalk tray. Ask children, *How many letters are in the word* found?

Draw five squares on the board.

Ask children to help spell the word *found.* Point to the word on the board and ask, *What letter comes first?* Instruct children to say the letter and draw it in the air. Ask a volunteer to find the letter, write the letter in the first box on the board, and face the group holding the card. Repeat the procedure for the remaining letters, asking, *What letter comes next?* Have volunteers stand side-by-side with the Letter Cards to spell the word *found.* Ask the group to read the word aloud together. Repeat the procedure for the remaining words.

Practice

Instruct children to write each high-frequency word on a large index card. Write the following sentences on the board:

> In the morning, I do not climb out of bed.
>
> I like to sleep as long as I can.
>
> Mom and Dad come by with a shout.
>
> "Show us you are up! We found you!
> It is time to go out!"

Read the sentences aloud and point to the words as you read. Next, read without pointing, and instruct children to raise their word cards when they hear those words in the sentences.

Check each child's ability to pronounce *morning, found, shout, by, out, show,* and *climb* as the child reads each sentence.

178   THEME 6: **Animal Adventures**

Apply

Have children write the sentences from the previous activity on sentence strips. Then have them cut up the sentence strips and then rebuild the sentences.

LITERATURE FOCUS: 10–15 MINUTES

Review *Legs Gets His Lunch*

Reread the story together with children. Have children take turns reading aloud.

Have children look through *Legs Gets His Lunch* to find the following high-frequency words: *out, climb*. Have them read the sentences that contain these words.

Suggestions for grouping and planners for coordinating small group instruction can be found in the *Classroom Management Handbook*, along with selection-based independent activities.

Literature Preview

The Anthology selection walkthrough is targeted at the day's reading in the core program, and follows the previewing suggestions in the Teacher's Edition.

Theme 1

All Together Now

Day 1

Objectives

- associate the /m/ sound with the letter *m*
- associate the /t/ sound with the letter *t*

Materials

- Teaching Master ES1-1

Technology

Education Place

www.eduplace.com
Mac the Cat

Audio CD

On the Go!
Mac the Cat
Audio CD for **All Together Now**

Lexia Phonics
CD-ROM

Primary Intervention

SKILL FOCUS: PHONICS   10-15 MINUTES

Consonants *m* and *t*

Teach

Recite and repeat the chant shown. Have children join in as they are able.

> CHANT
> Mike likes milk.
> Mmm, mmm, milk!
> Ted likes tea.
> T-t-tea!

Say *milk*, stretching out and emphasizing the /m/. If needed, model for children the /m/ mouth position. Then say: *Get your mouth ready to say milk. Now say it.* Have children say *milk* several times.

Print *m* on the board, and tell children that the letter *m* stands for the /m/ sound. Ask what sound children hear at the beginning of *milk*. (/m/) Ask what letter stands for this sound. (m) Follow a similar procedure for /t/t/, using the word *tea*.

Blend

Have children listen as you say three sounds: /m/ /ă/ /t/. Use Blending Routine 1 to model how to blend the sounds together to make *mat*. Then have children blend the sounds and say the word with you. Repeat the process with : /t/ /ĭ/ /m/ *(Tim)*; /m/ /ĕ/ /t/ *(met)*; /t/ /ŏ/ /m/ *(Tom)*; /m/ /ĭ/ /t/ *(mitt)*.

Guided Practice

Display or **distribute** Teaching Master ES1-1 and discuss the illustrations with children.

Ask children to tell you which pictures begin with /m/. Help children circle those pictures.

Repeat the procedure, crossing out the pictures that begin with /t/.

Check children's work to be sure they understand the difference between the two sounds.

SKILL FOCUS: PHONICS | 10–15 MINUTES

Short a

Teach

Recite and repeat the chant, asking children to join in.

> **CHANT**
> A my name is Andy.
> My friend's name is Ann.
> We live in Atlanta.
> And we sell apples.

Say *apple*, stretching out the short *a* sound. If needed, model for children the /ă/ mouth position. Have children say *apple* several times.

Print *apple* on the board, and underline the *a*. Tell children that the letter *a* can stand for the /ă/ sound.

Blend

Hold up the *a* card. Have children listen as you say its sound. Then hold up the *t* card and say its sound. Use Blending Routine 1 to model how to blend the sounds to form *at*. Then have children blend the sounds and say the word with you. Repeat the process with these words: *am, mat, sat, cat, Sam.*

Practice/Apply

Distribute Practice Master ES1-1. Read the directions with children. After they have completed the page, have children read the words aloud.

Check as children read the words to be sure they are blending them correctly.

LITERATURE FOCUS: | 10–15 MINUTES

Preview *Tam Cat*

Walk children through *Tam Cat* and discuss the illustrations. Use the following words from the story as you talk with children: *cat, mat, sat.* Explain that the cat's name is Tam.

Objectives

- associate the /ă/ sound with the letter *a*
- blend and read words with *m, s, c, t,* and short *a*

Materials

- Letter Cards: *a, c, m, s, S, t*
- Practice Master ES1-1
- Phonics Library: *Tam Cat*

Teaching Master ES 1–1

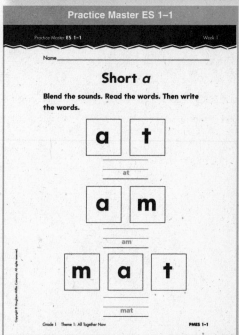

Practice Master ES 1–1

Day 2

SKILL FOCUS: COMPREHENSION 25-30 MINUTES

Sequence of Events

Objectives
- identify the beginning, middle, and end of activities and events
- sequence story events

Materials
- Teaching Master ES1–2
- Practice Master ES1–2
- Anthology: *On the Go!*

Teach

Ask children to act out brushing their teeth. Have them think about what they do first, next, and last.

Guide children to identify the sequence of events using the words *first* (put toothpaste on the toothbrush), *next* (brushed teeth), and *last* (rinsed mouth).

Have children use the words *first*, *next*, and *last* to describe other familiar routines. Then explain that many stories also happen in a certain order. Tell children that what happens first in a story is the *beginning*, what happens next is the *middle*, and what happens last is the *end*.

Guided Practice

Display or **distribute** Teaching Master ES1–2 and explain that these pictures tell a story, but that the pictures are not in the correct story order.

Have children describe what is happening in each picture.

Ask children to identify the picture that shows what happens at the beginning of the story. Help children write the number *1* next to the picture of the bird building a nest.

Tell children to name the picture that shows what happens in the middle of the story. (bird sits on eggs) Help children write the number *2* next to the picture of the bird sitting on her eggs.

Ask children what happens at the end of the story. (bird feeds new babies) Help children write the number *3* next to the picture of the bird feeding the baby birds.

Guide children in summarizing the story: *In the beginning of the story, the bird builds a nest. In the middle of the story, she sits on her eggs. At the end of the story, she feeds her babies.*

Practice/Apply

Distribute Practice Master ES1–2 to children and discuss the pictures to make sure they understand what is happening in each one.

Tell children that the pictures on this page tell a story, but that they are not in the correct order. Read the directions with children.

Have children cut out the pictures and put them in story order. Encourage children to try ordering the pictures in different ways before pasting them into the numbered boxes.

Check children's work to be sure they understand the concept of sequencing events.

LITERATURE FOCUS: 10-15 MINUTES

Preview *On the Go!*

Walk children through *On the Go!* Discuss the illustrations, using words such as *sat*, *cat*, and *go*. Explain that the dog's name is *Sam*.

Ask, *What are Sam and the cat doing at the beginning of the story?* (sitting beside a swimming pool) *In the middle of the story?* Sam is jumping into the pool. The cat is falling into the pool because a bee made a hole in her inner tube.) *At the end of the story?* (The cat is sitting on Sam in the pool.)

Day 3

Objective
- read and write new high-frequency words *go, on, the*

Materials
- High-Frequency Word Cards
- Anthology: *Mac the Cat*

High-Frequency Words

Teach

Ask children to listen to the sounds in the word as you say *go*. Draw two lines on the board to represent the two sounds in *go*. Work through the word, writing the appropriate letter or letters for each sound. Say:

The first sound in go *is /g/. The letter g spells the sound /g/ we hear at the beginning of the word* go. *I'll write g here on the first line.*

The next sound in go *is /ō/. The letter o spells the sound /ō/. I'll write o on the second line.*

Now help me spell go. *Say it with me:* g-o, go!

Lead children in a cheer to remember the word. Clap on each letter and syllable as you spell and say the word: *g-o, go!* Repeat the procedure for *on*.

Say *the*. Draw two lines on the board. Write *th* on the first line. Tell children that the letters *th* together stand for the first sound in *the*. Explain that the second sound in *the* is spelled *e*, and write *e* on the second line. Lead children in a cheer to remember *the*: *t-h-e, the!*

Write on the board the sentence *Go on the bus,* and read it together with children. Check each child's ability to pronounce *go, on,* and *the* as the child reads the sentence.

Practice

Have children copy the sentence starter *Go on the* _____. Then have them illustrate an ending to the sentence. For example, children may draw an airplane, a playground slide, or a bike. Ask children to exchange papers and read one another's sentences.

Apply

Have children match High-Frequency Word Cards to words on the Word Wall.

LITERATURE FOCUS: 10-15 MINUTES

Preview *Mac the Cat*

Walk children through *Mac the Cat*, on pages 21–31 in their Anthology.

Discuss the illustrations, identifying objects and words from the story such as *rug, ham, jam, hat, bat* and *bug*.

Note the suggestions in the Extra Support boxes on Teacher's Edition pages T57, T59, and T61.

Day 4

SKILL FOCUS: PHONICS 10-15 MINUTES

Consonants *m, s, c, t*

Objectives

- recognize *m, s, c,* and *t* and the sounds they represent
- independently read words with *m, s, c,* and *t*

Materials

- Letter Cards: *c, m, s, t*
- Picture Cards: *cab, can, car, cat, coins, cot, cow, cube, cup, cut, farm, kiss, lock, man, map, mask, mat, milk, mix, mop, mouth, mug, mule, net, sad, salt, seal, sit, six, soup, sun, tag, tape, ten, toast, tooth, top, toys, tub, tube*
- Anthology: *Mac the Cat*

Teach

Display the Letter Cards one at a time. Have children name each letter with you and say the letter sound: *m*/m/, *s*/s/, *c*/k/, *t*/t/. Distribute Picture Cards to children for initial *m*, initial *s*, initial *c*, and initial *t*. Say:

Find other children whose picture names begin with the same sound as your picture. Everyone whose picture name begins the same, stand together.

Have children in each group name their cards, say the beginning sound, and name the letter that stands for that sound.

Help children differentiate among the consonant sounds by pointing out the position of their lips, teeth, and tongue, and have them feel for vibration of the voice box.

- /m/— lips together; vibration
- /s/— tongue on roof of the mouth behind upper teeth; no vibration
- /k/— back of tongue against roof of the mouth; no vibration
- /t/— tip of tongue behind top teeth; no vibration

Practice

Display the *milk* Picture Card and have children identify it. Call on a child to tell what sound he or she hears at the beginning of *mmmilk*. Write the word *milk* on the board and have a child underline the *m*. Repeat with Picture Cards for *sun, car,* and *top*. Then display Picture Cards for *farm, kiss, lock,* and *net* and ask children what sound they hear at the end of each word.

Apply

Pin Letter Cards for *m, s, c,* and *t* on chart paper. Have children look for words that begin with *s* and *c* or end with *m* and *t* in *Mac the Cat*. Each time they find a word, ask them to say it so you can write it under the appropriate letter. When the search is complete, choose children to read the words on the list.

SKILL FOCUS: PHONICS 10-15 MINUTES

Blending Short *a* Words with *m*, *s*, *c*, and *t*

Teach

Display the Letter Card *a* and remind children of the sound the letter *a* makes: /ă/. Have them say the sound after you, /ă/. Then repeat for the letters *m* /m/, *s* /s/, *c* /k/, and *t*, /t/.

Hold up the Picture Card for *ten* and ask children to identify the picture and the sound they hear at the beginning of the word *ten*. Follow the procedure with Picture Cards for *ant*, *mat*, *cat*, and *seal*.

Use the Letter Cards to model how to blend the word *mat* using Blending Routine 2. Have children say the sound for *m*, /m/, then the sound for *a*, /ă/, and blend /mmm ăăă/. Have them say the sound for *t*, /t/, blend /mmm ăăă t/, and say *mat*. Repeat with the words *sat* and *cat*.

Practice

Display Letter Card *a* on the chalkboard ledge. Remind children that short *a* has the /ă/ sound. Add the Letter Cards *c* and *t* and say *caaat*, *cat*. Then take away the *c* and have children choose a letter to place in front of *-at*. Tell children to blend the letter sound with *-at* to read the new word. Continue replacing initial or final letters until three or four words have been made.

Apply

Have partners take turns finding short *a* words with *m*, s, c, and *t* in *Mac the Cat*. Each time a child finds a word with short *a*, he or she should read the word so that you can write it on a word list on the board.

Objectives

- listen to and blend phonemes
- associate the short *a* sound with the letter *a*
- independently read short *a* words with *m*, *s*, *c*, and *t*

Materials

- Letter Cards: *a, c, m, s, t*
- Picture Cards: *ant, cat, mat, seal, ten*
- Anthology: *On the Go!, Mac the Cat*

LITERATURE FOCUS: 10-15 MINUTES

Review *Mac the Cat*

Reread the story with children. Together, make a list of short *a* words. Then have partners find and read story words with *m*, s, c, and *t*.

Day 5

Objectives
- use order words *first, next,* and *last*
- sequence story events

Materials
- Phonics Library: *Tam Cat, Cat on the Mat*
- Anthology: *On the Go!, Mac the Cat*

SKILL FOCUS: COMPREHENSION   25-30 MINUTES

Sequence of Events

Teach

Ask children what they do each morning before arriving at school. Then ask them to identify the order in which they do those things, asking:

- *What do you do first? Then what do you do next?*
- *What other steps do you take to get ready for school?*
- *What words do you use to tell about the order of events?*

Use words like *first, next, then,* and *last,* as you talk with children. Tell children that events happen in order. Explain that saying *First, we got out of bed and next we got washed* is a sequence because it tells the order in which the events took place. Tell children that authors often tell stories by putting events in the order in which they happen.

Practice

Discuss the story *Mac the Cat* by Nadine Bernard Westcott, using terms such as *first, next, last* or *beginning, middle,* and *end* to indicate the story sequence and structure. Point out that first Mac the cat sits on the rug, and that next Mac tugs on a piece of yarn and unravels the rug. Then have children identify the next event that happens. Continue until children identify all of the story events in sequence. You might want to have children look at the book to help them identify events.

Apply

Assign each line of the story to a pair or small group of children. Let each group practice reading its line together, then ask children to stand in the order in which their lines occur in the story and read them in sequence. Reinforce the sequence of events by asking questions such as the following: *Where is Mac the Cat at the* beginning *of the story? What does he do* next? *What does he do at the* end?

Reread the story, coaching children to recognize the sequence of events.

Revisit *Tam Cat, Cat on the Mat, On the Go!* and *Mac the Cat*

Page through the stories with children. Discuss the sequence of events in each of the stories.

Ask children to look for words with the short *a* sound in each of the stories.

Tell children to look through *On the Go!* and *Mac the Cat* for the following high-frequency words: *go, on, the*.

Have children read aloud selected sentences or pages from the stories.

Day 1

Objectives

- associate the /f/ sound with the letter *f*
- associate the /p/ sound with the letter *p*

Materials

- Sound/Spelling Cards: *fish, pig*
- Teaching Master ES1-3

Education Place
www.eduplace.com
A Day at School

Audio CD
Cam and Pat
A Day at School
Audio CD for **All Together Now**

Lexia Phonics
CD-ROM
Primary Intervention

PRETEACH

SKILL FOCUS: PHONICS   10-15 MINUTES

Consonants *f* and *p*

Teach

Recite and repeat the chant. Have children join in as they are able.

> **CHANT**
> Pam picks a pet.
> It's a p-p-pig!
> Fred finds five.
> They're f-f-fish!

Display the Sound/Spelling Card *pig*. Say *pig*, stretching out the /p/ sound. If needed, model the mouth position for /p/. Then say: *Get your mouth ready to say* pig. *Are you ready? Say it.* Have children repeat *pig* several times.

Print *p* on the board, and tell children that *p* stands for the /p/ sound.

Follow a similar procedure for /f/ *f*, using the Sound/Spelling Card *fish*.

Blend

Print *Pam* on the board. Use Blending Routine 1 to model how to blend the sounds, stretching each sound and then saying the word. Then have children blend and say the word with you. Finally, have children blend the word on their own.

Repeat the process with the word *fat*.

Guided Practice

Display or **distribute** Teaching Master ES1-3. Discuss the illustrations.

Direct children's attention to the first sentence. Tell them to use what they know about sounds as they read the sentence with you.

Repeat for the next two sentences. Then have children point out and read words that begin with /p/ or /f/.

Check that children are accurately blending the words.

SKILL FOCUS: PHONICS · 10-15 MINUTES

Blending Short *a* Words

Teach

Recite and repeat the chant. Tell children to join in.

> CHANT
> What can Nan do?
> Nap, nap, nap!
> What can Pam do?
> Tap, tap, tap!

Say *nap*, stretching out and isolating each sound. Then have children say *nap* with you, again stretching out the sounds. Repeat for *tap*.

Blend

Give the word card *an* to one child. Use Blending Routine 1 to model how to blend the word. Then have children blend and say the word with you. Repeat with *can* and *man*, having children blend the words on their own as a final step.

Practice/Apply

Distribute Practice Master ES1-3, and discuss the illustrations with children. Read the directions aloud, and be sure children understand what to do.

Tell children to use what they know about sounds as they read the sentences and then match the sentences to the pictures.

Check children's responses to be sure they know how to blend the sounds.

LITERATURE FOCUS: · 10-15 MINUTES

Preview *Nan Cat*

Walk children through *Nan Cat* and discuss the illustrations, using words from the story such as *Cam*, *sat*, *can*, *pat*, and *Nan*.

Objectives

- associate /ă/ with *a*
- read short *a* words

Materials

- word cards: *an*, *can*, *man*
- Practice Master ES1-3
- Phonics Library: *Nan Cat*

Teaching Master ES 1–3

Teaching Master **ES 1–3**   Week 2

Consonants *f* and *p*

Pam sat.

Fat Pat sat.
Pat sat on Pam!

TMES 1-3   Grade 1   Theme 1: All Together Now

Practice Master ES 1–3

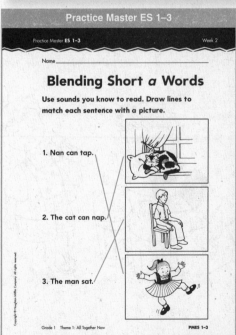

Practice Master **ES 1–3**   Week 2

Name_____

Blending Short *a* Words

Use sounds you know to read. Draw lines to match each sentence with a picture.

1. Nan can tap.

2. The cat can nap.

3. The man sat.

Grade 1   Theme 1: All Together Now   PMES 1-3

Day 2

PRETEACH

SKILL FOCUS: COMPREHENSION   25-30 MINUTES

Compare and Contrast

Teach

Hold up a penny and a nickel for children to see. Explain that the two objects are alike in some ways and different in others.

Draw two large overlapping circles on the board to create a Venn diagram. Label the left circle *penny* and the right circle *nickel*.

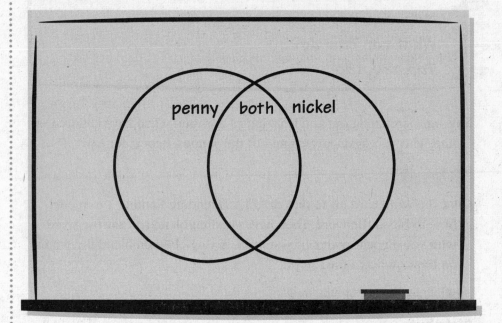

Tell children that they can use these two circles to show how the two objects are alike and different. Explain that you will write the things that are different about the two objects in the outer parts of the circles. Then direct attention to the middle, where the two circles overlap. Tell children that you will write the things that are the same about the objects in the middle part.

Brainstorm with children ways in which the two objects are alike and different and complete the diagram. (Possible answers: **Alike:** coins, made of metal; **Different:** brown vs. silver, smaller vs. larger)

Objectives

- identify similarities and differences
- use a Venn diagram to compare and contrast

Materials

- Teaching Master ES1–4
- Practice Master ES1–4
- Anthology: *Cam and Pat*

Guided Practice

Display or **distribute** Teaching Master ES1-4. Remind children that this is a diagram to show how things are alike and different.

Hold up a red pencil and a red pen. Ask children how the pen and pencil are alike and help children record the likenesses in the overlapping section of the circles. Then ask how the pen and pencil are different. Help children record the differences in the outer sections of the circles.

Practice/Apply

Distribute Practice Master ES1–4 to children and tell them that they will use the pictures on this page to practice looking for things that are the same and different.

Read the directions with children. Make sure they understand that they are to mark an *X* on the things that are different in each picture.

Have children complete the page independently or with a partner.

Check children's responses to be sure they understand the concepts of alike and different.

Preview *Cam and Pat*

Take a picture walk of *Cam and Pat* with children. Point to the characters and name them for children: *Cam* and *Pat*.

Direct children's attention to Cam and Pat. Ask children to tell how Cam and Pat are alike and how they are different.

Tell children that they will read this story with the rest of the class.

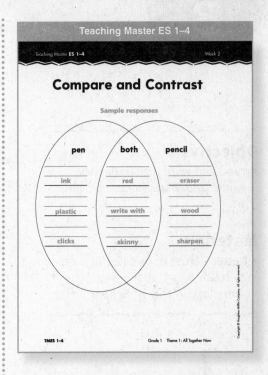

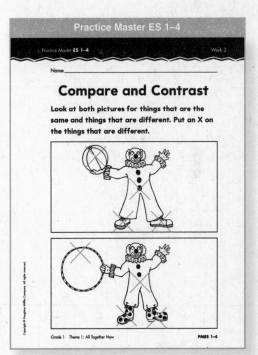

SKILL FOCUS: 25-30 MINUTES

High-Frequency Words

Teach

Write *and*, *here*, *jump*, *not*, *too*, and *we* on the board and read each word. Then distribute the Letter Cards. Draw three squares on the board and tell children that you need their help to spell the word *and*. Say:

The first letter in the word and is a. *Who has* a? *Stand up here and I'll write the letter* a *in the first box. What sound does* a *stand for?* (/ă/)

The next letter in the word and *is* n. *Who has* n? *Come up here and I'll write the letter* n *in the second box. What sound does* n *stand for?* (/n/)

The last letter in the word and *is* d. *Who has* d? *Come up here and I'll write the letter* d *in the third box. The letter* d *stands for the /d/ sound.*

Have the three children holding Letter Cards *a*, *n*, and *d* stand side by side to make the word *and*.

Lead children in a cheer to help them remember the word. Clap on each letter as you spell and say the word: *a-n-d, and!*

Repeat this procedure for the remaining words.

Write the following sentences on the board, and read them together with children:

We can jump here and not there.

Can you jump here too?

Check each child's ability to pronounce *and*, *here*, *jump*, *not*, *too*, and *we* as the child reads each sentence.

Objective

- read and write high-frequency words *and*, *here*, *jump*, *not*, *too*, *we*

Materials

- Letter Cards: *a, d, e* (2), *h, j, m, n, o* (2), *p, r, t, u, w*
- Anthology: *A Day at School*

Practice

Write the following sentence on the board:

Nan and Ann can jump here.

Ask children to read the sentence with you. Next, have children copy the following sentence frame:

_____ can jump here too.

Ask children to complete the sentence by drawing or writing to fill in the blank.

Apply

Have children show and read their sentences to the class. Then ask children to exchange papers and read one another's sentences.

LITERATURE FOCUS: 10-15 MINUTES

Preview *A Day at School*

Walk children through *A Day at School*, on pages 47–63 in their Anthology.

Discuss the illustrations and use words from the story such as *Pam*, *Nat*, *Jen*, *can*, *tap*, *fan*, *cat*, *pat*, and *nap*.

Note the suggestions in the Extra Support boxes on Teacher's Edition pages T127, T128, and T132.

Day 4

Consonants *n, f, p*

Teach

Display the Letter Cards one at a time. Have children name each letter with you and say the letter sound: *n* /n/; *f* /f/; *p* /p/. Give children Picture Cards for initial *n*, initial *f*, and initial *p*. Say:

Find other children whose picture names begin with the same sound as your picture. Everyone whose picture name begins the same, stand together.

Have children in each group name their cards, say the beginning sound, and name the letter that stands for that sound.

Help children differentiate among the consonant sounds by pointing out the position of their lips, teeth, and tongue, and have them feel for vibration of the voice box.

- /n/ — tongue tip at the top of the mouth; vibration

- /f/ — upper teeth on your lower lip; no vibration

- /p/ — lips together, tongue at the bottom of the mouth; no vibration

Practice

Display the *nest* Picture Card and have children identify it. Call on a child to tell what sound he or she hears at the beginning of *nnnest*. Write the word *nest* on the board and have a child underline the *n*. Repeat with Picture Cards for *fox* and *pan*, asking children what sound they hear at the beginning of each word. Then display Picture Cards for *cup* and *man* and *scarf* and ask children what sound they hear at the end of each word.

Apply

Pin Letter Cards for *n, f,* and *p* on chart paper. Have children look for words that begin with *n, f,* and *p* or end with *n* and *p* in *A Day at School.* Each time they find a word, ask them to say it so you can write it on a word list under the appropriate letter. When the search is complete, choose children to read the words on the list.

Objectives
- recognize *n, f,* and *p* and the sounds they represent
- independently read words with *n, f,* and *p*

Materials
- Letter Cards: *f, n, p*
- Picture Cards: *cup, fish, feet, fork, fox, man, nest, nose, nurse, nut, pan, pig, pot, pup, scarf*
- Anthology: *A Day at School*

SKILL FOCUS: PHONICS   10-15 MINUTES

Blending Short *a* Words with *n*, *f*, and *p*

Teach

Display the Letter Card *a* and remind children of the sound the letter *a* makes. Have them repeat it after you, /ă/–/ă/–/ă/. Then repeat the procedure for the letters *n*, /n/, *f*, /f/, and *p*, /p/.

Hold up the Picture Card for *ant* and ask children to identify the picture. Ask them which sound ant begins with, /ă/, /n/, or /t/. Follow the same procedure with the Picture Cards for *can*, *pan*, and *fan*.

Use the Letter Cards to model how to blend the word *fan* using Blending Routine 2. Have children say the sound for *f*, /f/, then the sound for *a*, /ă/, then have them blend /fff ă ă ă/. Finally, have them say the sound for *n*, /n/, blend /fff ă ă ănnn/, and say *fan*. Repeat with the words *man*, *nap*, and *pan*.

Practice

Display the Letter Cards. Remind children that *a* has the /ă/ sound. Show children how to add Letter Cards *p* and *n* to *a* to make the word *pan*. Then remove the *p* and have a child choose a letter to place before *-an*. Tell the child to blend the sounds on the Letter Cards to make a new word. Repeat the procedure.

Apply

Work with the children to make a list of short *a* words with *n*, *f*, and *p* in *A Day at School*. Then give partners a piece of paper divided in half vertically. Have each partner choose one of the words and illustrate it on either side of the center line.

LITERATURE FOCUS: 10-15 MINUTES

Review *A Day at School*

Reread the story with children. Together, make a list of short *a* words. Then have partners find and read story words with *n*, *f*, and *p*.

Objectives

- blend phonemes
- associate the short *a* sound with the letter *a*
- independently read short *a* words with *n*, *f*, and *p*

Materials

- Letter Cards: *a, f, m, n, p, r, t*
- Picture Cards: *ant, can, fan, pan*
- word cards: *can, fan*
- Anthology: *A Day at School*

Day 5

Objectives

- compare and contrast objects
- compare and contrast story ideas

Materials

- Phonics Library: *Nan Cat, Fat Cat*
- Anthology: *Cam and Pat, A Day at School*

SKILL FOCUS: COMPREHENSION   25–30 MINUTES

Compare and Contrast

Teach

Display leaves in varying sizes and shapes. Use real leaves or cut-out leaf patterns. Ask children to tell how the leaves are alike and how they are different. You might ask questions such as the following:

> *Which leaves are the same sizes?*
> *Which leaves are big? Which are small?*
>
> *Which leaves are the same colors?*
> *Which leaves have different colors?*

Explain to children that when they tell how the leaves are the same, they are comparing them and that when they tell how the leaves are different, they are contrasting them.

Practice

Discuss the story *A Day at School* using the terms *same* and *different*. Ask children to name all of the activities that Jen, Pam, and Nat do the same in the story. (read, sing, add, cut, play) When children look at the similarities in a story, the children are comparing the story events or characters.

Walk children through the story, encouraging them to look carefully at the pictures as you go along. Have children look at pages 54–55. Ask, *What is the same about what the children are doing? What is different?* (They are cutting out art: Pam is cutting a fan and Jen is cutting a cat) Tell children that when they look at the differences in a story, they are contrasting the story events or characters.

Apply

Have children observe common classroom activities. Have them compare and contrast their activities. Ask, *How is what you are doing the same as what another child is doing? How is it different?* On the chalkboard, write sentences that tell about the children's activities.

Thomas is reading.

Alicia is reading, too.

Jonathan writes on paper.

Sasha writes on the computer.

LITERATURE FOCUS: 10–15 MINUTES

Revisit *Nan Cat, Fat Cat, Cam and Pat,* and *A Day at School*

Page through the stories with children. Have children compare and contrast the different characters and pictures.

Tell children to look through all of the stories to find short *a* words.

Ask children to look at *Cam and Pat* and *A Day at School* in their Anthology to find the following high-frequency words: *and, here, jump, not, too, we.*

Have children read aloud selected sentences or pages from the stories.

SKILL FOCUS: PHONICS 10-15 MINUTES

Consonants *b* and *r*

Objectives

- associate the /b/ sound with the letter *b*
- associate the /r/ sound with the letter *r*

Materials

- Teaching Master ES1-5
- Sound/Spelling Cards: *bear, rooster*

Technology

Education Place

www.eduplace.com
Pigs in a Rig

Audio CD

A Big Hit
Pigs in a Rig
Audio CD for **All Together Now**

Lexia Phonics
CD-ROM

Primary Intervention

Teach

Recite and repeat the chant. Tell children to join in as they are able.

> **CHANT**
> Benny Bear is in his bed.
> Rudy Rooster crows.
> Benny Bear is out of bed,
> Reaching for his clothes.

Display the Sound/Spelling Card *bear*. Say *bear*, stretching out the /b/ sound. If needed, model the mouth position for /b/. Then say: *Get your mouth ready to say* bear. *Are you ready? Say it.* Have children repeat *bear* several times.

Print *b* on the board, and tell children that *b* stands for the /b/ sound.

Follow a similar procedure for /r/ *r*, using the Sound/Spelling Card *rooster*.

Blend

Print *bag* on the board. Use Blending Routine 1 to model how to blend the sounds, and then say the word. Then have children blend and say the word with you. Finally, have children blend the word on their own. Repeat the process with the word *ran*.

Guided Practice

Display or **distribute** Teaching Master ES1-5. Discuss the illustrations.

Direct attention to the first sentence. Read the sentence aloud. Have children find the three words that begin with /b/ *b*. Read the first two words with children. Then ask them to blend and read *bat* on their own.

Read the second sentence with children. Have them find the two words that are the same. Ask children to read the words.

Check that children are blending *ran* correctly.

SKILL FOCUS: PHONICS   10-15 MINUTES

Blending Short *i* Words

Teach

Recite and repeat the chant, telling children to join in.

> CHANT
> Iggy Iguana lives in an igloo.
> Iggy Iguana writes in ink.
> I-I-Iggy, I-I-Iguana

Display the Sound/Spelling Card *igloo*, and help children identify the object pictured. Say *igloo* stretching out and isolating the /ĭ/. Then have children say *igloo* with you, again stretching out the initial /ĭ/. Ask what sound children hear at the beginning of *igloo*. (/ĭ/) Ask what letter stands for this sound. (*i*)

Blend

Give the word card *it* to one child. Use Blending Routine 1 to model how to blend the word, stretching out the sounds. Then have children blend and say the word with you. Finally, have children blend the sounds and say the word on their own. Follow a similar procedure for the words *bit*, *hit*, *in*, *fin*, and *tin*.

Practice/Apply

Distribute Practice Master ES1-5, and discuss the illustrations with children. Read the directions aloud. Remind children to use what they know about the short *i* sound to read the sentences.

Check children's answers to be sure they read the sentences correctly.

LITERATURE FOCUS: 10-15 MINUTES

Preview *Can It Fit?*

Walk children through *Can It Fit?* Discuss the illustrations, helping children identify the animal characters, as needed. Use words from the story such as *hat*, *fit*, *big*, and *it*. Ask children to find and point to the pig in each picture.

Objectives
- associate /ĭ/ with *i*
- read short *i* words

Materials
- Practice Master ES1-5
- Sound/Spelling Card: *igloo*
- word cards: *bit*, *fin*, *hit*, *in*, *it*, *tin*
- Phonics Library: *Can It Fit?*

Teaching Master ES 1–5

Teaching Master ES 1-5   Week 3

Consonants *b* and *r*

Bear has a big bat.

Bear ran and ran!

TMES 1-5   Grade 1 · Theme 1: All Together Now

Practice Master ES 1–5

Practice Master ES 1-5   Week 3

Name_____

Blending Short *i* Words

Use sounds you know to read. Draw lines to match each sentence with a picture.

1. Big Pig can sit.

2. Big Pig ran.

3. Big Pig can hit.

Grade 1 · Theme 1: All Together Now   PMES 1-5

Day 2

SKILL FOCUS: COMPREHENSION   25-30 MINUTES

Cause and Effect

Teach

Position a book or other item on a bookshelf just out of children's reach. Call on a volunteer to get the book for you. Ask children to tell why the child couldn't reach the book. Say:

Yes. (Child's name) can't reach the book because it is on a high shelf.

Place a stool by the bookshelf. Then ask the same child to retrieve the book. Ask children to tell what happened and why. Say:

Yes. (Child's name) was able to reach the book because he/she stood on the stool.

Explain that people sometimes use the word *because* to tell why things happen.

Guided Practice

Display or **distribute** Teaching Master ES1–6 and direct children's attention to the first picture and set of sentences.

Read the sentences with children.

Have them answer the question with a *because* sentence. (Nan is glad because she is tall enough to go on the ride.)

Repeat the procedure with the second picture and set of sentences. (Nat is sad because he is not tall enough to go on the ride.)

Objectives

- identify cause-and-effect relationships
- recognize *because* as a signal to causes and effects

Materials

- Teaching Master ES1–6
- Practice Master ES1–6
- Anthology: *A Big Hit*

Practice/Apply

Distribute Practice Master ES1–6 and tell children that they will now practice what they have learned. They will think about what happened and why it happened.

Read the directions with children. Discuss the pictures as needed to make sure they understand what is happening in each.

Have children complete the page independently or with a partner.

Check children's responses to be sure they understand the concept of cause and effect.

LITERATURE FOCUS: 10-15 MINUTES

Preview *A Big Hit*

Walk children through *A Big Hit*. Have them use the title and illustrations to predict that the story is about pigs who play tennis.

Ask children to think about what happens in tennis and why it happens. Have children turn to page 74 and ask, *Why do you think the pigs are running?* (They are running because they want to hit the tennis ball.)

Tell children that they will find out what happens in the story when they read it with the rest of the class.

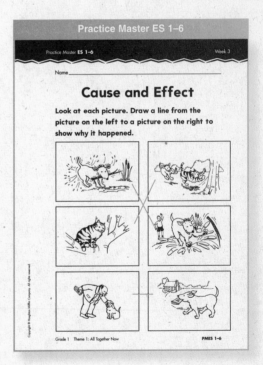

High-Frequency Words

Teach

Write *a*, *find*, *have*, *one*, *to*, and *who* on the board and read each word. Then distribute the Letter Cards. Draw two squares on the board and tell children that you need their help to spell the word *to*.

Who has t? *Stand up here and I'll write the letter* t *in the box. Who has* o? *Stand up here and I'll write the letter* o *in the box.*

Have the child holding Letter Cards for *t* and *o* stand next to each other so all children can see the word.

Lead children in a cheer to help them remember the word. Clap on each letter as you spell and say the word: *t, o, to!* Then tell the child to jump when you point to his or her card. Lead a new "hop it" cheer *t - o, to!*

Repeat the procedure, working with additional children and drawing one-, three-, and four-letter word boxes on the board for the words *a*, *find*, *have*, *one*, and *who*.

Write the following sentences on the board, and read them together with children:

Let's go to the park.
Who can find a ball?
I have one here.

Check each child's ability to pronounce *a*, *find*, *have*, *one*, *to*, and *who* as the child reads each sentence.

Objective

• read and write high-frequency words *a*, *find*, *have*, *one*, *to*, *who*

Materials

• Letter Cards: *a*, *d*, *e*, *f*, *h*, *i*, *n*, *o*, *t*, *v*, *w*
• Anthology: *Pigs in a Rig*

Practice

Give children the sentence frames below. Have them complete the
sentences by drawing or writing to fill in the blanks.

> Who can go to _____?
>
> Can _____ have one, too?
>
> Nat can find a big _____.

Apply

Have children show and read their sentences to the class. Then ask
children to exchange and read one another's sentences.

LITERATURE FOCUS: 10-15 MINUTES

Preview *Pigs in a Rig*

Walk children through *Pigs in a Rig*, on pages 79–95 in their Anthology.

Discuss the illustrations and use words from the story such as *Sid*, *Fig*,
rig, *fix*, *mess*, and *win*.

Note the suggestions in the Extra Support boxes on Teacher's Edition
pages T197, T199, T201, T202, and T204.

Day 4

Objectives
- independently read words with *b, r, h, g*
- associate the sounds /b/, /r/, /h/, /g/ with the letters *b, r, h, g*

Materials
- Letter Cards: *b, g, h, r*
- Picture Cards: *bat, book, box, cab, car, flag, gate, goat, guitar, hat, hen, house, hug, jar, pig, rake, rock, rug, tub, under*
- Anthology: *Pigs in a Rig*

RETEACH

SKILL FOCUS: PHONICS   10-15 MINUTES

Consonants *b, r, h, g*

Teach

Hold up the Letter Cards one at a time. Have children name each letter with you and say the letter sound: *b*/b/; *r*/r/; *h*/h/; *g*/g/.

Give some of the children Picture Cards for initial *b* and the remaining children Picture Cards for initial *r*. Say:

Find other children whose picture names begin with the same sound as your picture. Everyone whose picture name begins the same, stand together.

Have the children in each group name their cards, say the beginning sound, and name the letter that stands for that sound.

Give some of the children Picture Cards for final *b* and the remaining children Picture Cards for final *r*. Say:

Find other children whose picture names end with the same sound as your picture. Everyone whose picture name ends the same, stand together.

Repeat this procedure with Picture Cards for initial *g* and initial *h*, and then final *g*.

Help children differentiate among the consonant sounds by pointing out the position of their lips and tongue, and have them feel for vibration of the voice box.

- /b/ — lips together, tongue at the bottom of the mouth; vibration
- /r/ — tongue tip at the top of the mouth; vibration
- /h/ — lips open; no vibration
- /g/ — back of tongue at the top of the mouth; vibration

Practice

Display the Picture Cards *bat, cab, rug, hat, gate,* and *pig* and write those words on the board. Have children underline the *b, r, h,* or *g* in each word and say the sound and then read the word aloud. Call on children to find the matching Picture Card for each word.

Apply

Have children find words with *b, r, h,* and *g* in *Pigs in a Rig* and read them aloud while you write them on the board. Have volunteers underline the *b, r, h,* or *g* in each word.

Blending Short *i* Words

Teach

Display the Letter Card *i* and remind children of the sound the letter *i* makes: /ĭ/. Have them repeat it after you, /ĭ/–/ĭ/–/ĭ/. Hold up the Picture Card for *ink* and ask children to identify the picture. Ask them which sound *ink* begins with, /ĭ/ or /ă/. Follow the same procedure with the Picture Cards for *ant, astronaut* and *igloo*.

Remind children that they know the sounds for the following letters and say the sounds with them: *b*, /b/, *r*, /r/, *h*, /h/, *g* /g/.

Use the Letter Cards to model how to blend the word *big* using Blending Routine 2. Have children say the sound for *b*, /b/, the sound for *i*, /ĭ/, then blend /b ĭ ĭ/. Finally, have them say the sound for *g*, /g/, blend /b ĭ ĭ ĭg/, and say *big*. Remind children that they can make more words by adding different sounds before and after short *i*. Have children blend these words using Blending Routine 2: *sit, him, pin, rig*.

Practice

Display the Letter Card *i* on a chalk ledge. Write *bit* on the chalkboard. Have a volunteer find the correct Letter Cards to make the word and read it aloud. Repeat the procedure for the words *pig, hit,* and *rim*.

Apply

Have partners take turns finding short *i* words in *Pigs in a Rig*. Each time a child finds a word, he or she should read aloud the word while you write the word in a column on the board labeled short *i* words.

Review *Pigs in a Rig*

Reread the story with children. Ask, *Who can find a word with the short* i *sound?* Repeat with consonants *b, r, h,* and *g*.

Objectives
- blend phonemes
- associate the short *i* sound with the letter *i*
- independently read short *i* words

Materials
- Letter Cards: *b, g, h, i, m, n, p, r, s, t*
- Picture Cards: *ant, astronaut, igloo, ink*
- Anthology: *Pigs in a Rig*

Cause and Effect

Teach

Demonstrate a cause-and-effect situation for children. Roll a large ball into a small stack of small blocks. Have children watch as the ball knocks over the stack of blocks. Ask, *What happened?* Elicit from children that the ball caused the blocks to be knocked down. Explain to children that when one event causes another event to happen, that is called a cause and effect. The rolling of the ball was the cause, and the blocks being knocked down was the effect.

Provide other examples from common experiences in children's lives, such as the following:

Cause	Effect
I fall down.	I hurt my knee.
I am tired.	I go to sleep.

Practice

Discuss the story *Pigs in a Rig* by Helen Lester. Remind children that in the story, the pigs fall out of the rig and get very messy. Use a chart similar to the following to help children organize and understand cause-and-effect relationships. Encourage children to use questions when identifying causes (Why did this happen?) and effects (What happened?).

Cause	Effect
Sid falls in the mud.	Sid gets messy.
Pal finds the jam.	Pal gets messy.
Fig gets in the bag.	Fig gets messy.

Objectives

- answer the questions *Why did this happen?* to identify causes and *What happened?* to identify effects
- identify cause-and-effect relationships

Materials

- Phonics Library: *Can It Fit? Who Can Hit?*
- Anthology: *A Big Hit, Pigs in a Rig*

Apply

Have children look at pages 82 and 83 of the story and identify the cause-and-effect relationships on their own. If needed, guide them with questions such as the following:

* What are the pigs doing? (riding in the rig)

* What happens? (Sid falls out of the rig and into the mud.)

* Why does this happen? (The rig hit a big bump.)

Lead children to identify the cause (the rig hit a bump) **and the effect.** (Sid falls out of the rig and into the mud.)

LITERATURE FOCUS: 10-15 MINUTES

Revisit *Can It Fit? Who Can Hit? A Big Hit,* and *Pigs in a Rig*

Page through the stories with children. Have children find words with the consonants *b, r, g,* and *h*. Then have children look through the stories again for words with the short *i* sound.

Tell children to look at pages 94–95 of their Anthology. Ask, *Why did the pigs get ribbons?* (because they won the best pig contest)

Have children read aloud selected sentences or pages from the stories.

Theme 2

Surprise!

Consonants *d* and *l*

Teach

Recite and repeat the chant shown, having children join.

> ### CHANT
> Dance, Duck, dance!
> Dance all day long.
> Leap, Lion, leap!
> Leap all night long.

Display the Sound/Spelling Card *duck*. Say *duck*, stretching out the /d/ sound. If needed, model the mouth position for /d/. Have children repeat *duck* several times. Say the chant again, having children raise their hands when they hear a word that begins with /d/. Print *d* on the board, and tell children that *d* stands for the /d/ sound.

Follow a similar procedure for /l/ *l*, using the Sound/Spelling Card *lion*.

Blend

Print *dig* on the board. Using Blending Routine 1, model how to blend the sounds and then say the word. Then have children blend and say the word with you. Finally, have children blend and say the word on their own. Repeat the process with the word *lip*.

Guided Practice

Display or **distribute** Teaching Master ES2-1, and discuss the illustrations.

Direct attention to the first frame, and read aloud what Dad and Dan say. Help children find words that begin with /d/ and read them. Ask children to read both sentences with you.

Follow a similar procedure for the second frame. Focus on words that begin with /l/.

Check that children understand how to blend the sounds correctly in *Dad, Dan,* and *lap.*

Objectives

- associate the /d/ sound with the letter *d*
- associate the /l/ sound with the letter *l*

Materials

- Teaching Master ES2-1
- Sound/Spelling Cards: *duck, lion*

Education Place
www.eduplace.com
A Party for Bob

Audio CD
A Lot! A Lot!
A Party for Bob
Audio CD for **Surprise!**

Lexia Phonics
CD-ROM
Primary Intervention

Blending Short o Words

Teach

Recite and repeat the chant, asking children to join in.

> **CHANT**
>
> Ollie is an ostrich.
>
> Oscar is an octopus.
>
> /ŏ/-/ŏ/-Ollie, /ŏ/-/ŏ/-Oscar

Display the Sound/Spelling Card *ostrich*, and help children identify the bird pictured. Say *ostrich*, stretching out and isolating the short *o* sound. Then have children say *ostrich* with you.

Ask what sound children hear at the beginning of *ostrich*. (/ŏ/) Ask what letter stands for this sound. (o)

Blend

Give the Word Card *ox* to a child. Using Blending Routine 1, model how to blend the word, stretching out the sounds. Then have children blend and say the word with you. Finally, have children blend the sounds and say the word on their own. Follow a similar procedure with *dot*, *hop*, *log*, and *box*.

Practice/Apply

Distribute Practice Master ES2-1, and discuss the illustrations. Read the directions aloud, and be sure children understand what to do. Have them complete the Practice Master independently.

Check children's responses to be sure they understand and are able to read short *o* words.

Preview *Dot Fox*

Walk children through *Dot Fox* and discuss the illustrations. Point out that Dot Fox is the character in the story. Use words from the story such as *hot*, *got*, and *lot*.

Objectives

- associate /ŏ/ with *o*
- read short *o* words

Materials

- Practice Master ES2-1
- Sound/Spelling Card: *ostrich*
- Word Cards: *box, dot, hop, log, ox*
- Phonics Library: *Dot Fox*

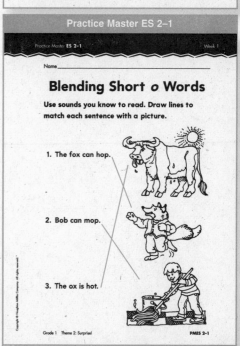

Day 2

PRETEACH

SKILL FOCUS: COMPREHENSION 25-30 MINUTES

Objectives
- note important details in pictures
- note important details in story text

Materials
- Teaching Master ES2-2
- Practice Master ES2-2
- Anthology: *A Lot! A Lot!*

Noting Details

Teach

Display three similar objects, such as backpacks, for children to examine. Call on children to point out a detail, or a small part, that sets each backpack apart from the others. A child might say: *This backpack has a key chain on it.*

Point out that details, such as the key chain, give a clear picture of how each backpack is different. Then explain that writers and illustrators often include details, or small parts of information, in their stories or pictures to help readers get a clear picture of story characters and events.

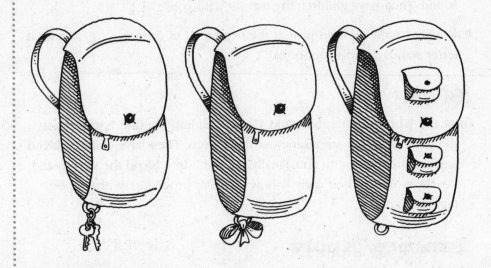

Guided Practice

Display or **distribute** Teaching Master ES2-2, and call on a child to name the place pictured.

Ask children what details in the picture helped them know that the place was a library. (Possible answers: bookshelves, books, tables and chairs)

Work with children to create the word web. Begin the web using the details children noticed. Then have them add details about libraries, based on their own experiences.

Practice/Apply

Distribute Practice Master ES2-2 to children. Read the directions and discuss the picture. Be sure children understand that they need to add one detail from each sentence to complete the picture.

Have children complete the Practice Master independently.

Have children share their completed pictures.

Check children's pictures to be sure that they understand how to find details in sentences. For example, ask, *Why is the word* big *in the first sentence important?* (because it tells which cat should be wearing the hat)

Preview *A Lot! A Lot!*

Take children on a picture walk of *A Lot! A Lot!*

Discuss the illustrations, having children note details in the pictures. Help children count the number of cats in each set.

Tell children that they will read this story with the rest of the class.

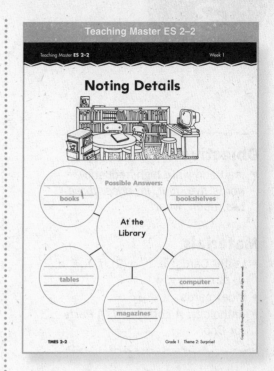

Day 3

Objective

- read and write high-frequency words *five, four, in, once, three, two, upon, what*

Materials

- Letter Cards: *a, c, e* (2), *f, h, i, n, o, p, r, t, u, v, w*
- index cards
- Anthology: *A Lot! A Lot!, A Party for Bob*

SKILL FOCUS: 25–30 MINUTES

High-Frequency Words

Teach

Write *five, four, in, once, three, two, upon,* and *what* on the board. Read each word aloud while pointing to that word. On a second reading, encourage children to read along with you.

Place the Letter Cards in the chalk tray below the words. Ask, *How many letters do we need to spell the word* five? Assign one letter to each of four children, and tell them to come up and hold their letters for classmates to see. Have classmates spell the word together, clapping for each letter.

Write a sentence from the story, *A Party for Bob* that contains the word *five,* for example, *Five kids fit.* Have children read the sentence together, and clap their hands together when they read the word *five.* Repeat this procedure for the remaining words.

Write the following sentences on the board, and read them together with children:

I once saw five big boxes.

What was in them?

I saw four gifts and three kids.

I saw two kids upon one box!

Check each child's ability to pronounce *five, four, in, once, three, two, upon,* and *what* as the child reads each sentence.

Practice

Ask the children to name the number words. If necessary, remind them that these words tell how many. Write each word on a large index card.

Tell children you want to sort the words into two groups: words that *tell how many* (five, four, three, two) and words that *do not tell how many.* (in, once, upon, what)

Have children read each word card and decide which group the card belongs in. Tape the words in two columns. When finished, have children read the lists together.

Apply

Have children match the high-frequency word cards to the words in the stories *A Lot! A Lot!* or *A Party for Bob.*

Preview *A Party for Bob*

Walk children through *A Party for Bob* on pages 113–129 in their Anthology.

Discuss the illustrations, and tell children that the characters' names are Bob, Tom, Ben, Dot, and Tim.

Use words from the story such as *got, box, wet, hid,* and *lit.*

Note the suggestions in the Extra Support box on Teacher's Edition page T57.

Day 4

SKILL FOCUS: PHONICS

10-15 MINUTES

Consonants *d, w, l, x*

Objectives

- recognize *d, w, l,* and *x* and the sounds they represent
- independently read words with *d, w, l, x*

Materials

- Letter Cards: *d, l, w, x*
- Picture Cards: *bed, box, cloud, desk, dime, dog, doll, fox, girl, hand, lamp, leaf, leg, lemon, lion, mix, ox, pad, sad, seal, watch, wave, web, wig*
- Anthology: *A Party for Bob*

Teach

Display the Letter Cards. Have children name each letter with you and say the letter sound: *d* /d/; *w* /w/; *l* /l/; *x* /ks/. Give some children Picture Cards for initial *d*, some initial *l*, and some initial *w*. Say:

Find other children whose picture names begin with the same sound as yours and stand with them.

Have children name their cards, say the beginning sound, and name the letter that stands for it.

Give some children Picture Cards for final *d*, some final *l*, and some final *x*. Have children find others whose picture names end with the same sound and stand with them.

Help children differentiate among the consonants, by pointing out the position of their lips and tongue, and have them feel for vibration of the voice box.

- /d/ — tongue tip starts behind upper teeth, then moves back; vibration
- /w/ — rounded lips, tongue behind lower teeth; vibration
- /l/ — tongue tip behind upper teeth; vibration
- /ks/ — combines /k/ and /s/; begin with back of tongue on top of mouth, no vibration and end with tongue at top of mouth, no vibration

Practice

Display the Picture Card for *dog* and have children identify it. Call on a child to tell what sound he or she hears at the beginning of *dog*. Write *dog* on the board and have a child underline the *d*. Repeat with Picture Cards for *web* and *leg*. Then display Picture Cards for *bed, girl,* and *fox* and ask children what sound they hear at the end of each word.

Apply

Pin Letter Cards for *d, w, l,* and *x* on chart paper. Have children look for words that begin with *d, w,* and *l* or end with *d, l,* or *x* in *A Party for Bob*. Each time they find a word, ask children to say it aloud so you can write it on a word list under the appropriate letter. Have children read the words on the list.

Blending Short *o* Words

Teach

Display the Letter Card *o* and have children repeat after you the sound the letter *o* makes, /ŏ/ - /ŏ/ - /ŏ/. Be sure that children have their mouths in the correct position as they say the sound. Hold up the Picture Card for *otter* and ask children to identify the picture. Ask them which sound *otter* begins with, /ŏ/ or /ă/.

Use the Letter Cards to model how to blend the word *pot* using Blending Routine 2. Have children say the sounds for *p*, /p/ and *o*, /ŏ/. Then have them blend /pŏŏ/. Finally, have them say the sound for *t*, /t/, blend /pŏŏŏt/, and say *pot*.

Remind children that they can make words by adding different letter sounds they know to the beginning and end of /ŏ/. Have children blend the following sounds using Blending Routine 2: /kŏŏŏd/, /fffŏŏŏx/, /lllŏŏŏt/, /bŏŏŏx/, /rrrŏŏŏd/.

Practice

Place Letter Card *o* on the chalk ledge and explain to children that they will spell some short *o* words. Then place the Picture Card for *box* on the chalk ledge and have a child choose the correct consonant Letter Cards to spell the word *box*. Repeat this procedure with Picture Cards for *cot, dot, fox, ox, hop, log,* and *pot*.

Apply

Have partners take turns finding words with short *o* in *A Party for Bob*. Each time children find a word with short *o* they should read it aloud while you write it in a column labeled short *o* words.

Review *A Party for Bob*

Reread the story with children. Together, make a list of short *o* words. Then have partners find and read story words with *d, w, l,* and *x*.

Objectives

- blend phonemes
- associate the short *o* sound with the letter *o*
- independently read short *o* words

Materials

- Letter Cards: *b, c, d, f, g, h, l, o, p, t, x*
- Picture Cards: *box, cot, dot, fox, hop, log, otter, ox, pot*
- Anthology: *A Party for Bob*

Day 5

Objectives

- note details in a story
- identify details in pictures

Materials

- Phonics Library: *Dot Fox, Bob Pig and Dan Ox*
- Anthology: *A Lot! A Lot!, A Party for Bob*

SKILL FOCUS: COMPREHENSION   25–30 MINUTES

Noting Details

Teach

Begin the lesson by using three similar but not identical items to discuss the skill of noting details. For example, you might ask three children to volunteer the use of their jackets, book bags, or lunch boxes. As you display the items, ask children to look closely as you describe details about the jackets, for example: *I am looking at a jacket that has a zipper. Which jacket is it? I am looking at a jacket that has brown trim around the sleeves.*

Explain to children that writers often create small details to help the reader get a picture of story characters and events. Explain that illustrators often do the same thing. They include details in their art to help the viewer further understand a character or event.

Practice

Discuss the story *A Party for Bob* by Angela Shelf Medearis. Begin by having children look at the illustration on pages 114 and 115. Tell them to describe what they see in the drawing and ask what details help them to know that the story takes place in a house. (walls, floor, table) Have children read the text on the page together. Ask, *How can you tell that story is about a birthday party?* Lead them to understand that the word *party* and the picture clues (birthday cake, balloons, streamers) can help them understand that the story is about a birthday party.

Explain to children that looking at picture clues and reading words carefully can help them note details when they read.

Apply

Have children work in small groups. Ask children to look carefully at the illustrations in the story *A Party for Bob* and to find details in the drawings. Ask *How does the artist use details to show that each friend is bringing a gift for Bob? What features does the artist give each gift?* Tell each group of children to choose one of the kids in the story and to draw a picture of him or her with their present for Bob. Tell the children to pay close attention to the details the artist uses in the drawings as they draw their own pictures.

Revisit *Dot Fox, Bob Pig and Dan Ox, A Lot! A Lot!*, and *A Party for Bob*

Page through the stories with children. Note important details that have been included in the pictures of the different stories.

Have children look for short *o* words in each of the stories.

Tell children to look through *A Lot! A Lot!* and *A Party for Bob* for the following high-frequency words: *five, four, in, once, three, two, upon, what*.

Have children read aloud selected sentences or pages from the stories.

Day 1

Objectives

- associate the /y/ sound with the letter *y*
- associate the /v/ sound with the letter *v*

Materials

- Teaching Master ES2-3

Education Place
www.eduplace.com
The Bunnies and the Fox

Audio CD
Val Can Help
The Bunnies and the Fox
Audio CD for **Surprise!**

Lexia Phonics
CD-ROM
Primary Intervention

PRETEACH

SKILL FOCUS: PHONICS   10–15 MINUTES

Consonants *y* and *v*

Teach

Recite and repeat the chant shown, having children join in.

> **CHANT**
> You like *violets*,
> Yes, *you* do!
> *Violets* in a *vase*,
> From me to *you*!

Say *violets*, stretching out the /v/ sound. If needed, model the mouth position for /v/. Have children repeat *violets* several times. Repeat with *vase*.

Follow a similar procedure for /y/, using the words *yes* and *you*.

Blend

Print *yam* on the board. Tell children that this word names a vegetable. Using Blending Routine 1, model how to blend the sounds, stretching the sound for *y* and then saying the word. Then have children blend and say the word with you. Finally, have children blend and say the word on their own. Repeat the process with the word *vet*, pointing out that *vet* is short for *veterinarian*.

Guided Practice

Display or **distribute** Teaching Master ES2-3. Discuss the illustrations and what is happening in each.

Direct attention to the first frame, and read aloud the caption with children. Help them draw a line under all the words that begin with /v/. Read these words again and then have children read them. Repeat the procedure for the second frame, focusing on words that begin with *y*. Ask children if they can think of other words that begin with /y/.

Check that children are forming the /v/ and /y/ sounds correctly.

SKILL FOCUS: PHONICS   10–15 MINUTES

Blending Short *e* Words

Teach

Recite and repeat the chant, telling children to join in.

> **CHANT**
>
> Ed is an elephant,
>
> Stepping on the eggs.
>
> /ĕ/-/ĕ/elephant, /ĕ/-/ĕ/eggs

Say *elephant*, stretching out the initial short e sound. Then have children say *elephant* with you, again stretching out the /ĕ/. Display the Sound/Spelling Card *elephant*. Ask what sound children hear at the beginning of *elephant*. (/ĕ/) Ask what letter stands for this sound. *(e)*

Blend

Print *Ed* on the board. Using Blending Routine 1, model how to blend the name, stretching out the short e sound. Then have children blend and say it with you. Finally, have children blend the name on their own. Repeat with y*et, vet, den,* and *hen.*

Practice/Apply

Distribute Practice Master ES2-3, discuss the illustrations, and read the directions with children. Have them complete the Practice Master independently. Have children read the sentences aloud and share their answers.

Check that children understand how to blend short *e* words.

LITERATURE FOCUS: 10–15 MINUTES

Preview *Not Yet!*

Walk children through *Not Yet!* As you discuss the illustrations, use the words *kit* and *van.* You may need to tell children that the word *kit* refers to the big bags that Peg Hen is trying to put into the van.

Objectives

- associate /ĕ/ with *e*
- read short *e* words

Materials

- Practice Master ES2-3
- Sound/Spelling Card: *elephant*
- Phonics Library: *Not Yet*

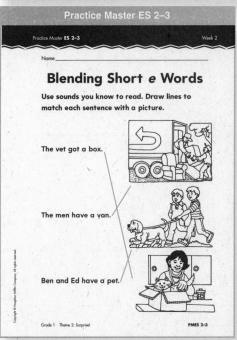

Day 2

Fantasy and Realism

Objectives

- distinguish between fantasy and realism
- identify elements of fantasy in a story

Materials

- Teaching Master ES2–4
- Practice Master ES2–4
- Anthology: *Val Can Help*

Teach

Tell children that you are going to say two sentences. Explain that they need to listen carefully because you are going to ask them which sentence could really happen and which could not. Say:

Sentence 1: *After school, Tom walked home.*

Sentence 2: *After school, Tom flew in a rocket to his house on the moon.*

Discuss which sentence children think could really happen. Say:

Yes, the sentence: After school, Tom walked home *could really happen. It tells about something that is real.*

Repeat the second sentence. Ask children why they think this sentence could not happen in real life. Say:

Yes, the sentence: After school, Tom flew in a rocket to his house on the moon *could not really happen. It is make-believe. Something that is make-believe is also called a fantasy.*

Point out that some stories tell about things that could happen in real life and other stories tell about things that could not.

Guided Practice

Display or **distribute** Teaching Master ES2–4 and invite children to look at the illustrations. Have them read the sentences under the pictures.

Help children circle the sentence that tells a story about a real fox. (the second sentence)

Discuss with children what it is about the second sentence that is real. (Sample answer: Real foxes walk on four paws and live in homes called dens.)

Ask children why they think the first picture and sentence tells a make-believe story about a fox. (Sample answer: Real foxes cannot talk; only make-believe or fantasy foxes can talk.)

Practice/Apply

Distribute Practice Master ES2–4 and preview the pictures to make sure children understand what is happening in each one. Tell children that two of the pictures and sentences on this page tell stories about real story characters, but that the other two tell stories about make-believe story characters.

Read the directions with children. Make sure they understand that they are to circle only the pictures that tell about things that could really happen.

Have children work independently to complete the page. Encourage them to discuss why they chose to circle, or not circle, the pictures on the page.

Check children's work to be sure they understand the differences between fantasy and reality in stories.

Preview *Val Can Help*

Walk children through *Val Can Help*. Discuss the illustrations, pointing out the characters and naming them for children: Val and Rob. Then ask children to look at the pictures to predict whether this story could be real or whether it is a fantasy story.

Tell children that they will read this story with the rest of the class.

Day 3

SKILL FOCUS: 25–30 MINUTES

High-Frequency Words

Teach

Write *do, for, I, is, me, my, said,* and *you* on the board. Read each word aloud while pointing to that word. On a second reading, encourage children to read along with you.

Place the Letter Cards in the chalk tray below the words. Ask, *How many letters do we need to spell the word* do? Assign one letter to each of two children, and tell them to come up and hold their letters for classmates to see. Have classmates spell the word together, clapping for each letter.

Write a sentence from the story *The Bunnies and the Fox* that contains the word *do*. For example, write: *We have a job to do.* Have children read the sentence together, and clap their hands when they read the word *do*. Repeat this procedure for the remaining words.

Write the following sentences on the board, and read them together with children:

"My dog is lost," I said.

"Do you want me to help?" she said.

"We can look for him."

"I can see him!" I said.

Check each child's ability to pronounce *do, for, I, is, me, my, said,* and *you* as the child reads each sentence.

Practice

Write each High-Frequency Word on a large index card and distribute the cards to children. Write a sentence on the board from one of the stories that uses each new word. Leave a blank for the word from the high-frequency list. Have children read each sentence along with you. Have the children decide who has the missing word. Have that child bring up the word and tape it in the blank space.

Apply

Have children match high-frequency word cards to the words in the stories *Val Can Help* or *The Bunnies and the Fox.*

Objective

- read and write high-frequency words *do, for, I, is, me, my, said, you*

Materials

- Letter Cards: *a, d, e, f, i, I, m, o, r, s, u, y*
- index cards
- Anthology: *Val Can Help, The Bunnies and the Fox*

Preview *The Bunnies and the Fox*

Walk children through *The Bunnies and the Fox,* on pages 145–161 in their Anthology.

Discuss the illustrations, and tell children that the characters' names are Kev and Viv.

Use words from the story such as *den, yet, get, yes,* and *help*.

Note the suggestions in the Extra Support box on Teacher's Edition page T129.

Consonants *y, k, v*

Teach

Display the Letter Cards one at a time. Have children name each letter with you and say the letter sound: *y*/y/; *k*/k/; *v*/v/. Give some children Picture Cards for initial *y*, some initial *k*, and some initial *v*. Say:

Find other children whose picture names begin with the same sound as yours. Everyone whose picture name begins the same, stand together.

Have children in each group name their cards, say the beginning sound, and name the letter that stands for that sound.

Display the Picture Card for *hook* and have children identify the picture. Ask a volunteer to tell what sound he or she hears at the end of *hook*. Write the word *hook* on the board and have a volunteer underline the final *k*.

Help children differentiate among the consonants by pointing out the position of their lips and tongue, and have them feel for a vibration of the voice box.

- /k/ — back of tongue against roof of mouth; vibration

- /v/ — upper teeth on your lower lip; vibration

- /y/ — combination of vowel sounds long e and short u; begins with tongue at the middle of the mouth, vibration and ends with tongue at the bottom of the mouth, vibration

Practice

Display the Picture Cards y*ak, yarn, key, kite, hook, vet,* and *van* and write those words on the board. Have children underline the *y, k,* and *v* in each word and say the sound and then the word aloud. Call on children to find the matching Picture Card for each word.

Apply

Have children find words with *y, k,* and *v* in *The Bunnies and the Fox.* Each time a child finds a word with *y, k,* or *v,* he or she should read the word aloud while you write it on the board. Have children come to the board to underline the *y, k,* or *v* in each word.

Objectives

- recognize *y, k,* and *v* and the sounds they represent
- independently read words with *y, k, v*

Materials

- Letter Cards: *k, v, y*
- Picture Cards: *hook, key, king, kiss, kit, kite, van, vane, vase, vest, vet, vine, yak, yam, yard, yarn, yellow, yolk, yo-yo*
- Anthology: *The Bunnies and the Fox*

Blending Short *e* Words

Teach

Display the Letter Card *e* and remind children of the sound the letter *e* makes: /ĕ/. Have them repeat it after you. Hold up the Picture Card *egg* and ask children to identify the picture. Ask them which sound *egg* begins with, /ĕ/ or /ŏ/.

Use the Letter Cards to model how to blend the word *vet* using Blending Routine 2. Have children say the sounds for *v*, /v/ and *e*, /ĕ/. Then have them blend /vĕ ĕ ĕ/. Finally, have them say the sound for *t*, /t/, blend /vĕ ĕ ĕt/, and say *vet*.

Remind children that they can make more words by adding different sounds to the beginning and end of short *e*. Have children blend the following sounds: /jĕ ĕ ĕt/, /hĕ ĕ ĕn/, /nĕ ĕ ĕt/, /pĕ ĕ ĕn/.

Practice

Place Letter Card *e* on a chalk ledge and explain to children that they will spell some short *e* words. Then place the Picture Card for *hen* on the chalk ledge and have a child choose the correct consonant Letter Cards to spell *hen*. Repeat this procedure with Picture Cards for *pen*, *pet*, *ten*, *vet*, *net*, and *bed*.

Apply

Have partners look for words with short *e* in *The Bunnies and the Fox*. Have a child say the word aloud so that you can write it on a short *e* word list on the board. Then give each pair a piece of paper divided in half vertically. Have partners each choose a different word from the word list and illustrate it on either side of the center line. Children can share their short *e* "partner pictures" with the group.

Review *The Bunnies and the Fox*

Reread the story together with children. Ask, *Who can find a word with the short* e *sound?* Repeat with consonants *y*, *k*, and *v*.

Objectives
- blend phonemes
- associate the short *e* sound with the letter *e*
- independently read words with short *e*

Materials
- Letter Cards: *b, d, e, h, j, n, p, t, v*
- Picture Cards: *bed, egg, hen, net, pen, pet, ten, vet*
- Anthology: *The Bunnies and the Fox*

Day 5

Objectives

• identify what is real and what is make-believe
• give examples of fantasy and realism

Materials

• Phonics Library: *Not Yet! Big Ben*
• Anthology: *Val Can Help, The Bunnies and the Fox*

Fantasy and Realism

Teach

Explain to children that you are going to tell them two short stories and that they should listen carefully to see if they can tell which one is real and which one is make-believe.

Story 1: *This morning I woke up, got dressed, and ate breakfast. I fed my goldfish and my dog.*

Story 2: *Two hundred years ago, I lived on the Planet Jupiter. When I was hungry, I reached out and ate some stars.*

Ask children which story they think is real and could happen in real life. Ask them why it might be true. (We wake up in the morning, we get dressed and eat breakfast. We feed our pets. These are things that happen every day.) Then ask them which story is not true. Repeat the story if necessary. Ask them why they think the second story is not true. (People don't live to be 200 years old. We live on Earth. We can't eat stars.) Explain that the second story is make-believe. Tell children that another word for make-believe is *fantasy*. And another word for stories with events that could happen in real life, and with characters who act and talk like we do in real life, is *realism*.

Practice

Revisit the story *The Bunnies and the Fox* by David McPhail. Direct the children to look at the illustrations and listen as you read pages 146 and 147. Ask them to tell you which parts of the story are realistic, that is, what parts could really happen. (bunnies live in a den, fox is dangerous) Then ask them what makes this story fantasy or make-believe. (bunnies wear clothes, bunnies own furniture, bunnies talk) Continue through the story, identifying elements of fantasy and realism.

Apply

Have children act out some of the story actions by taking the parts of Kev, Viv, Mom, and Fox. Provide cards for each child with the words *Yes* on one and *No* on the other. As volunteers act out the roles of the story animals, have classmates tell whether the action could really happen or not by holding up their cards.

Revisit *Not Yet! Big Ben, Val Can Help,* and *The Bunnies and the Fox*

Page through the stories with children. Discuss various aspects of the stories that could be real or that are definitely fantasy.

Have children look for short *e* words in each of the stories.

Tell children to look through *Val Can Help* and *The Bunnies and the Fox* for the following high-frequency words: *do, for, I, is, me, my, said,* and *you.*

Have children read aloud selected sentences or pages from the stories.

Day 1

Objectives

- associate the /j/ sound with the letter *j*
- associate the /z/ sound with the letter *z*

Materials

- Teaching Master ES2-5
- Sound/Spelling Cards: *jumping Jill, zebra*

Technology
Education Place

www.eduplace.com
A Surprise for Zig Bug

Audio CD

Quit It, Bug!
A Surprise for Zig Bug
Audio CD for **Surprise!**

Lexia Phonics
CD-ROM

Primary Intervention

Consonants *j* and *z*

Teach

Recite and repeat the chant shown. Have children join in.

> **CHANT**
>
> Jackets have zippers;
>
> Jungles have trees;
>
> Zoos have zebras.
>
> Zookeepers have knees!

Display the Sound/Spelling Card *zebra*. Say *zebra*, stretching out the /z/ sound. If needed, model the mouth position for /z/. Have children repeat *zebra* several times. Say the chant again, having children raise their hands whenever they hear a word that begins with /z/.

Print *z* on the board, and tell children that *z* stands for the /z/ sound.

Repeat the procedure for /j/, using the Sound/Spelling Card *jumping Jill*.

Blend

Print *jet* on the board. Use Blending Routine 1 to model how to blend the sounds, stretching the *j* sound and then saying the word. Then have children blend and say the word with you. Finally, have children blend the word on their own.

Repeat the process with the words *jog, zip,* and *zap*.

Guided Practice

Display or **distribute** Teaching Master ES2-5. Discuss the illustrations.

Direct attention to the first picture, and read the sentence with children. Then help children find and point to the words *Jan* and *zoo*. Read the next two sentences with children. Ask if they can find the zebra. Then read the sentences again, having children join you.

Check that children are blending the sounds correctly and are able to read and understand the words.

SKILL FOCUS: PHONICS | 10–15 MINUTES

Blending Short *u* Words

Teach

Recite and repeat the chant, asking children to join in.

> CHANT
>
> Umbrellas go up;
>
> Umbrellas go down.
>
> Now my umbrella is upside-down!

Say *umbrella*, stretching out the initial /ŭ/. Then have children say it with you. Ask what sound children hear at the beginning of *umbrella*. (/ŭ/) Ask what letter stands for this sound. (*u*) Display the Sound/Spelling Card *umbrella*, and ask if the umbrella in the picture is up or down. Then turn the card upside-down, and ask children to describe the umbrella now.

Blend

Print *up* on the board. Using Blending Routine 1, model how to blend the word, stretching out the short *u* sound. Then have children blend and say it with you. Finally, have children blend the sounds and say the word on their own. Repeat with *us, but,* and *jug*.

Practice/Apply

Distribute Practice Master ES2-5, and discuss the illustrations. Read the directions with children. Have them complete the Practice master independently. Have children share their answers and read the sentences aloud.

Check that children are blending short *u* words correctly.

LITERATURE FOCUS: | 10–15 MINUTES

Preview *The Bug Kit*

Walk children through *The Bug Kit*. Discuss the illustrations and use words from the story. Ask children to look at the picture on page 29 and tell what they think a bug kit is for.

Objectives

- associate /ŭ/ with *u*
- read short *u* words

Materials

- Practice Master ES2-5
- Sound/Spelling Card: *umbrella*
- Phonics Library: *The Bug Kit*

Teaching Master ES 2–5

Practice Master ES 2–5

Story Structure

Teach

Explain to children that most stories follow a plan. Every story includes parts that tell *who the story is about, where the story takes place,* and *what happens.*

Have children think about the story of *The Three Little Pigs.* Ask, *Who is the story about?* (three little pigs and a wolf) Then ask, *Where does the story take place?* (in the pigs' houses) Finally, ask, *What happens?* (First, the wolf blows down the house of straw, then the wolf blows down the house of sticks, but in the end he couldn't blow down the house of bricks.)

Call on children to share information about their favorite stories. Have them answer the questions *Who? Where?* and *What happens?*

Guided Practice

Display or **distribute** Teaching Master ES2-6 and tell children that these pictures tell a short story. Invite children to look at the story with you to see if it answers the questions *Who? Where?* and *What happens?*

Direct attention to the first picture. Ask, *Who is in this story?* (a boy named Sam) Explain that Sam is a character in the story.

Ask, *Where does this story take place?* (in Sam's yard) Ask how children can tell the story takes place in Sam's yard. (from the picture clues) Explain that Sam's yard is the setting for the story.

Remind children that a story has a beginning, a middle, and an end. Point to the first frame of the story. Ask, *What happens at the beginning of this story? What problem does Sam have?* (Sam's kite is caught in a tree and he can't get it down.)

Point to the second frame. Ask, *What happens in the middle of the story?* (Sam's dad tries to reach the kite, but he can't.)

Objectives

- identify story characters, setting, plot
- complete a simple story map

Materials

- Teaching Master ES2–6
- Practice Master ES2–6
- Anthology: *Quit It, Bug!*

Direct attention to the third frame. Ask, *What happens at the end of the story?* (Sam sits on his dad's shoulders to reach the kite.)

Point out the story map under the pictures. Explain that children can use a map like this to help them show the plan a story follows. Work with children to complete the story map.

Practice/Apply

Distribute Practice Master ES2-6 to children and read the directions with them. Be sure children understand that they need to tell who is in the story and where it takes place. They also need to tell what happens at the beginning, in the middle, and at the end of the story.

Have partners work together to complete story maps.

Check children's work to be sure they understand the concepts of character, setting, and story events.

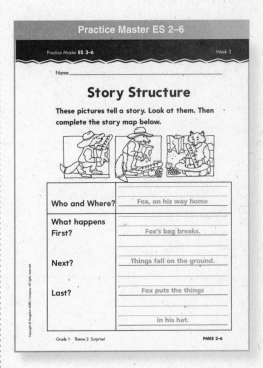

LITERATURE FOCUS: 10–15 MINUTES

Preview *Quit It, Bug!*

Walk children through *Quit It, Bug!* Ask children who the characters in the story are. (a boy, a girl, and a bug) Tell children that the boy's name is Dan and the girl's name is Meg.

Ask children if they can tell from the pictures what the setting of the story is. Then call on children to use picture clues to tell what happens in this story. Ask if children think Dan and Meg still have a problem at the end of the story, and if not, why.

Tell children that they will read this story with the rest of the class.

Day 3

Objective

- read and write high-frequency words *are*, *away*, *does*, *he*, *live*, *pull*, *they*, *where*

Materials

- Letter Cards: *a* (2), *d*, *e* (2), *h*, *i*, *l* (2), *o*, *p*, *r*, *s*, *t*, *u*, *v*, *w*, *y*
- Anthology: *A Surprise for Zig Bug*

RETEACH

SKILL FOCUS: 25–30 MINUTES

High-Frequency Words

Teach

Write *are*, *away*, *does*, *he*, *live*, *pull*, *they*, and *where* on the board and read each word. On a rereading, have children read the words along with you. Then distribute the Letter Cards. Draw three squares on the board, and tell children that you need their help to spell the word *are*. You might want to emphasize the use of *are* in a sentence to be certain they understand the word's meaning. For example, say, *We are learning to read lots of new words.* Say:

The word are *has three letters. Who will come up and help me identify the letters in the word? Who has the letters* a, r, *and* e? *Stand up here and I'll write the word* are *in the boxes.*

Lead children in a cheer to help them remember the word. Clap on each letter and syllable as children spell and say the word together: *a-r-e, are!* Then tell children to jump when you point to each of their cards. Lead a new "hop-it" cheer *a-r-e, are!*

Repeat the procedure for the words *away*, *does*, *he*, *live*, *pull*, *they*, and *where*.

Write the following sentences on the board, and read them with children:

Where does he live?

Pull the door shut.

They are away.

Check each child's ability to pronounce *are*, *away*, *does*, *he*, *live*, *pull*, *they*, and *where* as the child reads each sentence.

Practice

Give children these sentence frames. Have them complete the sentences by drawing or writing to fill in the blanks.

> Are you_____?
>
> Where does_____ live?
>
> They are away in the_____.
>
> He is_____.

Apply

Have children show and read their sentences to the class. Then ask children to exchange and read one another's sentences.

LITERATURE FOCUS: 10–15 MINUTES

Preview *A Surprise for Zig Bug*

Walk children through *A Surprise for Zig Bug*, on pages 177–193 in their Anthology. Discuss the illustrations with children. Explain that the characters' names are Zig Bug, Kip Bug, and Zag Bug.

Use words from the story such as *bug*, *hut*, *tug*, *jug*, and *quit*.

Note the suggestions in the Extra Support box on Teacher's Edition page T201.

Day 4

SKILL FOCUS: PHONICS 10-15 MINUTES

Consonants *q, j, z*

Teach

Display the Letter Cards *q, u, j,* and *z.* Have children name each letter with you. Tell them that *q* is always followed by *u* in a word and that letters *qu* together stand for the /kw/ sound. Say the letter sounds: *qu* /kw/; *j* /j/; *z* /z/.

Divide the Picture Cards for initial *qu, j,* and *z* among the children. Say:

Find other children whose picture names begin with the same sound as yours. Everyone whose picture name begins the same, stand together.

Have children in each group name their cards, say the beginning sound, and name the letter or letters that stand for that sound.

Help children differentiate among the consonant sounds by pointing out the position of their lips, teeth, and tongue, and have them feel for a vibration of the voice box:

- /kw/ — combination of /k/ and /w/ sounds; begins with back of tongue against roof of mouth, vibration, and ends with rounded lips, tongue behind lower teeth; vibration

- /j/ — tongue against the roof of the mouth; vibration

- /z/ — tongue in the middle of the mouth, teeth closed; vibration

Practice

Display Letter Cards for *q, u, j,* and *z* in random order on the chalk ledge, and post the *queen* Picture Card above the letters. Have children identify the picture. Call on a child to tell what sound he or she hears at the beginning of /kwēn/. Write the word *queen* on the board and have a child place the correct Letter Cards under the picture. Point out again that that the letters *qu* together stand for the /kw/ sound. Repeat with Picture Cards for *jam* and *zip*, asking children what sound they hear at the beginning of each word.

Apply

Have children look for words that begin with *qu, j,* and *z* in *A Surprise for Zig Bug.* Each time a child finds a word with *qu, j,* or *z,* he or she should read the word aloud as you write it on the appropriate place on a Word Pattern Board. Have children come to the chart to underline the *qu, j,* or *z* in each word.

Objectives

- recognize *q, j,* and *z* and the sounds they represent
- read words with *q, j,* and *z*

Materials

- Letter Cards: *q, u, j,* and *z*
- Picture Cards: *jam, jar, jeans, jeep, jet, jug, queen, quill, quilt, zebra, zigzag, zip, zoo*
- Anthology: *A Surprise for Zig Bug*

SKILL FOCUS: PHONICS   10–15 MINUTES

Blending Short *u* Words

Teach

Display the Letter Card *u* and remind children of the sound the letter *u* makes: /ŭ/. Have them repeat it after you: /ŭ/ - /ŭ/- /ŭ/. Be sure children have their mouth in the correct position as they say the sound. Hold up the Picture Card for *under* and ask children to identify the picture. Ask them which sound *under* begins with, /ŭ/ or /ĕ/. Do the same with the Picture Cards for *egg* and *up*.

Use the Letter Cards to model how to blend the word *nut* using Blending Routine 2. Have children say the sound for *n*, /n/, the sound for *u*, /ŭ/, then blend /nnnŭ ŭ ŭ/. Finally, have them say the sound for *t*, /t/ blend /nnnŭ ŭ ŭt/, and say *nut*.

Remind children that they can make words by adding different sounds to the beginning and end of short *u*. Have children blend the following sounds using Blending Routine 2: /kŭ ŭ ŭt/, /hŭ ŭ ŭg/, /bŭ ŭ ŭn/.

Practice

Write *nut* on the board. Have a volunteer find the matching Picture Card and Word Card and then read the word aloud. Repeat the procedure with the words *rug, hut, run, up, hug,* and *bug*.

Apply

Have children look for words with short *u* in *A Surprise for Zig Bug*. Each time a child finds a word, ask him or her to read the word aloud and help you to write it on the board. Have all children repeat the word as the child at the board circles the *u*.

LITERATURE FOCUS: 10–15 MINUTES

Review *A Surprise for Zig Bug*

Reread the story together with children. Have partners look through the story to find and read words with short *u* and the consonants *q, j,* and *z*.

Objectives
- blend phonemes
- associate the short *u* sound with the letter *u*
- independently read words with short *u*

Materials
- Letter Cards: *n, t, u*
- Picture Cards: *bug, egg , hug, hut, nut, rug, run, under, up*
- Word Cards: *bug, hug, hut, nut, rug, run, up*
- Anthology: *A Surprise for Zig Bug*

Day 5

Objectives

- identify the setting, characters, and plot of a story
- use a story map to identify the elements of a story

Materials

- Phonics Library: *The Bug Kit, Quit It, Zig!*
- Anthology: *Quit It, Bug!, A Surprise for Zig Bug*

Story Structure

Teach

Ask children if they know the well-known children's fairytale, *Goldilocks and the Three Bears*. If they don't know the story, tell it to them. Then ask them questions such as the following:

- *Who are the characters in the story?* (Goldilocks and the three bears)

- *Where does the story take place?* (the woods, the home of the three bears)

- *What happens in the story?* (Goldilocks explores the house of the three bears.)

Explain to children that many stories include these elements: *characters,* the people or animals; a *setting,* the place the story happens; and a *plot,* events in the story, often with a story problem and solution. You might want to write the words *Character* (Who?), *Setting* (Where?) and *Plot* (What happens?) on the chalkboard.

Practice

Discuss the story *A Surprise for Zig Bug* by Pam Muñoz Ryan. Begin by asking children to identify the characters in the story. Allow them to look through the pages of the story to be certain they have identified each of the characters. Write the word *Character* on the board or chart paper and list the names of the story characters. Continue in this same way as children identify the *Setting* and story *Plot*. If children are uncertain about the setting or plot, encourage them to look at the illustrations for clues.

Apply

Assign children the roles of Zig, Zag, and Kip. Have other children draw the setting on the chalkboard. Then ask a child to tell the plot of the story while the story characters act it out. When finished, work with children to complete a story map. Some children may want to draw pictures to indicate their responses.

Revisit *The Bug Kit, Quit It, Zig!, Quit It, Bug!,* and *A Surprise for Zig Bug*

Page through the stories with children. Discuss the different characters, settings, and story events in each of the stories.

Have children list all the short *u* words found in the stories.

Tell children to look through *Quit It, Bug!* and *A Surprise for Zig Bug* for the following high-frequency words: *are, away, does, he, live, pull, they, where.*

Have children read aloud selected sentences or pages from the stories.

Theme 3

Let's Look Around!

Day 1

PRETEACH

SKILL FOCUS: PHONICS 10–15 MINUTES

Double Final Consonants

Teach

Recite and repeat the chant shown, having children join in.

> CHANT
> All that stuff
> Makes such a mess!
> I pick some up,
> And now there's less.

Say *stuff*, emphasizing the final /f/. Print *stuff* on the board and underline the final consonants. Have children repeat *stuff* with you. Point out that the letters *ff* stand for one sound, /f/. Follow a similar procedure for *mess*, pointing out that the letters *ss* stand for one sound, /s/.

Say *pick*, emphasizing the final sound. Print *pick* on the board, underlining the letters *ck*. Tell children that the letters *ck* together stand for one sound, /k/. Have children repeat the word *pick* with you.

Blend

Print the name *Jill* on the board and underline the letters *ll*. Use Blending Routine 1 to model how to blend the sounds, stretching /l/. Have children blend and say the word with you. Then have children blend and say the word on their own. Repeat with *Jeff, Matt,* and *miss*.

Print the name *Jack* on the board, underlining the letters *ck*. Repeat the blending process stretching /k/. Repeat with *sock, tack,* and *lick*.

Guided Practice

Display or **distribute** Teaching Master ES3-1. Tell children that the wolf and the pig are from *The Three Little Pigs*.

Direct attention to the first frame, and ask children to find words that end with the same consonants. (will, huff, puff) Help children to use sounds they know to read the words and the wolf's dialogue.

Read the first sentence of the second frame with children. Help them find and read the word that ends with the letters *ck*. Follow a similar procedure for the second sentence, having children identify the words that end with the letters *ll*.

Objectives

- recognize double final consonants and their sounds
- associate final /k/ sound with the letters *ck*

Materials

- Teaching Master ES3-1

Technology

Education Place
www.eduplace.com
Seasons

Audio CD
Animals in the Cold, Seasons
Audio CD for **Let's Look Around!**

Lexia Phonics CD-ROM
Primary Intervention

SKILL FOCUS: PHONICS — 10–15 MINUTES

Plurals with -s

Teach

Recite and repeat the chant, telling children to join in.

> **CHANT**
> The boys are here.
> The girls are there.
> But the dogs and cats
> are everywhere!

Say *boys*, stretching out the final /s/. Then have children say it. Print *boy* and *boys* on the board. Help children compare the two words, letter by letter. Underline the -s ending on *boys*. Tell children that the -s ending makes this word mean "more than one boy." Repeat the chant again asking children to listen for other words that have the -s ending.

Blend

Distribute the Word Card *bat*. Using Blending Routine 1, model how to blend the word. Then have children blend and say the word. Give a card with the -s ending to another child. Have children hold the cards together and blend *bats*. Repeat with *leg, lock, pet*, and *dog*.

Practice/Apply

Distribute Practice Master ES3-1, discuss the illustrations, and read the directions with children.

Have children complete the page and then read the sentences aloud.

Check that children are reading the plural words correctly.

LITERATURE FOCUS: — 10–15 MINUTES

Preview *Cabs, Cabs, Cabs*

Walk children through *Cabs, Cabs, Cabs*. Ask children to look at the picture on page 6 and count the cabs. Write the word *cab* and ask children what you need to add to the word to make it more than one cab. *(s)*

Objective

- blend and read words with the plural ending -s as /s/ and /z/

Materials

- Practice Master ES3-1
- Word Cards: *bat, dog, leg, lock, pet*
- suffix card: *s*
- Phonics Library: *Cabs, Cabs, Cabs*

Day 2

Objective
- identify topic, main idea, and details of a story

Materials
- Teaching Master ES3-2
- Practice Master ES3-2
- Anthology: *Animals in the Cold*

SKILL FOCUS: COMPREHENSION   25–30 MINUTES

Topic, Main Idea, Details

Teach

Tell children that some authors write stories to help us learn information.

Write the following story on the board.

> ## School
> We do many things in school.
> We read in school.
> We play outside.
> We can draw in school too.

Read the story with children.

Point to the title and read it with children. Explain that the title of a story usually tells what the story is about.

Reread the first sentence with children. Explain that this is the most important idea of the story and is called the main idea.

Reread the remaining sentences. Point out that they tell more about the main idea, and that they are called details.

Guided Practice

Display or **distribute** Teaching Master ES3-2, and read the story with children.

Ask *What is this story about?* (playing outside) Help children write *playing outside* on the chart to identify the topic.

Ask *What is the most important idea of this story?* (There are many things to play outside.) Help children write *There are many things to play outside* on the chart to identify the main idea.

Ask *What do the details tell about playing outside?* (They list different outdoor games.) Help children add these details to the chart. When the chart is complete, have children identify:

- the topic of the whole story

- the main idea sentence

- three details that tell more about the main idea

Note: You may wish to leave the Teaching Master on display for children's reference as they complete the Practice Master.

Practice/Apply

Distribute Practice Master ES3-2 and read the directions with children. Have them complete the Practice Master independently.

Remind them to use sounds they know to read the story.

Check children's work to be sure they understand the concepts of topic, main idea, and details.

LITERATURE FOCUS: 10–15 MINUTES

Preview *Animals in the Cold*

Walk children through *Animals in the Cold*. Discuss the illustrations, naming the animals for children.

Ask children what they think the topic of this story will be. Ask them to name some of the details they may read about.

Tell children they will read this story with the rest of the class.

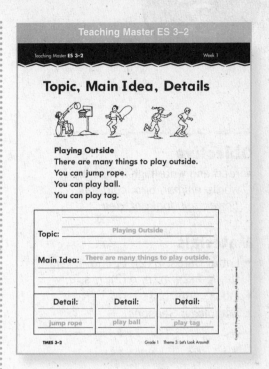

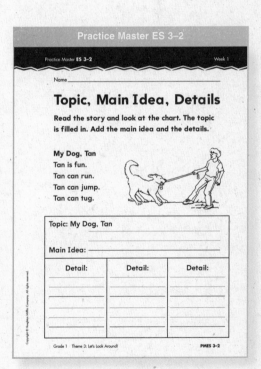

Day 3

SKILL FOCUS: 25–30 MINUTES

High-Frequency Words

Teach

Write the words *animal, bird, cold, fall, flower, full, look, of,* and *see* on the board. Read the words aloud, pointing to each as you go. Then have children read the words along with you.

Display the Letter Cards on the chalk tray. Ask the group, *How many letters are in the word animal?*

Draw six squares on the board.

Ask two children to come up. Ask one child to find the letters *a, n,* and *i,* and the other to find the letters *m, a,* and *l.* Ask the children to help you spell *animal.* Say, *show me the letter I should write in the first box, the second box, and so on. How many different letters did I write? How many times did I write the letter* a? *How many times did I write the letter* l?

Tell the children to put the letters back on the chalk tray with the other cards. Have them help lead the cheer to remember the word. Tap your right index finger in your left palm for each letter and syllable as you spell and say the word: *a-n-i-m-a-l, an-i-mal!*

Repeat the lesson procedure with the other words in the list. Remind children to use what they know about letters and sounds to help them remember the words.

Write the following sentences on the board, and read them together with children:

Fall is full of nice things.

See the animal by the flower?

Look at the bird fly!

It will not be cold.

Check each child's ability to pronounce *animal, bird, cold, fall, flower, fall, look, of,* and *see* as the child reads each sentence.

Objective

- read and write high-frequency words *animal, bird, cold, fall, flower, full, look, of, see*

Materials

- Letter Cards: *a* (2), *b, c, d, e* (2), *f, i, k, l* (2), *m, n, o* (2), *r, s, u, w*
- index cards
- Anthology: *Seasons*

Practice

Write the following sentence on the board: *I see a big animal*. Ask children if they can find the word *see* in the sentence. Point to each word and ask them if it is *see*. Tell children to slap their knees and say the word with you when you read the word *see*. Next have children find the word *animal*.

Repeat the procedure with each of these sentences: *It can be cold in the fall. Look at the bird. I have a flower. The vat is full of soup.*

Apply

Have children work in pairs. Give each pair nine large index cards and have them write the new words on them. Then have them go back to the story *Seasons* and find each of the words. When children match the word, have them read the sentence in the story that contains the word. Have them continue in this way until they have matched all of the words and read all the sentences.

LITERATURE FOCUS: 10–15 MINUTES

Preview *Seasons*

Walk children through *Seasons* on pages 21–39 in their Anthology.

Discuss the illustrations and use words from the story such as *grass, buds, eggs, kick, buzz, quack,* and *pass.*

Note the suggestions in the Extra Support boxes on Teacher's Edition pages T57 and T62.

Day 4

Objectives

- recognize *ck, ll, gg,* and *ss* and the sounds they represent at the end of words
- read words ending with *ck, ll, gg,* and *ss*

Materials

- Letter Cards: *c, g* (2), *k, l* (2), *s* (2)
- Sound/Spelling Card: *cat*
- 3 cups
- Anthology: *Seasons*

SKILL FOCUS: PHONICS   10–15 MINUTES

Double Final Consonants

Teach

Ask children to listen for the sound at the end of the word *lock.* (/k/) Hold up the *cat* Sound/Spelling Card and point out the _*ck.* Explain that sometimes two consonant letters together can stand for one sound. In *lock,* the two letters *c* and *k* stand for one sound, /k/. Write *lock* on the board, have a child circle the *ck.* Blend the word *lock* with children using Blending Routine 2. Have them say the sound for *l,* /l/, then the sound for *o,* /ŏ/, and blend /lllŏŏŏ/. Then have them say the sound for *ck,* /k/, and say /lllŏŏŏk/, *lock.*

Tell children that sometimes two of the same consonants can stand for one sound in a word, such as *ll,* /l/, *gg,* /g/, and *ss,* /s/. Have children listen for the ending sound in the words *bell, egg,* and *miss.* Write each word on the board. Have a child circle the double consonant in each word and have the class say the sound. Then help the class to blend each word using Blending Routine 2.

Practice

Place Letter Cards for *ck, ll, gg,* and *ss* on a chalk ledge. Write *pi_ _* on the board and say *pick.* Ask a child to say the sound at the end of *pick* and choose the letters from the chalk ledge that would complete the word. (*ck*) Then fill in the *ck* and have the class blend, /p ĭ ĭ ĭk/, *pick.* Repeat this process for the words *doll, egg,* and *kiss.*

Apply

Have children look for words that end with *ck* and double consonants in *Seasons.* Each time a child finds a word, he or she should blend and read the word aloud as you write it on the appropriate place on the Word Pattern Board.

Plurals with -s

Teach

Display one cup on a table. Place the Word Card for *cup* next to it and help children read the word. Place two cups on another part of the table. Explain that there is more than one cup, and have children say *cups*. Have them listen for the sound at the end of *cups*, /s/. Write *s* on a self-stick note and place it on the Word Card *cup* so that it now reads *cups*. Explain that when a naming word tells about more than one person, place, or thing it often ends in the letter *s*, /s/. Have children blend /cŭpsss/ emphasizing the *s*.

Display the Word Card *cup* and the self-stick *s* separately. Explain that *cup* is a base word and the *-s* that has been added to it is an ending.

Hold up the *zebra* Sound/Spelling Card. Explain that sometimes when an *s* is at the end of a word it is pronounced /z/. Have children listen for the /z/ sound in *cans*, write it on the board, and have a child circle the *s* while the group says /z/. Help children to blend *cans* using Blending Routine 2.

Practice

Draw a large dot on the board and write *dot* below it. Help children blend and say the word. Ask children how many dots are on the board. (one) Then ask a child to draw another dot and change the word *dot* to mean more than one. Have a volunteer underline the base word and circle the ending. Help children to blend and read the new words.

Apply

Have children look for plurals with *-s* in *Seasons*. Each time a child finds a plural with *-s*, he or she should read it aloud and write it in a column on the board. After the search is complete, have volunteers identify the singular base word for each plural and come to the board to circle it.

Review *Seasons*

Reread the story together with children. Ask children to make a list of words ending with a double consonant.

Objectives
- understand that adding *-s* to a naming word makes the word mean more than one
- blend and read words with the plural ending *-s* as /s/ and /z/

Materials
- Word Card: *cup*
- Sound/Spelling Card: *zebra*
- Anthology: *Seasons*

Day 5

RETEACH

SKILL FOCUS: COMPREHENSION   25–30 MINUTES

Topic, Main Ideas, Details/Summarizing

Teach

Begin a discussion of the story *Seasons* by Ashley Wolff by asking children what the story is mostly about. (seasons) Explain that the title of a story often tells us the topic. Have children name the four seasons.

Ask the children, *What is the main idea of the story?* If children have difficulty stating the main idea, that the seasons change, ask them, *What are the animals doing in each season?* Guide them to conclude that animals are engaged in different activities in different seasons because the weather changes. Explain that the main idea tells us the most important idea about the topic *Seasons*.

Ask the children about each season and what animals do in the story in different seasons. Explain to them that these story details are important because they explain the main idea, *The seasons change*.

Tell children that the topic, main ideas, and details make up the summary of the story.

Practice

Draw the graphic organizer shown here on the board or on chart paper.

Ask children to assist you in completing the graphic organizer for the story *Seasons*.

Objectives

- identify the topic, main ideas, details/summarizing
- use the topic, main ideas, and details/summarizing to understand a text structure

Materials

- Phonics Library: *Cabs, Cabs, Cabs; Fall Naps*
- Anthology: *Animals in the Cold, Seasons*

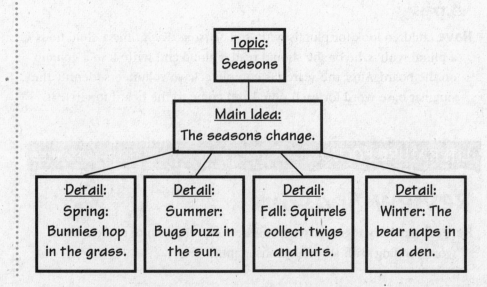

Apply

Complete a graphic organizer such as the one in the Practice activity for another nonfiction story children know, such as one about animals, holidays, or weather.

Revisit *Cabs, Cabs, Cabs; Fall Naps; Animals in the Cold;* and *Seasons*

Page through the stories with children. Then ask them to tell about the topic of each story.

Ask children to make a list of words that have a plural *-s* at the end.

Tell children to look through *Seasons* to find the following high-frequency words: *animal, bird, cold, fall, flower, full, look, of, see.*

Have children read aloud their favorite sentences or pages from the stories.

Day 1

PRETEACH

SKILL FOCUS: PHONICS — 10–15 MINUTES

Verb Ending -ed

Teach

Recite and repeat the chant shown, having children join in.

> **CHANT**
> The dog can jump.
> Jump, dog, jump!
> The dog jumped, and jumped, and jumped.

Say *jumped*, emphasizing the /d/. Have children say *jumped* several times. Print *jump* and *jumped* on the board. Help children compare the two words, letter by letter, so that they see the *-ed* ending at the end of *jumped*. Underline the *-ed* ending in *jumped*. Tell children that *-ed* is an ending shows that the action happened in the past.

Blend

Give the word card *pull* to one child. Using Blending Routine 1, model how to blend the word. Then have children blend and say the word.

Give a card with the ending *ed* to another child. Have that child stand next to the child with *pull*. Have the children move the cards together to make *pulled*. Then have them blend the sounds and say *pulled*. Repeat with other action words, such as *fill* and *pack*.

Guided Practice

Display or **distribute** Teaching Master ES3-3, discuss the illustration, and read the sentences with children. Have them find the words with the *-ed* ending. *(packed, filled)* Help children to read the sentences aloud.

Monitor them to be sure they are reading the *-ed* words correctly.

Objective

- blend and read verbs with the ending *-ed*

Materials

- Teaching Master ES3-3
- word cards: *fill, pack, pull*
- suffix card: *ed*

Education Place

www.eduplace.com
Miss Jill's Ice Cream Shop

Audio CD

Ham and Eggs,
Miss Jill's Ice Cream Shop
Audio CD for **Let's Look Around!**

Lexia Phonics CD-ROM

Primary Intervention

SKILL FOCUS: PHONICS | 10–15 MINUTES

Possessives with 's

Teach

Recite and repeat the chant, asking children to join in.

> **CHANT**
> Mack's dog is big.
> Nan's cat is small.
> But nobody has seen
> Sam's pet at all.

Say *Mack's dog*, emphasizing the final /s/ on *Mack's*. Ask children who owns the dog. (Mack) Print *Mack* and *Mack's* on the board. Help children compare the two words, letter by letter, so that they see that one word ends with *'s*. Tell children that the *'s* shows that something belongs to Mack. Repeat the process for *Nan's* and *Sam's*.

Blend

Give the word card *Jack* to one child. Using Blending Routine 1, model how to blend the word. Then have children blend and say the word. Give a card with *'s* to another child. Have that child stand next to the child with *Jack*. Then have children move the cards together to make *Jack's*. Have them blend and say *Jack's*.

Practice/Apply

Distribute Practice Master ES3-3, discuss the illustrations, and read the directions with children. Have them complete the Practice Master independently.

Check children's responses to see if they know that *'s* shows ownership.

LITERATURE FOCUS: | 10–15 MINUTES

Preview *Lots of Picking*

Walk children through *Lots of Picking* and tell them that the girl is named Kim. Have children look at the picture of Kim's dad on page 18.

Objective

- read nouns with *'s*

Materials

- Practice Master ES3-3
- cards: *Jack, 's*
- Phonics Library: *Lots of Picking*

Teaching Master ES 3–3

Teaching Master **ES 3-3**   Week 2

Verb Ending -*ed*

Jack packed his bags.
He filled up three bags!

TMES 3-3   Grade 1   Theme 3: Let's Look Around!

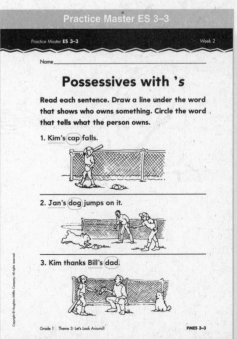

Practice Master ES 3–3

Practice Master **ES 3-3**   Week 2

Name_____

Possessives with 's

Read each sentence. Draw a line under the word that shows who owns something. Circle the word that tells what the person owns.

1. Kim's cap falls.

2. Jan's dog jumps on it.

3. Kim thanks Bill's dad.

Grade 1   Theme 3: Let's Look Around!   PMES 3-3

Day 2

Objective
- make predictions based on personal knowledge and story details

Materials
- Teaching Master ES3-4
- Practice Master ES3-4
- Anthology: *Ham and Eggs*

SKILL FOCUS: COMPREHENSION   25–30 MINUTES

Making Predictions

Teach

Call on a volunteer to look out the window and describe the weather. Then ask a question that requires the volunteer to make a prediction, for example: *Do you think it will rain today? Do you think the sun will come out today?*

Discuss with children how they can predict, or guess, what the weather might be like. Point out that they may know from their own experiences that dark clouds often bring rain.

Lead children to see that they make predictions many times throughout the day, often without thinking about it. Ask them to make predictions about tomorrow's school day based on classroom routines, for example:

What will we do first in the morning?

What will we do after reading?

When will we have recess?

Tell children that we can also make predictions when we read stories. Explain that making predictions can help readers to better understand a story.

Guided Practice

Display or **distribute** Teaching Master ES3-4, and have children look at the picture. Read the sentences under the picture with them.

Read the question to children, and help them jot down a word to predict what the weather is like at Gram's. Have them share their ideas. (Most children will suggest *cold* or *snowy*.)

Ask children how they were able to figure out that it is cold where Jim is going. If needed, point out these clues: the picture shows that Jim is packing warm things—mittens, hat, snow boots, pants, sweaters; the words say that *He will need warm things*.

Explain that children were able to make a prediction about what the weather will be like at Gram's by using what they know about warm clothing.

Practice/Apply

Distribute Practice Master ES3-4 to children and read the directions with them. Make sure children understand that they will cut out all of the pictures at the bottom of the page but that they will paste only two of them. Have them complete the Practice Master independently.

Have children share their predictions and tell what they were thinking when they made them.

Check children's responses to be sure they understand how to make predictions.

LITERATURE FOCUS: 10–15 MINUTES

Preview *Ham and Eggs*

Read aloud the title on page 47, and discuss the illustration. Then have children look at the illustrations on the next two pages of the story and discuss what is happening in each.

Ask children to predict what Dad and the children will do. If needed, remind children that Dad and the children are sitting in a diner, looking at menus.

Tell children they will find out if their predictions are correct when they read the story with the rest of the class.

Teaching Master ES 3–4

Practice Master ES 3–4

Day 3

| SKILL FOCUS: | 25–30 MINUTES |

High-Frequency Words

Teach

Write the words *all, call, eat, every, first, never, paper, shall,* and *why* on the board. Read the words aloud, pointing to each as you go.

Display the Letter Cards on the chalk tray. Ask the group, *How many letters are in the word* all?

Draw three squares on the board.

Ask two children to come up. Ask one to find the letter *a,* and the other to find the letter *l.* Ask the children to help you spell *all.* You might say, for example, *Show me the letter I should write in the first box* (in the second box, and so on). Once you have written the word, ask children to read it along with you.

Tell the children to put the letters back on the chalk tray with the other cards. Have them help lead the cheer to remember the word. Tap your right index finger in your left palm for each letter and syllable as you spell and say the word: *a-l-l, all!*

Repeat the lesson procedure with the other words in the list.

Write the following sentences on the board, and read them together with children:

We never eat together.

Why not call a friend?

First, put away your paper.

Now, shall we eat?

Check each child's ability to pronounce *all, call, eat, every, first, never, paper, shall,* and *why* as the child reads each sentence.

Practice

Write the following sentence on the board: *We shall eat.* Ask children if they can find the word *shall* in the sentence. Point to each word and ask them if it is *shall.* Tell children to tap their finger and say the word with you when you read the word *shall.* Read the sentence. Next have them find the word *eat.*

Repeat the procedure with each of these sentences: *Why was Pig the first to eat? Why do all of you call for the paper every day? I never get the paper.*

Objective

• read and write high-frequency words *all, call, eat, every, first, never, paper, shall, why*

Materials

• Letter Cards: *a, c, e* (2), *f, h, i, l* (2), *n, p* (2), *r, s, t, v, w, y*
• index cards
• Anthology: *Miss Jill's Ice Cream Shop*

Apply

Have children work in pairs. Give each pair nine large index cards and
have them write the new words on them. Then have them go back to
Miss Jill's Ice Cream Shop and find each of the words. When children
match the word, have them read the sentence in the story that contains
the word. Have them continue in this way until they have matched all
of the words and read all the sentences.

LITERATURE FOCUS: 10–15 MINUTES

Preview *Miss Jill's Ice Cream Shop*

Walk children through *Miss Jill's Ice Cream Shop* on pages 55–71 in
their Anthology.

Discuss the illustrations, naming the characters Miss Jill, Jack, and Bill.
Use words from the story such as *eating, fixed, likes, filled, licked,
falling,* and *bumped.*

Note the suggestions in the Extra Support box on Teacher's Edition
page T129.

Day 4

Objectives

- understand that -s, -ed, and -ing can be added to action words
- independently read action words with -s, -ed, and -ing

Materials

- Anthology: *Miss Jill's Ice Cream Shop*

Verb Endings -s, -ed, -ing

Teach

Write the word *lick* on the chalkboard and have children say it after you. Remind them that *lick* is an action word that tells what a person or animal does. Then point to the word *lick* and explain that *lick* is a base word to which different endings can be added. Then write *licks, licked,* and *licking* under *lick*. Point to the words *licks, licked,* and *licking,* and circle the base word *lick* in each word. Explain that this part of a word is called the base word and the letter or letters that have been added to it is called the ending.

Write the following sentences on the chalkboard:

[Jason] licks his ice cream cone.

[Lindsay and Bob] lick their ice cream cones.

Repeat each sentence and ask children to listen carefully for the word *lick* or *licks*. Then underline the *s* in *licks*.

Write these sentences on the chalkboard:

Today I am licking a strawberry ice cream cone.

Yesterday I licked a chocolate ice cream cone.

Underline the *ed* in *licked* and the *ing* in *licking*. Repeat the two sentences, emphasizing the endings in *licked* and *licking*.

Practice

Write the following base words on the board:

    walk   *jump*   *help*

Read the base words aloud, and have children repeat them after you. Then copy each word three times in columns. Have volunteers come to the board to add -s, -ed, and -ing to each base word and use each of the new words in a sentence.

Apply

Have pairs of children find words with -s, -ed, and -ing in *Miss Jill's Ice Cream Shop*. Each time children find an -s, -ed, or -ing word, he or she should read it aloud while you write the word on the board. Have volunteers come to the board, underline the base word, and circle the ending in each word.

Possessives with 's

Teach

Ask a volunteer to stand at the front of class with a pencil. Point to the pencil and say: *Whose pencil is this?* When someone says, *It's _____'s pencil*, write on the board, _____'s *pencil*. Circle the possessive noun and remind children that *'s* shows who something belongs to.

Write the title *Miss Jill's Ice Cream Shop* on the chalkboard. Circle the apostrophe and the *s* in the name. Remind children that adding *'s* to the name *Miss Jill* tells readers who the dinner belongs to. Remind children that another way to say the same thing is to say, *the ice cream shop of Miss Jill.* Write the following on the board:

The hat of Jim — Jim's hat   The book of the girl — the girl's book

Read the phrases aloud and remind children that they mean the same thing. Then have volunteers display something they own and ask children to tell to whom the items belong. Write each possessive noun on the board, and have the group read them aloud.

Practice

Write the following on the board:

the pigs wig   the cats hat   Sams ham   Dans van

Read each phrase aloud and ask to whom each item belongs. Ask children what is missing in each group of words. Have children add the missing apostrophe in each phrase.

Apply

Have pairs of children find possessives in *Miss Jill's Ice Cream Shop*. Each time children find a possessive, they should read it aloud while you write it on the board. Have volunteers come to the board to tell who owns what and to circle the apostrophe in each possessive.

Review *Miss Jill's Ice Cream Shop*

Reread the story together with children. Ask children to make a list of words from the story that have an *-s, -ed, -ing,* or *'s* ending.

Objectives

- understand that possessives are words that show ownership
- recognize that *'s* shows ownership
- independently read possessives

Materials

- Anthology: *Miss Jill's Ice Cream Shop*

Making Predictions

Teach

Ask children how they know when it is lunchtime. Encourage them to describe their understanding of lunchtime in terms of experience. (It is the same time every day, or We always eat lunch after ____.) Explain to children that they are making a prediction about what will happen based on what they already know and have experienced. Ask them what other events they can predict will happen today. Ask them, *What will happen tomorrow? Will you come to school? Why?* (It's Tuesday.) Or, ask *Why not?* (It will be Saturday.)

Explain to children that we can make predictions when we read stories, too. Making predictions helps us understand the story. We make predictions about story events and story characters based on details in the story and our own knowledge.

Practice

Discuss the story *Miss Jill's Ice Cream Shop* by Nancy Shaw, using the term "making predictions."

Ask the children, *What did Bill predict when he saw that Jack wanted every kind of ice cream?* (He predicted that Jack would never eat it all.) *Why did Bill predict that?* (Because it was too much ice cream for one pig.) Guide the children to understand that we make predictions based on what we know about someone or something.

Apply

Point out to children that in the story, Bill and Jack are very excited to eat ice cream at Miss Jill's shop. Ask children how they knew the characters were happy about the ice cream. (They look happy and excited; Jack orders every kind of ice cream.)

Tell children to use what they know about the story characters and the story events to tell whether they think Bill and Jack would go back to Miss Jill's shop. Have children draw a picture to show what they think would happen.

Objectives
- make predictions based on their knowledge
- apply what they have learned to make new predictions

Materials
- Phonics Library: *Lots of Picking, Bill Bird*
- Anthology: *Ham and Eggs, Miss Jill's Ice Cream Shop*

LITERATURE FOCUS: 10–15 MINUTES

Revisit *Lots of Picking, Bill Bird, Ham and Eggs,* and *Miss Jill's Ice Cream Shop*

Page through each of the stories, having children look for words with the endings *-s, -ed, -ing,* and *'s.*

Ask them to predict what Kim and her dad will do with all the apples they picked in *Lots of Picking.*

Tell children to look through *Miss Jill's Ice Cream Shop* to find the following high-frequency words: *all, call, eat, every, first, never, paper, shall, why.*

Have children read aloud selected sentences or pages from the stories.

Day 1

PRETEACH

SKILL FOCUS: PHONICS   10–15 MINUTES

Clusters with *r*

Teach

Recite and repeat the chant shown. Tell children to join in.

> **CHANT**
> Bears growl,
> Yes, they do.
> Gr-r-r, gr-r-r!
> Yes, it's true!

Say *growl*, stretching out and isolating /gr/. Then have children say *growl* several times. Also have them make growling sounds: *grr, grr!*

Print the letters *gr* on the board. Tell children that these letters stand for the /gr/ sounds. Ask what sounds children hear at the beginning of *growl*. (/g/, /r/)

Follow a similar procedure with the word *frog*, explaining that frogs sometimes make a croaking sound. Point out that the letters *fr* stand for the beginning sounds in *frog*, while the letters *cr* stand for the beginning sounds in *croak*. Tell children that all three words—*growl*, *frog*, and *croak*—begin with a consonant sound followed by /r/.

Blend

Give the word card *frog* to one child. Using Blending Routine 1, model how to blend the sounds, stretching the /fr/ sounds and then saying the word. Have children blend and say the word with you. Finally, have children blend the word on their own. Repeat the process with the words *trip*, *crab*, and *grass*.

Guided Practice

Display or **distribute** Teaching Master ES3-5 and discuss the illustrations.

Direct children's attention to the first sentence. Tell them to use what they know about sounds as they read the sentence with you. Repeat for the second sentence in the first set. Have children read the second set of sentences aloud.

Help children underline all of the words that begin with clusters with *r*.

Check that children are blending *r* cluster words correctly.

Objective

- blend and read words beginning with clusters with *r*

Materials

- Teaching Master ES3-5
- word cards: *crab, frog, grass, trip*

Technology

Education Place

www.eduplace.com
At the Aquarium

Audio CD

The Trip,
At the Aquarium
Audio CD for **Let's Look Around!**

Lexia Phonics
CD-ROM

Primary Intervention

SKILL FOCUS: PHONICS   10–15 MINUTES

Contractions with 's

Teach

Recite and repeat the chant, having children join in as they are able.

> **CHANT**
>
> Now where's Jack?
>
> He's out with Jill.
>
> It's time for them
>
> To climb the hill.

Say *where's*, emphasizing the final sound. Tell children that *where's* is a short way to say *where is*. Print *where is* and *where's* on the board. Help children compare *where is* and *where's*. Point out that in *where's*, the apostrophe takes the place of the letter *i* in *is*. Demonstrate how to write an apostrophe. Repeat with *he's* and *it's*.

Blend

Give the word card *it* to one child. Using Blending Routine 1, model how to blend the word. Then have children blend and say *it*. Give a card with *'s* to another child. Have children move their two cards together to make *it's*. Have the group blend and say *it's*.

Practice/Apply

Distribute Practice Master ES3-5, and discuss the illustrations. Have children find in each sentence a word that ends with *'s*. Then have them read the two choices below the sentence and circle the one that means the same thing as the word with the *'s*.

Check children's ability to read contractions with *'s*.

LITERATURE FOCUS: 10–15 MINUTES

Preview *Let's Trim the Track!*

Walk children through *Let's Trim the Track!* Tell them that the track in this story is a place where people can run. Ask if they know another kind of track. Help children find words with clusters with *r*.

Objective

- blend and read contractions with *'s*

Materials

- Practice Master ES3-5
- cards: *it*, *'s*
- Phonics Library: *Let's Trim the Track!*

Teaching Master ES 3–5

Practice Master ES 3–5

Day 2

SKILL FOCUS: COMPREHENSION   25–30 MINUTES

Categorize and Classify

Teach

Tell children to look around the classroom and observe the way in which things in the classroom are organized. Ask children why the classroom might be set up in such a way. For example:

Why do you think we keep all the books in one corner?

Why do we keep all the art supplies together?

Why do we keep blocks in a different area from board games?

Help children see that keeping things that are the same together in the classroom can help keep order in the classroom and make it easier for children to know where they can do different activities.

Explain that categorizing things can also help them remember some details and see how things are alike and different.

Guided Practice

Display or **distribute** Teaching Master ES3-6 and have children look at the pictured animals. Then direct attention to the chart beneath the pictures and read the headings with children.

Ask children to look at the pictures and suggest animal names for each category. When the chart is complete, discuss how the chart helps children to see how the animals are alike and different.

Objectives

- categorize and classify objects in the classroom
- categorize and classify objects in stories

Materials

- Teaching Master ES3-6
- Practice Master ES3-6
- Anthology: *The Trip*

Practice/Apply

Distribute Practice Master ES3-6 to children. Read the directions and the category headings with children. Make sure children understand that they will write the animal name under the correct category heading. Have them complete the Practice Master independently.

Have children share their completed papers. Allow them time to explain their reasoning. Accept alternate answers if children can justify them.

Check children's work to be sure they understand the concept of categorizing and classifying.

LITERATURE FOCUS: 10–15 MINUTES

Preview *The Trip*

Walk children through *The Trip*.

Ask children to think about things they might group together. Children might, for example, put the characters together as family members or group the cats by color.

Tell children they will read this story with the rest of the class.

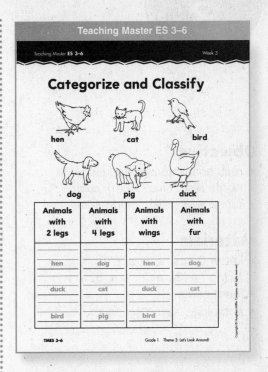

Categorize and Classify

hen   cat   bird

dog   pig   duck

Animals with 2 legs	Animals with 4 legs	Animals with wings	Animals with fur
hen	dog	hen	dog
duck	cat	duck	cat
bird	pig	bird	

TMES 3–6   Grade 1   Theme 3: Let's Look Around!

Name

Categorize and Classify

Read each animal name. If it names a farm animal, write it under Farm Animals. If it names a pet, write it under Pets.

dog   cat   hen   frog   ox   pig

Farm Animals	Pets
hen	dog
ox	cat
pig	frog

Grade 1   Theme 3: Let's Look Around!   PMES 3–6

Day 3

SKILL FOCUS: 25–30 MINUTES

High-Frequency Words

Teach

Write *also, blue, brown, color, funny, green, like, many*, and *some* on the chalkboard. Read the words aloud, pointing to each as you go.

Display the Letter Cards on the chalk tray. Ask the group, *How many letters are in the word* also?

Draw four squares on the board.

Ask four children to come up and find each letter in the word *also*. Ask the children to help you spell *also* as you write the word in the four squares.

Tell the children to put the letters back on the chalk tray with the other cards. Have them help lead the cheer to remember the word. Tap your left foot for each letter and then each syllable as you spell and say the word: *a-l-s-o, al-so!*

Repeat the procedure with the other words in the list.

Write the following sentences on the board, and read them together with children:

Some fish are just one color.

Some are many colors.

I like that funny blue fish.

I also like that green and brown one.

Check each child's ability to pronounce *also, blue, brown, color, funny, green, like, many*, and *some* as the child reads each sentence.

Practice

Write a sentence from *At the Aquarium* that contains the word *also:* *A brown otter also lives here.* Ask the children to help you read the sentence. Tell them you want them to read the word *also* together when it occurs in the sentence. Point to each word in the sentence as you read. Pause before the word *also* and resume reading after the group has supplied the word.

Repeat this activity for each high-frequency word.

Objective
- read and write high-frequency words *also, blue, brown, color, funny, green, like, many, some*

Materials
- Letter Cards: *a, b, c, e* (2), *f, g, i, k, l, m, n* (2), *o* (2), *r, s, u, w, y*
- index cards
- Anthology: *At the Aquarium*

Apply

Have children work in pairs. Give each pair nine large index cards and have them write the new words on them. Then have them go back to *At the Aquarium* and find each of the words. When children match the word, have them read the sentence in the story that contains the word. Have them continue in this way until they have matched all of the words and read all the sentences.

Preview *At the Aquarium*

Walk children through *At the Aquarium* on pages 87–105 in their Anthology.

Discuss the photographs, and use words from the story such as *trip, let's, frills, trick, grass, grab, crabs, brown,* and *it's.*

Note the suggestions in the Extra Support box on Teacher's Edition page T201.

Day 4

Objectives

- associate the /br/ sound with the letters *br*, /cr/ sound with the letters *cr*, /dr/ sound with the letters *dr*, /fr/ sound with the letters *fr*, /gr/ sound with the letters *gr*, /pr/ sound with the letters *pr*, /tr/ sound with the letters *tr*
- read words beginning with consonant clusters with *r*

Materials

- Letter Cards: *b, c, d, f, g, p, r, t*
- Picture Cards: *braid, brown, crow, dress, frog, gray, prize, train, tray*
- Anthology: *At the Aquarium*

RETEACH

SKILL FOCUS: PHONICS   10–15 MINUTES

Clusters with *r*

Teach

Display the Letter Card *f*, and remind children of the sound the letter *f* makes. Have them repeat it after you, /f/-/f/-/f/. Be sure children have their mouth in the correct position as they say the sound. Repeat the procedure with Letter Card *r*.

Hold up the Picture Cards for *frog, train,* and *braid,* and ask children to identify the pictures. Remind students that when a consonant and an *r* are side by side, such as *fr* in *frog, tr* in *train,* and *br* in *braid,* the sounds for each consonant and *r* are so close they almost seem to be one sound.

Use the Letter Cards *f* and *r* to model how to blend /f/ and /r/. Hold the Letter Cards apart, and, as you say /fr/, move the Letter Cards together until they touch. Have children repeat /fr/ as you move the Letter Cards next to each other a few times. Follow the same procedure with /trrr/, /brrr/, /grrr/, /drrr/, /crrr/, and /prrr/.

Write *frog* on the chalkboard. Blend the word *frog* aloud using Blending Routine 2 as you run your finger under each letter. Have children say the sound for *f*, /f/ and the sound for *r*, /r/ and blend /fffrrr/. Then say the sound for *o*, /ŏ/ and blend /fffrrrŏŏŏ/. Finally, say the sound for *g*, /g/, blend /fffrrrŏŏŏg/, and say *frog*. Repeat with other words with *r* clusters, such as *brown, crow, dress, gray, prize,* and *tray.*

Practice

Write *br, cr, dr, fr, gr, pr,* and *tr* in a column on the board. Next to the column, write _ _ *ab*. Say that you have written part of the word *crab* on the board. Have children repeat *crab* after you. Then have a child come to the board and circle the consonant cluster that completes the word *crab.* Have everyone say /cr/, *crab* as the child fills in the blank spaces with the letters *cr.* Repeat with the words *brim, drip, from, grab, prim,* and *trip.*

Apply

Have partners work together to find words with clusters with *r* in *At the Aquarium.* Have one child say the sounds of the consonant cluster and read the word aloud, and have his or her partner read the sentence with the word in it.

Contractions with 's

Teach

Write the words *she* and *is* on the chalkboard. Then write the contraction *she's* and remind children that the words *she* and *is* are joined to form the contraction *she's*. Circle the word *she* in the contraction *she's*. Then point to the apostrophe and remind children that it takes the place of the letter *i* in the word *is*. Point out that the letter *i* in the word *is* has been dropped to make the contraction *she's*. Say the contraction *she's* aloud and have children repeat it after you. Remind children that *she's* is a shorter way of saying *she is*.

Write *He's sad*. Then write *he is* above the contraction. Remind children that the words *he is* mean the same as *he's*. Remind them that the letter *i* is missing in the contraction. Point to the apostrophe and tell them that the apostrophe takes the place of the missing letter *i*. Have children say *he's* and remind them that *he's* is a shorter way of saying *he is*. Repeat the procedure for the contraction *it's*.

Practice

Write the following sentences on the board.

> *It* *is* big.   *She* *is* mad.   *He* *is* a man.   *It* *is* a ham.

Read the sentences aloud and point out the underlined words. Have volunteers say the contraction that can be formed by each pair of words, and write that contraction above each pair. Have partners work together to make up other sentences using each of the contractions.

Apply

Have pairs of children find contractions with *'s* in *At the Aquarium*. Ask children to read them aloud while you write them on the board. Have children tell you the pair of words that form the contraction. Then children can come to the board and circle the apostrophe and tell what letter it replaces.

Review *At the Aquarium*

Reread the story together with children. Have them take turns reading aloud. Tell children to make a list of words that have contractions with *'s*.

Objectives

- understand that contractions with *'s* are formed by joining two words
- recognize that an apostrophe replaces the letter *i* in a pair of words that form a contraction with *'s*
- independently read contractions with *'s*

Materials

- Anthology: *At the Aquarium*

Day 5

Objectives

- categorize and classify information
- identify information in stories by category

Materials

- Phonics Library: *Let's Trim the Track!, Brad's Quick Rag Tricks*
- Anthology: *The Trip, At the Aquarium*

Categorize and Classify

Teach

Gather a variety of writing tools including pencils, crayons, and markers. Collect three small boxes, bins, or cans for sorting the items. Explain that all of the tools can be used to write or draw. Hold up a pencil, a crayon, and a marker. Say, *We can use all of these to write or draw, but are they different from each other in any way?*

Accept all answers, for example, one is smaller, one has a top, and so on. Discuss the differences. Ask children how they might sort the objects so the things that are alike are in the same container. Put the pencils in one container, the crayons in another, and the markers in the last container. Explain that putting things that are *alike* in some way together is called *categorizing* or *classifying*.

Practice

Make a T chart on the board or chart paper. Write the headings *Animals that live on land* and *Animals that live in the water*. Tell children that when we separate things into different categories, we sometimes make a chart. The chart is a kind of picture that helps us see what belongs in each category. Ask children to name animals for each list. Write the names of the animals on the chart.

Apply

Draw a new T chart on the board or chart paper. Label the two columns *Things that live on land* and *Things that live in water*. Tell children you are going to read the story *At the Aquarium.* Tell them you want them to help you find all of the things that they see or read in the story that live on land and all the things that live in water. Explain the new chart headings. Ask them to help you fill in the chart with information from the story.

Revisit *Let's Trim the Track!*, *Brad's Quick Rag Tricks*, *The Trip*, and *At the Aquarium*

Page through each of the stories, asking children to look for words with consonant clusters with *r*.

Have children look through *At the Aquarium*. Discuss the different ways they could categorize the fish. (Possible answers: by color, by size, by what they eat, by texture)

Tell children to look through *At the Aquarium* to find the following high-frequency words: *also, blue, brown, color, funny, green, like, many, some*.

Have children read aloud selected sentences or pages from the stories.

Theme 4

Family and Friends

Day 1

PRETEACH

SKILL FOCUS: PHONICS 10-15 MINUTES

Clusters with *l*

Teach

Recite and repeat the chant shown, having children join in.

> **CHANT**
> A big glob of blue glue
> Is slipping through the door.
> Hurry please, to clean it up,
> Or it'll land upon the floor!

Say *glob*, emphasizing the beginning sounds /gl/. Then have children say *glob* with you several times. Print *glob* on the board and underline the *gl*. Tell children that these letters stand for the /gl/ sounds at the beginning of *glob*. Explain that the letter *l* sometimes appears with another consonant at the beginning of words.

Repeat the chant asking children to listen for other words that begin with a consonant and *l*. Write the *l* cluster words on the board.

Blend

Display the letters *g, l, a,* and *d* in front of the class. Use Blending Routine 1 to model how to blend the sounds, emphasizing the initial consonant cluster, and then say the word *glad*.

Blend and say the word with children before having children blend the sounds and say the word on their own. Repeat the process with the words *black, clap, flip, plug,* and *slot*.

Guided Practice

Display or **distribute** Teaching Master ES4-1, and discuss the illustrations with children. Tell them to use what they know about clusters with *l* as they read the sentences with you.

Help children underline any words that begin with clusters with *l*.

Check that they are blending *l* cluster words correctly.

Objective
- associate sounds with the clusters *bl, cl, fl, gl, pl,* and *sl*

Materials
- Teaching Master ES4-1
- Letter Cards: *a, b, c, d, f, g, i, k, l, o, p, s, t, u*

Technology

Education Place
www.eduplace.com
Go Away, Otto!

Audio CD
Fluff Is Missing!
Go Away, Otto!
Audio CD for **Family and Friends**

Lexia Phonics
CD-ROM
Primary Intervention

SKILL FOCUS: PHONICS · 10-15 MINUTES

Blending More Short o Words

Teach

Recite and repeat the chant shown. Tell children to join in.

> CHANT
> Don't drop the block
> Upon the clock,
> Or it will start
> To flip and flop.

Write *block* on the board, underlining the *o*. Remind children that the *o* can stand for /ŏ/. Say *block*, stretching the /ŏ/. Have children repeat *block* several times. Repeat with the word *flop*.

Blend

Give five children the Letter Cards *b*, *l*, *o*, *c*, and *k*, and ask them to stand holding the cards together to form *block*.

Use Blending Routine 1 to model how to blend the word, emphasizing the short *o* sound. Next, tell children to chant their letter sound when you point to them. Then have them blend the sounds together to make *block*. Repeat with the words *clog*, *flop*, *glob*, *plot*, and *slot*.

Practice/Apply

Distribute Practice Master ES4-1, discuss the illustrations, and read the directions with children.

Have children complete the Pratice Master independently.

Check children's responses to be sure they can read short *o* words.

LITERATURE FOCUS: · 10–15 MINUTES

Preview *Hot Dog*

Walk children through *Hot Dog* and discuss the illustrations. Tell children that *Floss* is the name of the girl in the story and *Hot Dog* is the name of her dog. Use words from the story such as *flips*, *flop*, and *glad*.

Objectives

- associate the /ŏ/ sound with the letter *o*
- blend and read words with short *o*

Materials

- Practice Master ES4-1
- Letter Cards: *b, c, f, g, k, l, o, p, s, t*
- Phonics Library: *Hot Dog*

Day 2

Drawing Conclusions

Teach

Tell children that sometimes they can use things they already know to figure out what people will say or do. Explain that this is called *drawing conclusions*.

Present situations that call for children to use their own experiences to draw conclusions:

What conclusion can you draw if the fire bell goes off? (There is a fire drill or a fire.)

What conclusion can you draw if the clock shows three o'clock and the bell rings? (It is time to go home.)

What conclusion can you draw if I point to the job chart and ask the napkin, cup, and juice helpers to do their jobs? (It is time for snack.)

Lead children to see that they can use their own experiences to help them draw conclusions about story characters and events as they read. Explain that this will help them better understand and enjoy stories.

Objective
- use details and personal experience to draw conclusions

Materials
- Teaching Master ES4-2
- Practice Master ES4-2
- Anthology: *Fluff Is Missing!*

JOB CHART

JOB	MON.	TUES.	WED.	THURS.	FRI.
(cup) Ann					
(BERRY'S JUICE) Ted					

Guided Practice

Display or **distribute** Teaching Master ES4-2, and discuss the illustration with children.

Remind children that they can use details from the picture and what they know about their own experiences to draw a conclusion about where Meg is going.

Discuss children's ideas about where they think Meg is going based on clues they used from the picture and their own experiences.

Practice/Apply

Distribute Practice Master ES4-2, and read the directions with children.

Tell them that they may write one word for each conclusion or that they may write longer conclusions. Have them complete the Practice Master independently.

Have children share their conclusions and tell what clues they used to make them.

Check children's responses to be sure they understand how to use the story, the pictures, and their own experiences to draw conclusions.

LITERATURE FOCUS: 10–15 MINUTES

Preview *Fluff Is Missing!*

Read aloud the first page of *Fluff Is Missing!* Identify the characters as Fluff the cat, Max, and his sister.

Ask children to use their own experiences and the details in the story to draw conclusions about how Max and his sister feel when Fluff runs away.

Tell children they will read this story with the rest of the class.

Teaching Master ES 4–2

Teaching Master **ES 4-2**   Week 1

Drawing Conclusions

Where is Meg going?

to school

Why do you think so?

Meg has a backpack. Meg is waving to her

mother. Meg is about to get on a school bus.

TMES 4-2   Grade 1 Theme 4: Family and Friends

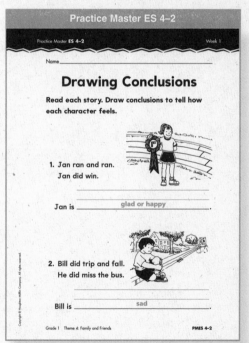

Practice Master ES 4–2

Practice Master **ES 4-2**   Week 1

Name _____

Drawing Conclusions

Read each story. Draw conclusions to tell how each character feels.

1. Jan ran and ran.
   Jan did win.

Jan is _____ glad or happy _____.

2. Bill did trip and fall.
   He did miss the bus.

Bill is _____ sad _____.

Grade 1 Theme 4: Family and Friends   **PMES 4-2**

Day 3

SKILL FOCUS: 25-30 MINUTES

High-Frequency Words

Teach

Write the words *children, come, family, father, love, mother, people, picture,* and *your* on the board. Point to each word as you read it aloud. Tell children to help you read the words aloud a second time.

Display Letter Cards on the chalk tray. Ask children, *How many letters are in the word* children?

Draw eight squares on the board.

Have the class name letters in the word *children.* As each letter is named, ask a volunteer to find the letter. Invite the class to help spell the word *children.* Point to the word on the board and ask, *What letter comes first?* Instruct children to say the letter and point to the letter card. Have the volunteer with the card write the letter in the correct box on the board. Repeat the procedure for the remaining letters asking, *What letter comes next?* Have children spell and read the word aloud together. When finished, put the letter cards back on the chalk tray.

Ask volunteers to help lead a cheer to remember the word. Have children find a partner and clap hands patty-cake style for each letter and syllable as you spell and say the word: *c-h-i-l-d-r-e-n, children!*

Repeat the lesson for the remaining words in the list.

Write the following sentences on the board, and read them together with children:

Come here, Tanya.

I would love to see your family picture.

Are these people your mother and father?

Tell me about the children in the picture.

Check each child's ability to pronounce *children, come, family, father, love, mother, people, picture,* and *your* as the child reads each sentence.

Objective

- read and write high-frequency words *children, come, family, father, love, mother, people, picture, your*

Materials

- Letter Cards: *a, c, d, e* (2), *f, h, i, l, m, n, o, p* (2), *r, t, u, v, y*
- index cards
- Anthology: *Go Away, Otto!*

Practice

Write the following sentences on the board: *Mother and father come for a family picture. People love children!* Ask children to help find the word *mother* in the first sentence. Read each word aloud and direct children to tap their pencil on the desk and say the word aloud when you read *mother*. You might want to point out that the word *mother* is capitalized because it is the first word in the sentence. Repeat the exercise for each high-frequency word.

Apply

Have children work in pairs to draw pictures of or make symbols for each of the high-frequency words. Instruct children to write each word on a large index card and draw a picture that helps them remember what the word is and what it means.

LITERATURE FOCUS: 10–15 MINUTES

Preview *Go Away, Otto!*

Walk children through *Go Away, Otto!* on pages 123–141 in their Anthology.

Discuss the illustrations and use words from the story such as *not, clean, plan, fluff, lots, blocks, black,* and *play*.

Note the suggestions in the Extra Support box on Teacher's Edition page T57.

Day 4

SKILL FOCUS: PHONICS   10-15 MINUTES

Clusters with *l*

Objectives

- independently read words beginning with consonant clusters with *l*
- associate sounds with the clusters *bl, cl, fl, gl, pl,* and *sl*

Materials

- Letter Cards: *b, c, f, g, l, p, s*
- Picture Cards: *blue, cloud, flag, globe, plug, sled*
- Sound/Spelling Cards: *fish, lion*
- Word Card: *flag*
- Anthology: *Go Away, Otto!*

Teach

Display the Sound/Spelling Card *fish* and remind children of the sound the letter *f* makes. Have them repeat it after you, /f/. Be sure children have their mouth in the correct position as they say the sound. Repeat the procedure with Sound/Spelling Card *lion*.

Hold up the Picture Cards *flag, blue, cloud, globe, plug,* and *sled,* and ask children to identify the pictures. Remind children that when a consonant and an *l* are side by side, such as *fl* in *flag,* and *sl* in *sled,* the sounds for each consonant and *l* are so close together they almost seem to be one sound.

Use the Letter Cards *f* and *l* to model how to blend /f/ and /l/. Hold the cards apart, and as you say /ffflll/, move them together until they touch. Have children repeat /ffflll/ as you move the Letter Cards next to each other a few times. Repeat for /b/ - /l/, /k/ - /l/, /g/ - /l/, /p/ - /l/ and /s/ - /l/.

Display the Word Card for *flag* on the chalk ledge. Help children use Blending Routine 2 to blend the word. Have children say the sound for *f*, /f/ and the sound for *l*, /l/ and blend the consonant cluster /ffflll/. Then have them say the sound for *a*, /ă/, and blend /ffflll ă ă ă/. Finally, have them say the sound for *g*, /g/, blend /fffllllă ă ă g/, and say *flag*.

Practice

Display the following Picture Cards on the chalk ledge: *flag, globe, plug, sled.* Write those words on the board above each card. Have children underline the cluster with *l* in each word and say the sounds of the consonant cluster and then read the word aloud. Have volunteers use each word in a sentence.

Apply

Have partners work together to find words with clusters with *l* in *Go Away, Otto!* Each time a child finds a word, he or she should read the word aloud while you write it on a Word Pattern Board.

SKILL FOCUS: PHONICS — 10-15 MINUTES

Blending More Short o Words

Teach

Display the Sound/Spelling Card *ostrich*, and remind children that the short sound of the letter *o* is: /ŏ/. Have them repeat it after you, /ŏ/. Be sure that children have their mouth in the correct position as they say the sound. Hold up Picture Card *box*, and ask children to identify the picture. Have them listen for the short *o* sound as you say *box*, and ask them to repeat it after you.

Hold up Picture Card *fox* and ask children to identify the picture. Ask them which sound they hear in *fox*, /ŏ/ or /ĭ/. Follow the same procedure with Picture Cards *cot*, *dot*, *fish*, *hop*, *pig*, *mop*, and *pit*.

Display the Word Card *box* next to its Picture Card and use Blending Routine 2 to help children blend the word. Have children say the sound for *b*, /b/, then the sound for *o*, /ŏ/, and blend /bŏŏ/. Finally, have them say the sound for *x*, /ks/, blend /bŏŏks/, and say *box*.

Practice

Display the Word Card *dot*. Distribute Letter Cards *c*, *g*, *h*, *l*, *n*, *p*, and *x*. Have volunteers choose a letter to place over the *d* or the *t* in *dot* and blend the letter sounds to make a new short *o* word. List the new words on a short *o* Word Pattern Board.

Apply

Draw a horizontal box that is divided into three squares on the board. In the middle square, print *o*. Have children look through *Go Away, Otto!* for short *o* words that have three letters. Each time they find a word, ask them to say the word aloud, and have a child write its other letters in the squares.

LITERATURE FOCUS: — 10-15 MINUTES

Review *Go Away, Otto!*

Reread the story together with children. Ask children to make a list of short *o* words and words with clusters with *l* that they find in the story.

Objectives

- blend phonemes
- associate the short *o* sound with the letter *o*
- independently read words with short *o*

Materials

- Letter Cards: *c, g, h, l, n, p, x*
- Picture Cards: *box, cot, dot, fish, fox, hop, mop, pig, pit*
- Sound/Spelling Card: *ostrich*
- Word Cards: *box, dot*
- Anthology: *Go Away, Otto!*

Day 5

SKILL FOCUS: COMPREHENSION   25-30 MINUTES

Drawing Conclusions

Teach

Act out for children the following examples of feelings. After each example, ask children to tell what feeling is expressed and what clues helped them figure it out.

- Yawn and say, *I stayed up late last night.* (tired)

- Clap your hands and say, *My mom is coming to visit me.* (happy)

- Wipe your eyes and say, *My cat is lost.* (sad)

Explain to children that when we can figure things out by what people say and how they act, we are drawing conclusions. Explain that when we look at the facts and details in a story and use what we know from our experiences, we are also drawing conclusions.

Practice

Review with children *Go Away, Otto!* by Pat Cummings. Draw attention to the following events in the story:

- Otto trying to fluff the pillows, making a mess

- Otto accidentally scattering pictures across the floor

Ask children to use the clues in the words and pictures and what they know from their experiences to draw conclusions about Otto. Children might say that Otto wants to help, but he is clumsy.

Apply

Have children reread the story and draw their own conclusions about what the authors tell us about the story characters. Invite children to discuss with a partner the conclusions they made and what details in the story they used to figure them out. Help children to see that, just as they were able to figure out that you were tired, happy, and sad, so they can figure out information about story events and story characters from what they read and what they already know from their experiences.

Have children draw a picture of the story characters doing something that they just discussed with their partner.

Objectives

- use details in the story and personal experience to draw conclusions
- talk about families

Materials

- Phonics Library: *Hot Dog, Tom's Plan*
- Anthology: *Fluff Is Missing!, Go Away, Otto!*

Revisit *Hot Dog, Tom's Plan, Fluff Is Missing!,* and *Go Away, Otto!*

Page through the stories with children. Then ask them to find short *o* words and words with clusters with *l*.

Have children look through *Hot Dog* and draw a conclusion as to whether Hot Dog is a friendly dog or an unfriendly dog.

Tell children to look through *Go Away, Otto!* to find the following high-frequency words: *children, come, family, father, love, mother, people, picture, your*.

Have children read aloud their favorite sentences or pages from the stories.

Day 1

Objective

- associate sounds with the clusters *sc, sk, sl, sm, sn, sp, st,* and *sw*

Materials

- Teaching Master ES4-3
- Letter Cards: *a, c, i, k, l* (2), *m, n, o, p, s, t, w*

Education Place

www.eduplace.com

Two Best Friends

Audio CD

Zack and His Friends
Two Best Friends
Audio CD for **Family and Friends**

Lexia Phonics

CD-ROM

Primary Intervention

Clusters with *s*

Teach

Recite and repeat the chant shown, telling children to join in.

> **CHANT**
> Stop, don't skip!
> I see a spill.
> Watch your step,
> Stand very still.

Have children repeat the first line after you. Write *stop* on the board. Underline the letters *st*, and tell children that these letters stand for the /s/ /t/ sounds at the beginning of *stop*. Read the word for children stretching the initial consonant sounds. Have them say *stop*. Tell children that the letter *s* sometimes appears with another consonant at the beginning of words.

Repeat the chant, asking children to listen for other words that begin with *s* and another consonant. Write the *s* cluster words on the board.

Blend

Distribute the Letter Cards *s, n, a,* and *p* to four volunteers. Have the children hold the cards close together to form the word *snap*.

Use Blending Routine 1 to model how to blend the sounds, emphasizing the initial consonant cluster, and then say the word *snap*. Have children blend the sounds and say the word *snap* on their own.

Repeat with the words *scan, skip, slap, smock, spin, still,* and *swim*.

Guided Practice

Display or **distribute** Teaching Master ES4-3, and discuss the illustrations with children. Tell children to use what they know about clusters with *s* as they read the sentences with you.

Help children underline and read any words that begin with clusters with *s*.

SKILL FOCUS: PHONICS 10-15 MINUTES

Blending More Short *e* Words

Teach

Recite and repeat the chant shown, asking children to join in.

> **CHANT**
> Meg can spell well,
> And I think that's swell.

Write *spell* on the board, underlining the *e*. Remind children that they have learned that the letter *e* can stand for /ĕ/, the short *e* sound. Say *spell* stretching the /ĕ/ sound. Have children repeat *spell* several times.

Repeat the procedure with the words *well* and *swell*.

Blend

Give four volunteers the Letter Cards *s, l, e,* and *d*. Point to each letter and have the child say its sound. Then have them move the cards close together to form *sled*.

Model how to blend the sounds, using Blending Routine 1 and stretching the short *e*. Have children blend the sounds, and then say the word *sled*. Repeat with *spell* and *stem*.

Practice/Apply

Distribute Practice Master ES4-3, and discuss the illustrations with children. Read the directions with them. Explain that they need to use what they know about the short *e* sound as they read the sentences and match the pictures.

Check children's responses to be sure they are able to read short *e* words.

LITERATURE FOCUS: 10–15 MINUTES

Preview *Knock, Knock*

Walk children through *Knock, Knock,* and discuss the illustrations. Explain that children will have a chance to read some short *e* words and some words with *s* clusters in this story.

Objectives
- associate /ĕ/ with *e*
- read words with short *e*

Materials
- Practice Master ES4-3
- Letter Cards: *d, e, l* (2), *m, p, s, t*
- Phonics Library: *Knock, Knock*

Day 2

SKILL FOCUS: COMPREHENSION   25-30 MINUTES

Compare and Contrast

Teach

Ask two children to volunteer to bring their backpacks to the front of the room. Explain that the two backpacks are alike in some ways and different in other ways.

Encourage children to find ways in which the backpacks are alike and different. You may want to make a list on the board of similarities and differences.

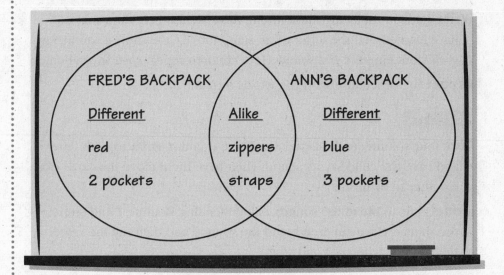

Objectives

- identify similarities and differences
- use a Venn diagram to compare and contrast

Materials

- Teaching Master ES4-4
- Practice Master ES4-4
- picture of lion
- picture of domestic cat
- Anthology: *Zack and His Friends*

Guided Practice

Display a picture of a lion beside a picture of a domestic cat, and call on volunteers to identify the animals. Then explain to children that the lion and the cat are alike in some ways and different in others.

Display or **distribute** Teaching Master ES4-4, and remind children that the two circles are called a Venn diagram. Explain that it can be used to help them show how cats and lions are alike and different.

Point out the labels *lion* in the left circle and *cat* in the right circle. Explain to children that you will write the things that are different about the two animals in these parts of the circles. Begin by writing the words *wild* under *lion* and *tame* under *cat*.

Tell children that in the middle, where the two circles overlap, you will write the things that are similar about a lion and a cat. Add the words *claws* in the space where the circles overlap.

Prompt children with questions to help them identify other similarities and differences, for example: *What sound does a lion make? What sound does a cat make? Is this the same or different? What should I write in the diagram?*

Continue until several more similarities and differences have been noted.

Practice/Apply

Distribute Practice Master ES4-4 to children, and read the directions.

Tell children that they will use the pictures and words on this page to practice looking for things that are the same and different. Make sure children understand that they will complete the Venn diagram by writing the words in the appropriate parts of the circle.

Have children work independently or with partners to complete the page.

Check children's responses to be sure they understand the concepts of comparing and contrasting.

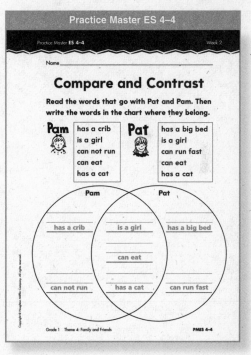

LITERATURE FOCUS: 10–15 MINUTES

Preview *Zack and His Friends*

Take a picture walk of *Zack and His Friends* with children. Ask them to identify the setting of the story.

Encourage children to tell how this school is similar to and different from their own.

Tell children that they will read this story with the rest of the class.

Day 3

SKILL FOCUS: 25-30 MINUTES

High-Frequency Words

Teach

Write the words *friend, girl, know, play, read, she, sing, today,* and *write* on the board. Point to each word as you read it aloud. Have children help you read the words aloud a second time.

Display Letter Cards on the chalk tray. Ask children, *How many letters are in the word* friend?

Draw six squares on the board.

Have the class name each letter in the word *friend*, and ask a volunteer to find that letter. Ask the class to help spell the word *friend*. Point to the word on the board and ask, *What letter comes first?* Instruct children to say the letter and point to the letter card. Have the volunteer with the card write the letter in the correct box on the chalkboard.

Repeat the procedure for the remaining letters, asking, *What letter comes next?* Have children spell and read the word aloud together, then put the letter cards back on the chalk tray.

Ask children to help lead a cheer to remember the word. Have them stomp their right foot for each letter and syllable as you spell and say the word: *f-r-i-e-n-d, friend!*

Repeat the lesson for the remaining words in the list.

Write the following sentences on the board, and read them together with children:

Do you know that girl?

She can read, write, and sing.

She is my friend.

We will play with her today.

Check each child's ability to pronounce *friend, girl, know, play, read, she, sing, today,* and *write* as the child reads each sentence.

Objective

• read and write high-frequency words *friend, girl, know, play, read, she, sing, today, write*

Materials

• Letter Cards: *a, d, e, f, g, h, i, k, l, n, o, p, r, s, t, w, y*
• index cards
• Anthology: *Two Best Friends*

Practice

Write the following sentences on the board:

> A girl and a friend play.
>
> They know how to read and write.
>
> Today she has a bell and they sing.

Ask children to help find the word *friend* in the first sentence. Read each word aloud and direct children to knock on the desk and say the word aloud when you read *friend*. Repeat the exercise for each high-frequency word.

Apply

Instruct children to write each high-frequency word on a large index card. Then have children work in pairs to draw pictures of or make symbols for each word to help them remember what the word is and what it means.

LITERATURE FOCUS: 10–15 MINUTES

Preview *Two Best Friends*

Walk children through *Two Best Friends* on pages 157–175 in their Anthology.

Discuss the illustrations, and use words from the story such as *last, rest, smile, still, felt, just, met,* and *best*.

Note the suggestions in the Extra Support box on Teacher's Edition page T129.

Day 4

SKILL FOCUS: PHONICS
10-15 MINUTES

Clusters with *s*

Teach

Display Sound/Spelling Card *seal*, and remind children of the sound the letter *s* makes. Have them repeat it after you. Be sure children have their mouths in the correct position as they say the sound. Repeat the procedure for the /m/ sound with Sound/Spelling Card *mouse*.

Hold up the Picture Cards for *smell, skate, snow,* and *spot,* and ask children to identify the pictures. Remind students that when *s* and another consonant are side by side, such as *sm* in *smell,* and *sp* in *spot,* the sounds for *s* and the other consonant are so close together they almost seem to be one sound.

Use the Letter Cards *s* and *m* to model how to blend /s/ and /m/. Hold the Letter Cards apart, and as you say /s/ - /m/, /sssmmm/ move the Letter Cards together until they touch. Have children repeat /sssmmm/ as you move the Letter Cards next to each other a few times. Follow the same procedure with /s/ - /p/, /s/ - /t/, /s/ - /n/, /s/ - /k/, and /s/ - /w/.

Write *smell* on the chalkboard, and blend it using Blending Routine 2. Have children say the sound for *s,* /s/ and the sound for *m,* /m/ and blend the consonant cluster, /sssmmm/. Then have them say the sound for *e,* /ĕ/, and blend /sssmmmĕĕĕ/. Finally, have them say the sound for double *l,* /l/, blend /sssmmmĕĕĕlll/, and say *smell.* Underline *sm.* Then write on the board other words with clusters with *s,* such as *scarf, skate, snow, spot, stem,* and *nest,* and underline the cluster with *s* in each of the words. Have children blend each word using Blending Routine 2. Remind children that clusters with *s* can be found at the beginning or end of a word.

Practice

Display Picture Cards *skate, smell, stem, swim, desk, mask, nest, vest,* and *wasp* on the chalk tray. Write those words on the board above each card. Have children underline the cluster with *s* in each word, say the sounds of the consonant cluster, and read the word aloud.

Apply

Have children find words with clusters with *s* in *Two Best Friends.* Have them read the words aloud while you write them on the board.

Objectives

- associate sounds with the clusters *sc, sk, sl, sm, sn, sp, st,* and *sw*
- independently read words beginning and ending with clusters with *s*

Materials

- Letter Cards: *c, k, m, n, p, s, t, w*
- Picture Cards: *desk, mask, nest, skate, smell, snow, spot, stem, swim, vest, wasp*
- Sound/Spelling Cards: *mouse, seal*
- Anthology: *Two Best Friends*

SKILL FOCUS: PHONICS 10–15 MINUTES

Blending More Short *e* Words

Teach

Display Sound/Spelling Card *elephant*, and remind children of the sound for short *e*: /ĕ/. Have them repeat it after you, /ĕ/. Be sure that children have their mouth in the correct position as they say the sound.

Hold up Picture Card *jet* and ask children to identify the picture. Ask them which sound they hear in *jet*, /ĕ/ or /ŏ/. Follow the same procedure with Picture Cards *pen, cot, pet, mop, log*, and *web*.

Display Word Card *bed* next to its Picture Card and help children to use Blending Routine 2 to blend the word. Have children say the sound for *b*, /b/, then the sound for *e*, /ĕ/, and blend /bĕĕ/. Finally, have them say the sound for *d*, /d/, blend /bĕĕd/, and say *bed*.

Practice

Place the Letter Card *e* on the chalk ledge and place consonant Letter Cards *b, h, j, n, p, t,* and *w* on a different part of the chalk ledge. Then, one at a time, show Picture Cards *hen, jet, net, pen, pet,* and *web* and name each picture. Have individuals come to the board, find the correct consonants to place before and after the *e* on the chalk ledge to spell the word, and then read it.

Apply

Make two horizontal boxes on the board, one divided into three squares, and the other into four squares. In the second square in both boxes, print *e*. Have children look for three-and four-letter words with short *e* in *Two Best Friends*. Each time they find a word, ask them to say it aloud and come to the board to write its letters in the squares. Keep the *e* in the second box as children change the initial and final letters to form these words from *Two Best Friends*: *Peg, pet, met, yes, rest,* and *best*.

Objectives

- blend phonemes
- associate the short *e* sound with the letter *e*
- independently read words with short *e*

Materials

- Letter Cards: *b, e, h, j, n, p, t, w*
- Picture Cards: *bed, cot, hen, jet, log, mop, net, pen, pet, web*
- Sound/Spelling Card: *elephant*
- Word Card: *bed*
- Anthology: *Two Best Friends*

LITERATURE FOCUS: 10–15 MINUTES

Review *Two Best Friends*

Reread the story together with children. Have them make a list of the *s* cluster words they find.

Day 5

Compare and Contrast

Teach

Tell children about an experience you had in the first grade, such as taking the wrong bus home or learning to ride a bike for the first time. Ask children, *Have you ever done anything like that?* Have children tell the class what happened. As children share experiences, say, *That happened to me, too.* Or say, *Unlike you, I…* Ask children to find similarities and differences in the experiences.

Explain to children that when they look for similarities, they are comparing and when they look for differences, they are contrasting.

Practice

Reread with children *Two Best Friends* by Eve Bunting. Have children tell how their experiences are similar to or different from events in the story.

Have children describe their friends. Ask children to tell how their friends are similar to or different from Kim. Use a Venn diagram to demonstrate the similarities and differences.

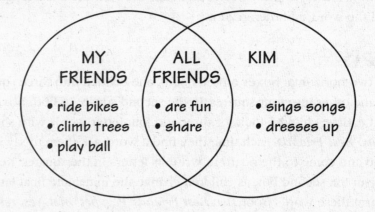

MY FRIENDS
• ride bikes
• climb trees
• play ball

ALL FRIENDS
• are fun
• share

KIM
• sings songs
• dresses up

Apply

Have children use the information from the Venn diagram to demonstrate their understanding of comparing and contrasting by completing sentence pairs such as the following:

Most friends_____.   Most friends_____.

But Kim_____.   And Kim does, too!

Objectives

• compare and contrast story events to personal experiences
• talk about pets

Materials

• Phonics Library: *Knock, Knock; Miss Nell*
• Anthology: *Zack and His Friends, Two Best Friends*

Revisit *Knock, Knock; Miss Nell; Zack and His Friends;* and *Two Best Friends*

Page through the stories with children, and ask children to compare and contrast the different settings.

Ask children to find short *e* words and words with clusters with *s* in each story.

Tell children to look through *Two Best Friends* to find the following high-frequency words: *friend, girl, know, play, read, she, sing, today, write.*

Have children read aloud their favorite sentences or pages from the stories.

Day 1

Objective
- associate sounds with the clusters *scr, spl, spr, str*

Materials
- Teaching Master ES4–5
- Letter Cards: *a, b, c, g, i, l, m, n, p, r, s, t, u*

Technology

Education Place
www.eduplace.com
Dog School

Audio CD
Dad's Big Plan,
Dog School
Audio CD for **Family and Friends**

Lexia Phonics
CD-ROM
Primary Intervention

PRETEACH

SKILL FOCUS: PHONICS   10-15 MINUTES

Triple Clusters

Teach

Recite and repeat the chant shown, having children join in.

> CHANT
> Spring rain,
> What a pain!
> Splash, sprinkle, splatter, stream,
> Why won't it stop?
> I want to scream!

Have children repeat the first line after you. Then write *spring* on the board. Say *spring* stretching the /s/, /p/, and /r/ sounds. Underline the letters *spr*, and tell children that these letters stand for the /s/ /p/ /r/ sounds at the beginning of *spring*. Have them say *spring* several times. Tell children that sometimes three consonants appear at the beginning of a word.

Blend

Write the following clusters on the board: *scr-, spl-, spr-, str-*. Tell children that many words begin with these letters.

Display the letters *s, c, r, u,* and *b* in front of the class. Use Blending Routine 1 to blend the sounds, stretching out the initial sounds of the consonant cluster, and then say the word, *scrub*. Have children blend the sounds, and say the word *scrub* with you, and then have them blend and say the word on their own. Repeat the process with the words *scrap, split, spring,* and *strum*.

Guided Practice

Display or **distribute** Teaching Master ES4-5, and discuss the illustrations with children. Tell them to use what they know about consonant clusters as they read the sentences with you.

Help children circle words that begin with a triple cluster, and read them.

Check that children are blending the words correctly.

SKILL FOCUS: PHONICS   10-15 MINUTES

Blending More Short *u* Words

Teach

Recite and repeat the chant shown, asking children to join in.

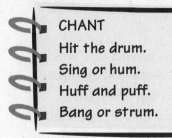

> **CHANT**
> Hit the drum.
> Sing or hum.
> Huff and puff.
> Bang or strum.

Write *drum* on the board. Call on a volunteer to read the word. Underline the *u* in *drum*. Explain to children that they have learned that the letter *u* can stand for the short *u*, /ŭ/ sound. Say *drum*, stretching the /ŭ/ sound. Have children repeat *drum* several times. Repeat with the words *hum, huff, puff,* and *strum*.

Blend

Give children the letters *d, r, u,* and *m*. Tell them to chant the letter sound when you point to them. Use Blending Routine 1 to model how to blend the sounds together to make *drum*. Then have children blend the sounds on their own. Repeat with the words *hum* and *strum*.

Practice/Apply

Distribute Practice Master ES4-5, discuss the illustrations, and read the directions with children. Point out the sentences beneath each picture. Tell children to use what they know about the short *u* sound to read the sentences. Have them complete the Practice Master independently. After they have circled the short *u* words, have them take turns reading aloud.

Check that they are blending short *u* words correctly.

LITERATURE FOCUS: 10-15 MINUTES

Preview *Buzzing Bug*

Have children read the title of the story with you. Take children on a picture walk of the story and discuss the illustrations. Use words from the story such as *buzz, splat,* and *stuck*.

Objectives
- associate /ŭ/ with *u*
- blend and read words with short *u*

Materials
- Practice Master ES4-5
- Letter Cards: *d, h, m, r, s, t, u*
- Phonics Library: *Buzzing Bug*

Day 2

SKILL FOCUS: COMPREHENSION 25–30 MINUTES

Sequence of Events

Teach

Call on volunteers to tell what they do when they eat a banana. Then restate children's descriptions, saying: *First, I peel the banana. Then I eat it.*

Ask what would happen if someone tried to eat the banana first, without peeling it. (They would bite into the peel; the banana wouldn't taste good.) Point out that people eat a banana in a certain order. Then remind children that they do many things in a certain order throughout the day.

Make a simple chart on the chalkboard to help children order the events of what they do in the morning before school. Your chart may resemble the following:

FIRST	NEXT	LAST
Get dressed	Eat breakfast	Get on the school bus

Remind children that stories also happen in a certain order. Tell them that what happens first in a story is the *beginning*. What happens next is the *middle*, and what happens last is the *end*.

Guided Practice

Display or **distribute** Teaching Master ES4-6 and point out that these pictures tell a story, but that the pictures are not in story order. Ask children to look at the pictures as you read the sentence under each one with them.

Ask children which picture and sentence tells what happens first, at the beginning of the picture story. Help children write the numeral *1* under the picture for *Mix it*.

Continue, having children name the pictures that show what happens next, in the middle of the story, and what happens last, at the end of the story.

Objectives
- identify the beginning, middle, and end of activities and events
- sequence story events

Materials
- Teaching Master ES4-6
- Practice Master ES4-6
- Anthology: *Dad's Big Plan*

Practice/Apply

Distribute Practice Master ES4-6 to children and discuss the pictures to make sure they understand what is happening in each one.

Tell children that the pictures on this page tell a story, but that the pictures are not in the right order.

Have children cut out the pictures and put them in story order. Encourage children to try ordering the pictures in different ways before pasting them into the numbered boxes.

Check children's responses to be sure they understand the concept of sequencing events.

LITERATURE FOCUS: 10–15 MINUTES

Preview *Dad's Big Plan*

Walk children through *Dad's Big Plan.* Discuss the illustrations, using words from the story such as *run, gulls, spritz,* and *scrub.*

Tell children to use picture clues to tell about the sequence of events in the story.

Explain to children that they will read *Dad's Big Plan* with the rest of the class.

Day 3

SKILL FOCUS: 25-30 MINUTES

High-Frequency Words

Teach

Write the words *car, down, hear, hold, hurt, learn, their, walk,* and *would* on the board. Point to each word as you read it aloud. Invite children to help you read the words aloud a second time.

Display Letter Cards on the chalk tray. Ask children, *How many letters are in the word* car?

Draw three squares on the board.

Have the class name the letters in the word *car.* As each letter is named, ask a volunteer to find the letter. Invite others to help spell the word *car.* Point to the word on the board and ask, *What letter comes first?* Instruct children to say the letter and point to the letter card. Have the volunteer with the card write the letter in the correct box on the board.

Repeat the procedure for the remaining letters asking, *What letter comes next?* Have children spell and read the word aloud together. When finished, put the letter cards back on the chalk tray.

Ask the volunteers to help lead a cheer to remember the word. Have children clap their hands over their head for each letter and syllable as you spell and say the word: *c-a-r, car!*

Repeat the lesson for the remaining words in the list.

Write the following sentences on the board, and read them together with children:

Hold my hand.

Don't walk so quickly.

Didn't you hear their car?

You must learn to slow down.

I would not want you to get hurt.

Check each child's ability to pronounce *car, down, hear, hold, hurt, learn, their, walk,* and *would* as the child reads each sentence.

Objective

• read and write high-frequency words *car, down, hear, hold, hurt, learn, their, walk, would*

Materials

• Letter Cards: *a, c, d, e, h, i, k, l, n, o, r, t, u, w*
• index cards
• Anthology: *Dog School*

Practice

Write the following sentences on the board:

> I want to learn to walk a dog.
> Let's go down to the pet shop to hear what they have to say.
> If you hold a dog well, it will not run into a car and get hurt.
> I would hold their dogs very well!

Ask children to help find the word *want* in the first sentence. Read each word aloud and direct children to knock on the desk and say the word aloud when you read *want*. Repeat the exercise for each high-frequency word in that sentence as well as the ones that follow in the remaining sentences.

Apply

Have children work in pairs to draw pictures of or make symbols for each of the high-frequency words. Instruct children to write each word on a large index card and draw a picture that helps them remember what the word is and what it means.

LITERATURE FOCUS: 10–15 MINUTES

Preview *Dog School*

Walk children through *Dog School* on pages 191–209 in their Anthology.

Discuss the illustrations, and tell children that the dog's name is Spritz. Use words from the story such as *scrub*, *tub*, *must*, and *just*.

Note the suggestions in the Extra Support box on Teacher's Edition page T201.

Day 4

RETEACH

SKILL FOCUS: PHONICS · · · · · · · · · 10-15 MINUTES

Triple Clusters

Teach

Point to a calendar and say: *Let's name the seasons of the year. There's summer, fall, winter, and …?* Ask children to name the fourth season. When someone says *spring*, repeat it, and have children say it after you. Remind children that when consonants at the beginning of words are side by side, their sounds can be so close together they almost seem to be one sound. Say the word *spring* again and have children listen for the consonant sounds at the beginning of the word, *spring*.

Display the Letter Card *s* and remind children of the sound the letter *s* makes. Be sure children have their mouths in the correct position as they say the sound. Repeat the procedure for the letter *p*, /p/ and the letter *r*, /r/. Then use the Letter Cards *s, p,* and *r* to model how to blend the sounds. Hold the Letter Cards apart, and, as you say /sssprrr/, move them together until they touch. Follow the same procedure for Letter Cards *s, c, r* (/s/ - /k/ - /r/), *s, p, l* (/s/ - /p/ - /l/), and *s, t, r* (/s/ - /t/ - /r/).

Write the word *sprig* on the board and explain that it is a small twig or piece of a plant. Help children to blend *sprig* using Blending Routine 2. Have them say the sound for *s*, /s/, the sound for *p*, /p/, and the sound for *r*, /r/, then blend the cluster, /sssprrr/. Have them say the sound *i*, /ĭ/ and blend /sssprrr ĭ ĭ ĭ/. Finally, have them say the sound for *g*, /g/, blend /sssprrr ĭ ĭ ĭg/, and say the word *sprig*. Repeat this procedure with the words *split, strap,* and *scrub*.

Practice

Write the four clusters, *scr, spl, spr,* and *str* on self-stick notes. Then write ___ *ap* on the board and say the word *scrap*. Have a child identify the correct cluster that comes at the beginning of *scrap* and come to the board to place the correct self-stick note in the blank at the beginning of the word. Have all children read *scrap*. If they need help, have them blend continuously, /ssscrrrăăăp/. Repeat this procedure with the words *splat, strum,* and *sprint*.

Apply

Have partners find words with triple clusters in *Dog School*. When children find the words, have them read each one aloud while you write it on a Word Pattern Board under the heading *scr* or *spl*.

Objectives

- independently read words beginning with triple clusters
- associate sounds with the clusters *scr, spr,* and *str*

Materials

- Letter Cards: *c, l, p, r, s, t*
- Anthology: *Dog School*

SKILL FOCUS: PHONICS | 10-15 MINUTES

Blending More Short *u* Words

Teach

Display the Sound/Spelling Card *umbrella* and remind children of the short *u* sound: /ŭ/. Have them repeat it after you, /ŭ/ - /ŭ/ - /ŭ/. Be sure that children have their mouths in the correct position as they say the sound. Hold up Picture Card *cup*, and ask children to identify the picture. Have children listen for the short *u* sound as you say *cup*, and ask children to repeat it after you.

Hold up Picture Card *rug* and ask children to identify the picture. Ask them which sound they hear in *rug*, /ŭ/ or /ĕ/. Follow the same procedure with Picture Cards *jet, leg, run*, and *sun*.

Display the Word Card *cup* next to its Picture Card. Use Blending Routine 2 to blend the word with children. Have children say the sound for *c*, /k/, then the sound for *u*, /ŭ/, and blend /cŭŭ/. Finally, have them say the sound for *p*, /p/, blend /cŭŭp/, and say *cup*.

Practice

Place the Letter Card *u* on the chalk ledge and place the Letter Cards *b, c, g, h, j, n, p* (2), *r*, and *t* on a different part of the chalk ledge. Then, one at a time, show Picture Cards *tub, cut, run, hut, jug, pup*, and *nut* and name each picture. Have children come to the board and find the correct consonants to place before and after the *u* to spell the word, then read it. If children need help reading the word, have them blend continuously. For example, /tŭŭŭb/, *tub*.

Apply

Have children look for words with short *u* in *Dog School*. Each time they find a word, ask them to say the word aloud so you can write it on a word list on the board. When the search is complete, choose volunteers to read the words on the list and use each word in a sentence.

LITERATURE FOCUS: | 10–15 MINUTES

Review *Dog School*

Reread the story together with children. Have children take turns reading aloud. Ask them to make a list of words with triple clusters that they find in the story.

Objectives

- blend phonemes
- associate the short *u* sound with the letter *u*
- independently read words with short *u*

Materials

- Letter Cards: *b, c, g, h, j, n, p* (2), *r, t, u*
- Picture Cards: *cup, cut, hut, jet, jug, leg, nut, pup, rug, run, sun, tub*
- Sound/Spelling Card: *umbrella*
- Word Cards: *cup*
- Anthology: *Dog School*

Day 5

Sequence of Events

Teach

Ask children to tell what things they do each day, and then tell the order in which they do them. Ask questions such as *What do you do first?* and *What do you do next?* to guide children's responses. Encourage children to use words like *first, next, then,* and *last.* Children might provide answers similar to the following:

First I go to school.

Then I come home and play.

Next I eat dinner.

Last, I get ready for bed and go to sleep.

Explain to children that the order in which they do things is called a *sequence.* Explain, too, that the sequence of events in a story is the order in which things happen.

Practice

Discuss with children events from *Dog School.* Have children recall what happens in the story. Children can look through the story to identify the events in the order in which they happen. Ask, W*hat happens first?* and *Then what happens?* Record children's suggestions in a sequence chart similar to the one that follows.

FIRST	NEXT	LAST
Spritz causes trouble.	Spritz goes to dog school.	Spritz passes the test.

Explain to children that knowing and recognizing the sequence of events can help us better understand what we read.

Objectives

- identify the order in which events happen
- use words like *first, then, next,* and *last* to tell the order of events
- record story events in a sequence chart

Materials

- Phonics Library: *Buzzing Bug, Duff in the Mud*
- Anthology: *Dad's Big Plan, Dog School*

Apply

Have children work in groups of four to dramatize the story. Children can play the following characters: Spritz, the boy, the mother, and the teacher. Remind children to keep the sequence of events in mind as they act out the story. Encourage them to refer to the sequence chart and the story to help them.

Revisit Buzzing Bug, Duff in the Mud, Dad's Big Plan, and Dog School

Page through the stories with children, and discuss the sequence of events in each story.

Ask children to look through the stories to find short *u* words and words with triple clusters.

Tell children to look through *Dog School* to find the following high-frequency words: *car, down, hear, hold, hurt, learn, their, walk, would.*

Have children read aloud their favorite sentences or pages from the stories.

Theme 5

Home Sweet Home

Day 1

Objectives

- associate the /sh/ sound with the letters *sh*
- blend and read words with *sh*

Materials

- Teaching Master ES5-1
- Letter Cards: *a, d, h, i, o, p, s, t*

Technology

**Get Set for Reading
CD-ROM**
Moving Day

Education Place
www.eduplace.com
Moving Day

Audio CD
Moving Day
Audio CD for **Home Sweet Home**

**Lexia Phonics
CD-ROM**
Primary Intervention

PRETEACH

SKILL FOCUS: PHONICS   10–15 MINUTES

Digraph *sh*

Teach

Recite and repeat the chant shown. Tell children to join in.

> CHANT
>
> Sh sh!
>
> Babies sleeping.
>
> Sh sh!
>
> People reading.

Say *ship*, isolating the /sh/ sound. Model the /sh/ mouth position. Have children say *ship* several times. Print *sh* and explain that these two letters stand for one sound, /sh/.

Blend

Give volunteers the letters *s, h, i,* and *p.* Point to *h, i,* and *p* and tell children to move the cards together as they say their sounds. Use Blending Routine 1 to model how to blend the sounds. Then have the group blend the sounds and say the word they have made, *hip.* Follow the same procedure with *sip.*

Give another child the *s* and *h* cards to hold together. Remind children *s* and *h* are two letters but together make one sound, /sh/. Have the children holding *s, h, i,* and *p* move the cards together to form *ship.* Have children blend the sounds, and then say the word. Repeat with *shop, shot, dish,* and *dash.*

Guided Practice

Display or **distribute** Teaching Master ES5-1 and discuss the illustration.

Tell children to use what they know about the /sh/ sound as they read the sentence with you.

Point to words from the sentence, and have children read them.

Check that children are blending the words correctly.

SKILL FOCUS: PHONICS   10–15 MINUTES

Digraph *ch*

Teach

Recite the chant shown. Have children join in as they are able.

> CHANT
>
> Ch ch ch
>
> Chocolate chips!
>
> Ch ch ch
>
> Chew, chew, chew!

Say *chip*, isolating the /ch/. Model the /ch/ mouth position. Have children say *chip* several times. Print *ch* and tell children that these letters stand for one sound, /ch/.

Blend

Spread out the letters *c, h, a, i, o, n* and *p* in front of the class. Have children make *ch* words using the letters. Use Blending Routine 1 to model how to blend the sounds. Then have children blend and say the word.

Practice/Apply

Distribute copies of Practice Master ES5-1, discuss the pictures, and remind children to use what they know about the /sh/ and /ch/ sounds as they read the story aloud.

Tell children to draw the last picture for the story in the space provided. Have them read the story to you and share their pictures.

Monitor children as they read aloud.

LITERATURE FOCUS: 10–15 MINUTES

Preview *The Shed*

Walk children through *The Shed* and discuss the illustrations. Name the characters and use words from the story. Ask children what each character might do to help fix up the shed.

Objectives
- associate /ch/ with *ch*
- blend and read words with *ch*

Materials
- Practice Master ES5-1
- Letter Cards *a, c, h, i, n, o, p*
- Phonics Library: *The Shed*

Teaching Master ES 5–1

Teaching Master **ES 5–1**   Week 1

Digraph *sh*

She shall mash the shed!

TMES 5–1   Grade 1   Theme 5: Home Sweet Home

Practice Master ES 5–1

Practice Master **ES 5–1**   Week 1

Name _____

Digraphs *sh* and *ch*

Use sounds you know to read the story.
Finish the story with a drawing of your own!

This is Chet.	Chet is hot.
He checks the tub.	Drawings will vary. Splash!

Grade 1   Theme 5: Home Sweet Home   PMES 5–1

Day 2

PRETEACH
SKILL FOCUS: COMPREHENSION 25–30 MINUTES

Compare and Contrast

Teach

Tell two volunteers to face the class standing shoulder to shoulder.

Have the volunteers hold erasers in their adjoining hands. In their outside hands, have one volunteer hold a piece of chalk and have the other hold a paper clip.

Ask the class what the volunteers have that are the same. (erasers)

Ask what things they have that are different. (piece of chalk, paper clip)

Objectives

• recognize similarities and differences
• compare and contrast using a Venn diagram

Materials

• Teaching Master ES5-2
• Practice Master ES5-2
• 2 erasers, a piece of chalk, a paper clip
• Anthology: *Moving Day*

Guided Practice

Display or **distribute** Teaching Master ES5-2 and read the story with children. Direct their attention to the first Venn diagram.

Point out the middle part of the Venn diagram and explain that it shows how Nat and Pat are alike. (they both have gloves)

Point out the differences shown in the outer parts of the diagram. (Nat has a bat, Pat has a ball)

Work with children to complete the Venn diagram at the bottom of the page.

Practice/Apply

Distribute Practice Master ES5-2 to children. Discuss the appearance of the characters and explain that the sentences describe how Pam and Ed are both alike and different.

Have children read the sentences independently or with a partner. Guide them as necessary.

Ask volunteers to tell what they will write on the first line of the Venn diagram and why.

Have children complete the Venn diagram independently or with a partner.

Check children's work to be sure they understand how to compare and contrast.

LITERATURE FOCUS: 10–15 MINUTES

Preview *Moving Day*

Walk children through *Moving Day* on pages 16–42 in their Anthology.

Discuss the illustrations and use words from the story such as *shell*, *big*, *small*, *long*, *wide*, *heavy*, *light*, *rough*, and *smooth*.

Note the suggestions in the Extra Support boxes on Teacher's Edition pages T49, T53, and T54.

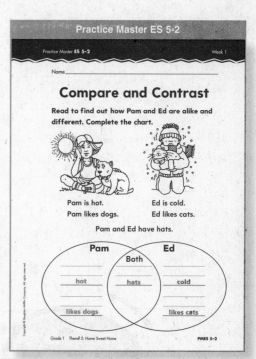

Day 3

Objective

- read and write high-frequency words *grow, light, long, more, other, right, room, small, these*

Materials

- High-Frequency Word Cards
- Letter Cards: *a, e, g, h, i, l (2), m, n, o (2), r, s, t, w*
- index cards
- Phonics Library: *Champ*

High-Frequency Words

Teach

Write the words *grow, light, long, more, other, right, room, small,* and *these* on the board. Point to each word as you read it aloud. Invite children to help you read the words aloud a second time.

Display the Letter Cards on the chalk tray. Ask children, *How many letters are in the word* grow?

Draw four squares on the board.

Ask children to help spell the word *grow*. Point to the word on the board and ask, *What letter comes first?* Instruct children to say the letter and draw it in the air. Ask a volunteer to find the letter among the Letter Cards, write the letter in the first box on the board, and face the group holding the card.

Repeat the procedure for the remaining letters, asking, *What letter comes next?* Have volunteers stand side by side with the Letter Cards to spell the word *grow*. Ask the group to read the word aloud together. Invite children to make up a charade to act out when they read the word *grow*. For example, children might start crouched on the floor and slowly stand up, spreading their arms.

Repeat the lesson for the remaining words in the list. Together, read aloud the words, and have children act out the charades they made up. Lead children in a silent exercise. Point to the words on the board, and have children act out each one.

Write on the board the following sentences, and read them together with children:

Small plants need room to grow.

Long plants need more light.

These other plants are just right.

Check each child's ability to pronounce *grow, light, long, more, other, right, room, small,* and *these* as the child reads each sentence.

Practice

Display this rhyme on the board. Instruct children to write each under-lined high-frequency word on a large index card.

> My Friend Hippo
> <u>These</u> are too <u>long</u>.
> The <u>other</u> is <u>small</u>.
> I have no <u>room</u> to
> <u>grow</u> at all.
> If I walk <u>more</u>
> and I am <u>light</u>,
> Then these you see,
> will fit me just <u>right</u>!

Read the poem aloud and point to the words as you read. Reread the poem, and instruct children to raise their word cards to match the high-frequency words you read. You may want to incorporate the charades for the words into a final reading of the poem.

Apply

Have children copy the poem and make an illustration to accompany it. Children can read the poem together and share their illustrations.

LITERATURE FOCUS: 10–15 MINUTES

Review *Champ*

Reread the story together with children.

Ask children to look through *Champ* to find the following high-frequency words: *light, long, these*. Have them read the sentences that contain these words.

Day 4

SKILL FOCUS: PHONICS   10–15 MINUTES

Digraphs *sh, th, wh*

Teach

Have children identify Letter Cards *s* and *h* and say the letter sounds: /s/; /h/. Display Sound/Spelling Card *sheep* and explain that *s* and *h* together can stand for the /sh/ sound. Have children identify initial /sh/ or /s/ in Picture Cards *sit*, *ship*, and *salt*, and final /sh/ or /s/ in *dress*, *fish*, and *leash*. Write *fish* on the board and help children use Blending Routine 2 to blend the word. Have children say the sounds for *f*, /f/ and *i*, /ĭ/, and blend /fff ĭ ĭ/. Finally, have them say the sound for the digraph *sh*, /sh/, blend /fff ĭ ĭsh/, and say *fish*.

Follow the procedure above for the digraph *th* using Letter Cards *t* and *h* and Sound/Spelling Card *thumb*. Then use Picture Cards to have children identify the /th/ or /t/ sound in *thorn*, *ten*, *top* for initial *th*, and *tooth*, *spot*, *mouth* for final *th*. Write the word *cloth* on the board and help children to blend it using Blending Routine 2.

Repeat for the digraph *wh* using Letter Cards *w* and *h* and Sound/Spelling Card *whale*. Use Picture Cards to have children identify the initial /wh/, /h/, or /w/ sound in *horse*, *wheel*, *white*, *wave*. Write *when* on the board. Help children blend it using Blending Routine 2.

Practice

Write *shop*, *dish*, *that*, *teeth*, *when*, *whale* on the board. Give each child three index cards on which you have written *sh*, *wh*, and *th*. Say each word and have children hold up the card. Have a child come to the board, circle the matching digraph, and blend the word.

Apply

Have partners take turns finding words with the digraphs *sh*, *th*, or *wh* in *The Shed*. Record the words. Have volunteers come to the board, underline the *sh*, *th*, or *wh* in each word, and read the word.

Help children differentiate the digraphs by pointing out the position of their lips and tongue. Have them feel for voice box vibration.

•/sh/— lips pursed, tongue is flat in the middle of the mouth; voiceless

•/th/— tip of tongue lightly against edges of the upper teeth; voiceless

•/wh/— rounded lips, tongue behind lower teeth; voiceless

Objectives

- associate the /sh/ sound with the letters *sh*, the /th/ sound with the letters *th*, and the /wh/ sound with the letters *wh*
- independently read words with digraphs *sh*, *th*, or *wh*

Materials

- Sound/Spelling Cards: *sheep*, *thumb*, *whale*
- Letter Cards: *h*, *s*, *t*, *w*
- Picture Cards: *dress*, *fish*, *horse*, *kiss*, *leash*, *mouth*, *salt*, *ship*, *sit*, *spot*, *ten*, *thorn*, *thumb*, *tooth*, *top*, *wave*, *wheel*, *white*
- index cards
- Phonics Library: *The Shed*

Digraphs *ch, tch*

Teach

Display Letter Cards *c* and *h*. Explain that the letters *c* and *h* together in a word stand for a new sound, /ch/. Say /ch/ and have children repeat it after you. Display the Sound/Spelling Card *chick*. Ask whether *chick* begins with /ch/ or /k/. Do the same with the Picture Cards *cab*, *chin*, and *car* for initial *ch*, and *peach* and *book* for final *ch*.

Write *chick* and help children decode it using Blending Routine 2. Have them say the sounds for *ch*, /ch/ and *i*, /ĭ/, then blend /ch ĭ ĭ/. Have them say the sound for *ck*, /k/ and blend and say the word, /ch ĭ ĭ k/, *chick*. Repeat for *tch*, using Picture Cards *watch* and *yak*. Help children blend *watch* using Blending Routine 2.

Distribute the Picture Cards *chain*, *chick*, *chin*, *ship*, *sheep*, *thorn*, *thumb*, *whale*, *wheel*, and *white* and say: *Find other children whose picture names begin with the same sound as your picture, and stand together with them.* Follow the same procedure with final digraphs, using the Picture Cards *fish*, *leash*, *mouth*, *peach*, *tooth*, and *watch*.

Help children pronounce the digraphs correctly by pointing out the position of their lips and tongue. Have them feel for voice box vibration.

Practice

Write *chip*, *pitch*, *bench*, *latch*, *chat* on the board. Point to a word and have a child underline the digraph as everyone blends the word.

Apply

Have children find and list words with the digraphs *ch* or *tch* in *The Shed*. Have them read each word aloud.

Review *Moving Day*

Reread the story together with children. Have them find words with *sh*, *th*, and *wh*.

Objectives

- associate the /ch/ sound with the letters *ch*, and the /tch/ sound with the letters *tch*
- independently read words with digraphs *ch* or *tch*

Materials

- Letter Cards: *c, h, t*
- Sound/Spelling Card: *chick*
- Picture Cards: *book, cab, car, chain, chick, chin, fish, leash, mouth, peach, sheep, ship, thorn, thumb, tooth, watch, whale, wheel, white, yak*
- Phonics Library: *The Shed*
- Anthology: *Moving Day*

Day 5

SKILL FOCUS: COMPREHENSION   25–30 MINUTES

Objectives

- find similarities and differences between objects
- make a chart that compares and contrasts objects

Materials

- Phonics Library: *The Shed, Champ*
- Anthology: *Moving Day*

Compare and Contrast

Teach

Place your chair and a student's chair side by side in the front of the classroom. Refer to the chairs as objects and ask children to describe first one object, and then the other. Next, ask children to tell what is the same about the two objects, and then what is different. Elicit from children that both objects are chairs with some similarities and some differences. Explain to children that when they tell how things are alike, they compare them. Explain that when they tell how things are different, they contrast them.

Practice

Remind children that in the story *Moving Day*, the hermit crab grows out of his shell and needs to find another one. Tell children that the hermit crab has to look at the shells very carefully to see which one would work for him now. Have children turn to pages 18 and 19. Ask them to describe the two shells. You might want to guide children's descriptions of the shells with questions such as *What is it? Where is it?* and *What is it like?*

Have children compare and then contrast the two shells. Ask, *How are the shells alike?* (They both have a spiral shape.) and then, *How are they different?* (One is bigger than the other.) Remind children to use clues from the words and pictures to find the answers. Record children's responses in a Venn diagram, substituting descriptive drawings for unfamiliar words.

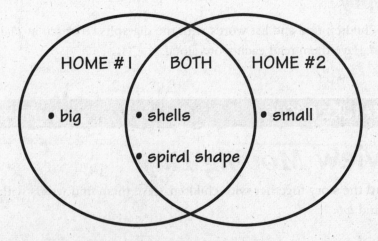

Have children compare and contrast other shells in the story, using the same steps.

Apply

Have children work with a partner to make a chart that compares and contrasts all of the homes the hermit crab looks at. Have children draw a picture and label each with a description, for example, *This shell is too big. This shell is too small.* Then have them write a description of the shell that is just right.

Revisit *The Shed, Champ,* and *Moving Day*

Page through the stories calling on children to compare the characters, settings, and the problems in the stories.

Ask children to point out words that begin and end with *sh, th,* or *wh.*

Have children read aloud selected sentences or pages from the stories.

Day 1

Objectives

- associate the /ā/ sound with the letters *a-e*
- blend and read *a-e* words

Materials

- Teaching Master ES5-3

Get Set for Reading CD-ROM

Me on the Map

Education Place

www.eduplace.com
Me on the Map

Audio CD

Me on the Map
Audio CD for **Home Sweet Home**

Lexia Phonics CD-ROM

Primary Intervention

SKILL FOCUS: PHONICS   10–15 MINUTES

Long *a* (CVCe)

Teach

Recite and repeat the chant shown. Have children join in.

> CHANT
>
> Bake, bake, bake.
> Cake, cake, CAKE!
> Who ate the cake?

Say *bake* with children, stretching the long *a* vowel sound.

Have them repeat the second line of the chant after you and stretch the /ā/ in *cake*.

Print *bake* and *cake* on the board. Underline the vowel letters *a* and *e* in each word. Explain that together, they make the long *a* /ā/ sound.

Blend

Print *late* on the board. Use Blending Routine 1 to model blending the sounds, stretching the long *a* sound, and saying the word. Point out that *late* has the *a*-consonant-*e* pattern, which gives the vowel *a* the long sound.

Blend and say *late* with children before having them blend it on their own. Then ask children to use it in a sentence. Repeat with the following words: *game*, *wave*, *cape*.

Check that all children can blend the sounds correctly.

Guided Practice

Display or **distribute** Teaching Master ES5-3 and discuss the illustration.

Tell children to use what they know about the long *a* sound as they read the sentences with you. Help children find and color the triangle-shaped part of the picture.

Point to words from the sentences, and have children read them.

SKILL FOCUS: PHONICS   10–15 MINUTES

Final *nk*

Teach

Recite and repeat the chant. Tell children to join in.

> CHANT
> Plink, plink, plink!
> It's raining in my sink.

Have children say the first line again with you. Repeat *plink*, emphasizing the final sounds. Ask if *plink* ends in the same way as *pin* or *sink*. Have children repeat *plink* several times. Print *plink* on the chalkboard. Underline the final *nk*.

Blend

Print *rink* on the board. Use Blending Routine 1 to model blending the sounds as you move your hand under each letter. Say *rink*, emphasizing the final /nk/ sound. Have children blend and say the word with you. Follow the same procedure for the words *dunk* and *honk*.

Check that children can blend the sounds correctly.

Practice/Apply

Distribute copies of Practice Master ES5-3, discuss the pictures, and remind children to use what they know about the /nk/ sound as they read the story. Have children draw the story's last illustration.

Ask children to read their completed story aloud and share their drawings.

Note children's ability to blend words correctly.

LITERATURE FOCUS: 10–15 MINUTES

Preview *Pets in a Tank*

Walk children through *Pets in a Tank*, and discuss the illustrations. Name the characters and use words from the story. Ask children what they think each character will do to get a pet.

Objectives

- associate /nk/ with *nk*
- read words with final *nk*

Materials

- Practice Master ES5-3
- Phonics Library: *Pets in a Tank*

Day 2

Objectives

- recognize common functions among items
- make generalizations

Materials

- Teaching Master ES5-4
- Practice Master ES5-4
- assorted pencils, crayons, pens, and markers
- paper
- Anthology: *Me on the Map*

SKILL FOCUS: COMPREHENSION   25–30 MINUTES

Making Generalizations

Teach

Display the pencils, crayons, pens, and markers. Have children identify what they are.

Have volunteers choose one of the objects. Give each a sheet of paper. Then tell each volunteer to write their name or draw something quickly. Have the volunteers show their drawings.

Make the point: *Max drew a picture with the pencil. Meg wrote her name with a crayon.*

Write the following generalization sentence on the board and ask children to complete it.

People use pencil, pens, crayons, and markers to _____. (write or draw)

Guided Practice

Display or **distribute** Teaching Master ES5-4. Have children look at the illustrations and follow along as you read.

Reread the sentences and have children listen for an action word that is the same in each sentence.

Have children supply the missing word to complete the generalization sentence.

Practice/Apply

Distribute Practice Master ES5-4 to children, discuss the three illustrations, and explain that the sentences tell about each picture.

Have children read the sentences aloud, using the illustrations for cues, as needed.

Ask them to circle the word that completes the generalization sentence. Then have them write the word in the sentence.

Check children's responses to be sure they can make generalizations.

LITERATURE FOCUS:
10–15 MINUTES

Preview *Me on the Map*

Walk children through *Me on the Map* on pages 55–79 in their Anthology.

Discuss the illustrations and use words from the story such as *state*, *make*, *place*, *something*, *find*, and *think*.

Note the suggestions in the Extra Support boxes on Teacher's Edition pages T135, T137, and T138.

Teaching Master ES 5-4

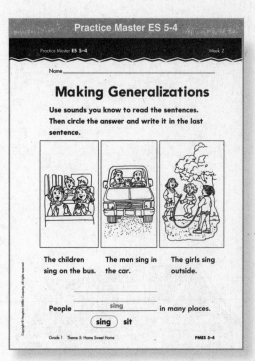

Practice Master ES 5-4

Day 3

Objective

• read and write high-frequency words *could, house, how, over, own, so, world*

Materials

• High-Frequency Word Cards
• Letter Cards: *c, d, e, h, l, n, o, r, s, u, v, w*
• index cards
• Phonics Library: *Gram's Trip*

RETEACH

SKILL FOCUS: 25-30 MINUTES

High-Frequency Words

Teach

Write the words *could, house, how, over, own, so,* and *world* on the board. Point to each word as you read it aloud. Invite children to read the words along with you a second time.

Display the Letter Cards on the chalk tray. Ask children, *How many letters are in the word* house?

Draw five squares on the board.

Ask children to help spell the word *house*. Point to the word on the board and ask, *What letter comes first?* Instruct children to say the letter and draw it in the air. Ask a volunteer to find the letter among the Letter Cards, write the letter in the first box on the board, and face the group holding the card.

Repeat the procedure for the remaining letters, asking, *What letter comes next?* Have volunteers stand next to each other with the Letter Cards to spell the word *house*. Ask the group to read the word aloud together. Invite children to make up a charade to act out when they read the word *house*. For example, children might hold their arms in a triangle over their head.

Repeat the lesson for the remaining words in the list. Then read aloud together the words from the list and have children act out the charades (where appropriate) that they made up. Lead children in a silent exercise. Point to the words on the board and have children act out each charade. For any words not acted out, have children silently mouth the letters with you.

Practice

Display these sentences on the board. Instruct children to write each underlined high-frequency word on a large index card.

> If I had my <u>own</u> jet,
>
> I <u>could</u> have a friend,
>
> From any place in the <u>world</u>,
>
> Come <u>over</u> to my <u>house</u> to play.
>
> <u>So</u> tell me! Tell me <u>how</u> I can get my own jet!

Read the sentences aloud and point to the words as you read. Reread the sentences, and instruct children to raise their word cards to match the high-frequency words you read.

Check each child's ability to pronounce *could, house, how, over, own, so,* and *world* as the child reads each sentence.

Apply

Have partners play a word game. Instruct children to pick a word from their word cards and give clues about it. Have their partner find the answer, show the card, and read the word aloud. Children can take turns providing clues and guessing.

LITERATURE FOCUS: 10-15 MINUTES

Review *Gram's Trip*

Reread the story together with children. Have children take turns reading aloud.

Ask children to look through *Gram's Trip* to find the following high-frequency words: *could, so.* Have them read the sentences that contain these words.

Day 4

SKILL FOCUS: PHONICS   10–15 MINUTES

Long *a* (CVCe)

Teach

Display the Sound/Spelling Card for *acorn*. Say *acorn*, and ask children to repeat it after you. Remind children that the long sound for *a* is the same sound as the letter's name and have them say /ā/ - /ā/ - /ā/. Be sure that children's mouths are in the correct position. Have them listen for the long *a* sound as you say /ā ā ācorn/ and they repeat it.

Hold up the Picture Card for *vane* and ask children to identify it. Ask them which *a* sound they hear in *vane*, the long *a* sound, /ā/, or the short *a* sound, /ă/. Follow the same procedure with the Picture Cards for *cat*, *game*, *gate*, *hat*, *jam*, *map*, *rake*, and *van*.

Display the Picture Card for *gate* and review that the word *gate* has the long *a* sound. Then write *gate* on the board and point out the consonant-vowel-consonant-*e* pattern. Circle the *a* and explain that this pattern stands for the long *a* sound, /ā/ and the *e* is silent.

Use Blending Routine 2 to help children blend the sounds in the word. Point to the *g* and have children say /g/. Then point to the *a* and have children say the long *a* sound, /ā/. Have them blend /gā ā ā/. Finally, point to the *t* and have children say /t/ and blend the whole word /gā ā āt/, *gate*.

Remind children that they can make new long a words by adding different consonants to the consonant-vowel-consonant-e pattern. Write _ a _ e on the board. Then say the following words and have children help you to fill in the correct consonants: *date*, *same*, *bake*, *wave*.

Practice

Place Letter Cards *a* and *e* on a chalk ledge with space between them: _ a _ e. Then hand out Letter Cards *c*, *p*, *l*, *k*, *t*, *v*, *s*, and *m*. Say the word *lake* and have the children holding the *l* and *k* Letter Cards place their cards on the chalk ledge with the *a* and *e* to spell *lake*. Repeat this procedure with: *cape*, *tape*, *vase*, *cave*, and *same*.

Apply

Have children look for words with long *a* in *Pets in a Tank*. Record the words children find. When the search is complete, choose children to read the words on the list.

Objectives

- associate the long *a* sound with the letter *a*
- blend phonemes
- independently read words with long *a*

Materials

- Sound/Spelling Card: *acorn*
- Letter Cards: *a, c, e, k, l, m, p, s, t, v*
- Picture Cards: *cat, game, gate, hat, jam, map, rake, van, vane*
- Phonics Library: *Pets in a Tank*

SKILL FOCUS: PHONICS 10–15 MINUTES

Final *nd, nk, ng*

Teach

Display the Letter Card *n*. Have children repeat after you the sound *n* makes. Repeat for the letter *d*.

Use the Letter Cards *n* and *d* to model blending /n/ and /d/. Hold the Letter Cards together, and say /nnnd/. Have children repeat /nnnd/.

Hold up the Picture Card for *hand*, and ask children to identify the picture. Ask them what they hear at the end of *hand*, /n/ or /nd/. Follow the same procedure with the Picture Card for *sun*. Repeat the procedure for final -*ng* and -*nk*, using the Picture Cards for *king* and *pan* for -*ng* and *ink* and *hen* for -*nk*.

Write *hand* on the board. Help children blend *hand* using Blending Routine 2. Have them say the sounds for *h*, /h/ and *a*, /ă/ and blend /hhhăăă/. Have them say the sound for -*nd*, /nd/, blend, and say the word: /hhhăăănnnd/, *hand*. Explain that when *n* and *d* are together, they are always found at the end of a word. Repeat with *band* and *end*. Follow the same procedure with the words *king*, *bang*, and *long* for -*ng*, and *ink*, *tank*, and *honk* for -*nk*.

Practice

Write -*nd*, -*ng*, and -*nk* on the board. Display the Picture Cards *hand*, *king*, and *ink*. Have children put each Picture Card under the correct heading. Write each word on the board and have children read it.

Apply

Have children look for words with -*nd*, -*ng*, and -*nk* in *Pets in a Tank*. Have them say each word they find aloud so that you can write them on the board. Give partners a piece of paper folded vertically into thirds. Have children write -*nd*, -*ng*, and -*nk* as headings and choose one word from the board to illustrate in each column.

LITERATURE FOCUS: 10–15 MINUTES

Review *Me on the Map*

Reread the story with children. Have them look for long *a* words.

Objectives

- associate /nd/ with the letters *nd*, /nk/ with the letters *nk*, /ng/ with the letters *ng*
- independently read words ending with -*nd*, -*nk*, and -*ng*

Materials

- Letter Cards: *d, g, k, n*
- Picture Cards: *hand, hen, ink, king, pan, sun*
- Phonics Library: *Pets in a Tank*
- Anthology: *Me on the Map*

Day 5

SKILL FOCUS: COMPREHENSION   25–30 MINUTES

Making Generalizations

Teach

Begin a discussion about how children arrive at school each day. Some children might walk to school; others might ride to school in a car, bus, or on a bicycle. Ask children if it would be true to say *All children ride to school or come on foot.* Have children think about a situation when the statement would not be true. (It would not be true if child swam to school.) You might want to ask children how many of them ride to school or come on foot. Then ask if there are any children that come to school in another way to help them see why the statement is true.

Give children another example: *Most rides are faster than going on foot.* Again, invite children to name a situation when the statement would not be true. (It would not be true if you were stuck in traffic, if you were riding a very old horse pulling a heavy cart uphill, or if you were just learning to ride a bicycle.) Explain that a statement that is true most of the time for most things is called a generalization.

Practice

Have children turn to pages 60 and 61 in *Me on the Map.* Read the pages aloud together. Ask children to name things you might find in a town. Encourage them to use facts from the story and what they know from their experiences to form answers. Record children's suggestions on a chart.

THINGS IN A TOWN

Most towns have _____.

All towns have _____.

Objectives

- use story facts and personal knowledge to make generalizations
- write generalizations about school

Materials

- Phonics Library: *Pets in a Tank, Gram's Trip*
- Anthology: *Me on the Map*

Make generalizations about things in a town using children's suggestions from the chart. For example, you might say:

- All towns have streets.

- All towns have houses.

- Most towns have a library.

Ask children if they agree or disagree with the generalizations. Ask, *Are the statements true most of the time for most towns?* Encourage children to suggest more generalizations about towns.

Apply

Have children work independently to write three to five generalizations about school. Encourage them to use facts and what they know from their experiences to make a list of things all schools have. When they have finished, ask children to share their responses. Lead children in a questioning routine to help them make generalizations by asking, *Do you think it is usually true that all schools have teachers?*

LITERATURE FOCUS: 10–15 MINUTES

Revisit *Pets in a Tank, Gram's Trip,* and *Me on the Map*

Page through all of the stories asking children to make generalizations about pets, trips, and maps. Then ask children to find words that end in *nk* or that have the long *a* vowel sound.

Tell children to look through *Me on the Map* to find the following high-frequency words: *could, house, how, over, own, so, world.*

Have children read aloud selected sentences or pages from the stories.

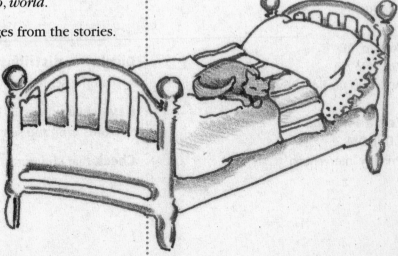

Day 1

Objectives
- associate the / ī / sound with the letters *i-e*
- blend and read *i-e* words

Materials
- Teaching Master ES5-5

Get Set for Reading CD-ROM
The Kite

Education Place
www.eduplace.com
The Kite

Audio CD
The Kite
Audio CD for **Home Sweet Home**

Lexia Phonics CD-ROM
Primary Intervention

Long *i* (CVCe)

Teach

Recite the chant shown. Have children join in.

> CHANT
>
> Slide, glide.
>
> Glide, slide.
>
> Nice ice.

Repeat the first line, stretching the vowel sound. Identify the sound as the long *i*. Have children repeat the word *slide*.

Tell children to listen carefully as you say the words *slip* and *glide*. Have them tell you which word has the long *i* sound they hear in *slide*. Say: *Yes. The words* slide *and* glide *both have the long* i *vowel sound.* Have children say the words *slide* and *glide* with you.

Print the words *slide*, *glide*, *nice*, and *ice* on the board. Underline the vowel letters *i* and *e* in each word. Explain that the two letters stand for one sound, the / ī / sound.

Blend

Print *side* on the board. Use Blending Routine 1 to model blending the sounds, stretching the long *i* sound, and saying the word. Have children blend and say *side* with you and then alone. Repeat the process with *five* and *shine*.

Guided Practice

Display or **distribute** Teaching Master ES5-5, discuss the illustration, and read the sentences with children.

Have children circle the picture of the animal with stripes. Point to words from the sentences, and have children read them.

Check that children are reading the words correctly.

SKILL FOCUS: PHONICS · 10–15 MINUTES

Contractions

Teach

Recite the chant. Tell children to join in.

> **CHANT**
>
> We'll do it. We will.
>
> We'll do it. We will.
>
> WE'LL do it!

Repeat the first line, emphasizing *we'll*. Tell children that *we'll* is a shorter way of saying *we will*. Print *we will* on the chalkboard and *we'll* below it. Compare the two words. Explain the use of the apostrophe to replace the missing letters. Have children read *we will* and then *we'll*.

Blend

Print *she'll* on the board. Use Blending Routine 1 to model blending the sounds as you move your hand under each letter. Say the word. Print *she will* above the contraction. Circle the apostrophe and ask what letters the apostrophe replaces. (wi). Continue with the contractions *I'll*, *he'll*, *you'll*, and *they'll*. Tell children to blend the contractions.

Practice

Distribute Practice Master ES 5-5, discuss the picture, and remind children to use what they know about sounds and letters to help them read the sentences.

Have children circle the contractions.

Check children's responses, having them say what each contraction means. Revisit the activity to have children identify and read /ī/ words.

LITERATURE FOCUS: · 10–15 MINUTES

Preview *Pine Lake*

Walk children through *Pine Lake* and discuss the illustrations. Name the characters, and use /ī/ words and contractions from the story.

Objectives

- recognize contractions
- understand the meaning of contractions

Materials

- Practice Master ES5-5
- Phonics Library: *Pine Lake*

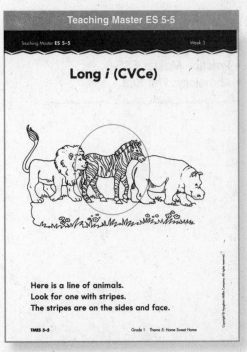

Teaching Master ES 5-5

Teaching Master **ES 5-5**   Week 3

Long *i* (CVCe)

Here is a line of animals.
Look for one with stripes.
The stripes are on the sides and face.

TMES 5-5   Grade 1 · Theme 5: Home Sweet Home

Practice Master ES 5-5

Practice Master **ES 5-5**   Week 3

Name _____

Contractions

Use sounds you know as you read.
Circle the contractions.

It's time to dine!

We'll have lunch.

I'll make a plate of chops and rice.

You'll like it!

Grade 1 · Theme 5: Home Sweet Home   PMES 5-5

Day 2

SKILL FOCUS: COMPREHENSION   25–30 MINUTES

Cause and Effect

Objective

- identify cause and effect relationships

Materials

- Teaching Master ES5-6
- Practice Master ES5-6
- Anthology: *The Kite*

Teach

Switch off the classroom lights. Ask children what happened. (You turned off the lights.)

Say: *Yes. The lights went off because I flipped the light switch.*

Have a volunteer flip the lights back on. Have children explain what happened and why.

Introduce the terms *cause* and *effect*, saying that what happens is called the *effect*; why it happens is called the *cause*. Use the terms *cause* and *effect* as you talk about turning the lights on and off.

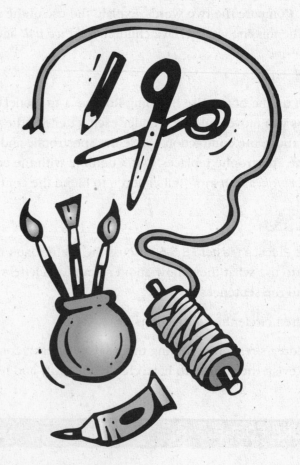

Guided Practice

Display or **distribute** Teaching Master ES5-6, and have children read the question with you and look at the illustration.

Help children read the response choices.

Discuss which cause statement makes sense, and help children to circle it. (It can do tricks.)

Reread with children the question and the circled cause statement.

Practice/Apply

Distribute Practice Master ES5-6 to children. Have them look at the illustration and talk about it.

Ask children to read the question independently or with a partner. Then have them read the response sentences independently.

Have children circle the cause statement that makes sense, using the illustration for clues, as needed.

Check children's responses to make sure they understand the concept of cause and effect.

LITERATURE FOCUS: 10–15 MINUTES

Preview *The Kite*

Walk children through *The Kite* on pages 88–101 in their Anthology.

Discuss the illustrations and use words from the story such *kite*, *like*, *she'll*, *doesn't*, *isn't*, *didn't*, *it's*, *can't* and *we've*.

Note the suggestions in the Extra Support boxes on Teacher's Edition pages T207, T208, and T209.

Teaching Master ES 5-6

Week 3

Cause and Effect

Why did the dog get a prize?

It can walk.   It can do tricks.

TMES 5–6   Grade 1 Theme 5: Home Sweet Home

Practice Master ES 5-6

Week 3

Name _____

Cause and Effect

Read what happens. Circle the sentence that tells why it happens.

The boy runs. Why?

He can race.   He hit the ball.

Grade 1 Theme 5: Home Sweet Home   PMES 5–6

Day 3

SKILL FOCUS: 25–30 MINUTES

High-Frequency Words

Teach

Write the words *give, good, her, little, try, was, fly,* and *our* on the board. Point to each word as you read it aloud. Invite children to help you read the words aloud a second time.

Display the Letter Cards on the chalk tray. Ask children, *How many letters are in the word* give*?*

Draw four squares on the board.

Ask children to help spell the word *give.* Point to the word on the board and ask, *What letter comes first?* Instruct children to say the letter and draw it in the air. Ask a volunteer to find the letter among the Letter Cards, write the letter in the first box on the board, and face the group holding the card.

Repeat the procedure for the remaining letters, asking, *What letter comes next?* Have volunteers stand side by side with the Letter Cards to spell the word *give.* Ask the group to read the word aloud together. Invite children to make up a charade to act out when they read the word *give.* For example, children might hold hands outstretched as if offering something.

Repeat the lesson for the remaining words on the list. Then read aloud together the words from the list, and have children act out the charades (where appropriate) that they made up. Lead children in a silent exercise. Point to the words on the board, and have children act out each charade. For any words not acted out, have children silently mouth the letters with you.

Write on the board the following sentences, and read them together with children:

Let's fly our kites.

Her kite is stuck.

Give it a little tug.

That was a good try!

Check each child's ability to pronounce *give, good, her, little, try, was, fly,* and *our* as the child reads each sentence.

Objective

• read and write high-frequency words *give, good, her, little, try, was, fly, our*

Materials

• High-Frequency Word Cards
• Letter Cards: *a, d, e, f, g, h, i,*
• index cards *l (2), o (2), r, s, t (2), u, v, w, y*
• Phonics Library: *Fun Rides*

Practice

Instruct children to write each high-frequency word from the board on a large index card. Display these sentences.

> <u>Our</u> <u>little</u> bird did not <u>fly</u>.
>
> We wanted to see <u>her</u> <u>give</u> it a <u>good</u> <u>try</u>.
>
> We let her go without a word.
>
> That <u>was</u> the last time I saw my little bird.

Read the sentences aloud, and point to the words as you read. Reread the sentences and instruct children to raise their word cards to match the high-frequency words you read. You may want to incorporate the charades for the words into a final reading of the poem.

Apply

Have partners play a word game. Instruct children to pick a word from their word cards and give clues about the word. Have their partner find the answer, show the card, and read the word aloud. Encourage children to take turns providing clues and guessing the words.

LITERATURE FOCUS: 10–15 MINUTES

Review *Fun Rides*

Reread the story together with children. Have children take turns reading aloud.

Tell children to look through *Fun Rides* to find the following high-frequency words: *little, try, our.* Have them read the sentences that contain these words.

Day 4

Objectives

• associate the long *i* sound with the letter *i*
• blend phonemes
• independently read words with long *i*

Materials

• Sound/Spelling Card: *ice cream*
• Letter Cards: *d, e, f, h, i, k, l, m, n, r, v*
• Picture Cards: *bike, kit, kite, lip, nine, sit, swim, vine, white*
• Phonics Library: *Pine Lake*

RETEACH

SKILL FOCUS: PHONICS   10–15 MINUTES

Long *i* (CVCe)

Teach

Display the Sound/Spelling Card for *ice cream*. Say *ice cream*. Have children repeat it. Remind them that the long sound for *i* is the same sound as the letter's name. Have them say the /ī/ sound after you, /ī/-/ī/ -/ī/. Be sure that children's mouths are in the correct position. Have them listen for the long *i* sound as you say *ice cream*, stretching out the vowel sound.

Hold up the Picture Card for *kite* and ask children to identify the picture. Ask them which *i* sound they hear in *kite*, the long *i* sound, /ī/, or the short *i* sound, /ĭ/. Repeat with the Picture Cards for *kit, lip, nine, sit, swim, vine,* and *white*.

Display the Picture Card for *bike,* noting that it has the long *i* sound. Write *bike* on the board and point out the consonant-vowel-consonant-*e* pattern. Circle the *i* and say that this pattern stands for the long *i* sound, /ī/ and the *e* is silent. Use Blending Routine 2 to help children blend the sounds. Point to the *b* and have children say /b/. Point to the *i* and have children say the long *i* sound, /ī/. Have them blend /bī ī ī/. Point to the k and have children say /k/ and blend the whole word, /bī ī īk/, *bike*.

Remind children that they can make new long *i* words by adding different consonants to the consonant-vowel-consonant-*e* pattern.
Write _ *i* _ *e* on the board. Then say the following words and have children help you fill in the correct consonants: *bite, dime, hide, wise*.

Practice

Place Letter Cards *i* and *e* on a chalk ledge. Hand out Letter Cards *r, d, f, v, l, h, k, n,* and *m*. Say the word *hike*. Have the children holding the *h* and *k* Letter Cards place them on the chalk ledge with the *i* and *e* to spell *hike*. Repeat this procedure with: *ride, five, lime, fine*.

Apply

Have children find long *i* words in *Pine Lake*. Have them say the words as they find them. List them on the board. Have volunteers read the words on the list.

Contractions

Teach

Write *he* and *is* on the board. Write the contraction *he's,* reminding children that *he* and *is* are joined to make *he's.* Circle the word *he* in the contraction *he's.* Point to the apostrophe, explaining that it takes the place of the letter *i* in the word *is.* Note that the letter *i* in the word *is* has been dropped to make the contraction *he's.* Say the contraction *he's* aloud. Have children repeat it after you.

Follow above for *he'll, she's, it's, I'm, can't, don't,* and *won't.*

Practice

Write the following sentences on the board.

> I <u>will</u> read the book.
>
> <u>We</u> <u>are</u> ready to go.
>
> <u>It</u> <u>is</u> a big bike.
>
> She <u>can</u> <u>not</u> walk yet.

Read the sentences aloud. Point out the pairs of underlined words. Have volunteers say the contraction formed by each pair as you write that contraction next to each pair. Have partners work together to make another sentence using each of the contractions.

Apply

Have partners find contractions in *Pine Lake.* Have children read aloud each contraction found. Write them on the board. Have volunteers say which two words take the place of each contraction.

Review *The Kite*

Reread the story together with children. Have them list long *i* words and contractions that they find.

Objectives

- understand that contractions are formed by joining two words
- recognize that an apostrophe replaces a letter or letters in a pair of words that form a contraction
- independently read contractions

Materials

- Phonics Library: *Pine Lake*
- Anthology: *The Kite*

Day 5

Objective
- identify causes and effects in a story

Materials
- Phonics Library: *Pine Lake, Fun Rides*
- Anthology: *The Kite*

SKILL FOCUS: COMPREHENSION   25–30 MINUTES

Cause and Effect

Teach

Draw a picture of a child with a big smile on his face as he is holding a kite string, with the kite flying high up in the sky. Ask, *Why do you think the child is so happy?* (The kite is flying high in the sky.) Invite children to talk about things that make them happy. You might want to record children's responses on the chalkboard.

_____ makes me happy because _____.

Ask *What happened?* (The child is happy.) *Why did this happen?* (Because John's cousin is coming to visit) Explain to children that the answer to the question *Why did this happen?* is the *cause* and the answer to the question *What happened?* is the *effect*.

Practice

Remind children that the whole story *The Kite* is based around good news and bad news. For every event, there is something that happens that causes the children to be happy or sad. As children read the story together, pause after every page and record the causes and effects.

CAUSE	EFFECT
Why did this happen?	What happened?
Mama wants to make a kite,	so the children are happy.
But Mama doesn't know how,	so the children are sad.
Mama can learn to make a kite,	so the children are happy.
But it is hard to make a kite,	so the children are sad.
Mama didn't give up,	so the children are happy.

Apply

Conduct a rereading of the story. Divide the children into two groups, asking one group to read the effects and one to read the causes. Children can refer back to the cause-and-effect chart if they need help. You might want to hold up cards with the words "Effect — What happened?" and "Cause — Why did this happen?" as children read each event.

LITERATURE FOCUS: 10–15 MINUTES

Revisit *Pine Lake, Fun Rides, and The Kite*

Page through the stories with children. Ask questions such as *In* Pine Lake, *what caused Mike and Rick to have to take different paths?* Then have children look for long *i* words and contractions in each of the stories.

Ask children to look through *The Kite* to find the following high-frequency words: *give, good, her, little, try, was, fly, our.*

Have children read aloud selected sentences or pages from the stories.

Theme 6

Animal Adventures

Day 1

Objectives

- associate the /ō/ sound with the letters o and o-e
- associate the /yo͞o/ sound with the letters u-e
- blend and read long o and long u words

Materials

- Teaching Master ES6-1

Get Set for Reading
CD-ROM
The Sleeping Pig

Education Place
www.eduplace.com
The Sleeping Pig

Audio CD
The Sleeping Pig
Audio CD for **Animal Adventures**

Lexia Phonics
CD-ROM
Primary Intervention

PRETEACH

SKILL FOCUS: PHONICS   10–15 MINUTES

Long o (CV, CVCe) and Long u (CVCe)

Teach

Recite and repeat the chant shown, having children join in.

> CHANT
>
> A cute little *doe*
>
> Was eating a rose.
>
> She had a huge bump
>
> On the side of her nose.

Say *doe*, stretching the long o sound. Identify the sound as the long o vowel sound. If necessary, explain that a doe is a female deer. Have children repeat *doe* several times. Repeat with *rose*. Print *rose* on the board. Underline the o and e and explain that together, these two letters make the long o sound. Repeat the process with the long u words *cute* and *huge*.

Blend

Print *no* on the board and use Blending Routine 1 to model how to blend the sounds, stretching each sound and then saying the word. Blend and say the word with children, before asking them to blend it on their own. Point out that *no* has the consonant-vowel pattern. Repeat the process with the words *note*, *broke*, and *rope*. Point out that these words have the o-consonant-e pattern.

Follow a similar procedure with the word *mule*, pointing out that it has the u-consonant-e pattern. Repeat with the words *rule*, *fume*, and *tube*.

Guided Practice

Display or **distribute** Teaching Master ES6-1 and discuss the illustrations with children. Tell them to use what they know about long o and long u vowel sounds as they read the sentences with you. Point to words from the sentences randomly, and have children read them.

Check that children are blending the words correctly.

SKILL FOCUS: PHONICS | 10–15 MINUTES

Final Cluster *nt*

Teach

Recite and repeat the chant shown, encouraging children to join in.

> **CHANT**
>
> An ant, an ant, an ant
>
> Sat on a plant, a plant, a plant.

Repeat the first line. Have children listen to compare *an* and *ant*. Ask, *Do these words end the same way?* Repeat the words, emphasizing the final /nt/ sounds in *ant*. Tell children that *ant* ends with two sounds. Say the sounds /n/ and /t/ and then blend them to form /nt/. Tell children to raise their hand each time they hear a word that ends with /nt/. Say: *hat, chant, spin, paint, get.*

Blend

Print *went* on the board, and use Blending Routine 1 to model how to blend the sounds, emphasizing the final /nt/ sounds. Have children blend and say *went* with you. Then have them blend it on their own. Repeat with *tent, grant,* and *grunt.*

Practice/Apply

Distribute Practice Master ES6-1, discuss the illustrations with children, and have them follow along as you read the directions with them. Tell children to read the sentences independently, and circle either *Yes* or *No* to answer each question.

Check children's responses to be sure they are able to read /nt/ words.

LITERATURE FOCUS: | 10-15 MINUTES

Preview *Duke's Gift*

Walk children through the story. Discuss the illustrations, naming the characters and using words from the story. Ask children why they think the dog wants to hide his bone.

Objectives

- associate /nt/ with *nt*
- blend and read word ending with *nt*

Materials

- Practice Master ES6-1
- Phonics Library: *Duke's Gift*

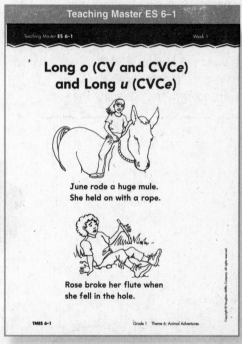

Day 2

Objectives

- identify story characters, problem, and solution
- complete a simple story map

Materials

- Teaching Master ES6-2
- Practice Master ES6-2
- Anthology: *The Sleeping Pig*

Story Structure

Teach

Ask a volunteer to help you act out a story for the group.

Place a pencil on the floor. Call the child by name and say, for example: *John, yesterday I hurt my back. Now I have a problem. I can't bend down to pick up my pencil. Can you help me solve my problem? Will you pick up the pencil?*

Have children retell the story. Then ask who the people, or characters, in the story were, what the problem was, and how it was solved.

Guided Practice

Display or **distribute** Teaching Master ES6-2. Tell children that they will read a story and then fill in the chart with you.

Read the story with children. Have them tell who the characters in the story are, what the problem is, and how it is solved. Help them write their responses in the chart.

Practice/Apply

Distribute Practice Master ES6-2. Discuss the illustrations and read the directions with children.

Ask them to read the sentences independently.

Have children circle the picture that shows Luke's problem and then draw a picture to show how Luke might solve the problem.

Check children's responses to be sure they understand what the problem in the story is and how it could be solved.

<table>
<tr><td>LITERATURE FOCUS:</td><td>10–15 MINUTES</td></tr>
</table>

Preview *The Sleeping Pig*

Walk children through *The Sleeping Pig* on pages 133-152 in their Anthology.

Discuss the illustrations and use words from the story such as *huge, home, went, use, lift, tune, woke, left,* and *whole*.

Note the suggestions in the Extra Support boxes on Teacher's Edition pages T47, T49, T51, T53, and T54.

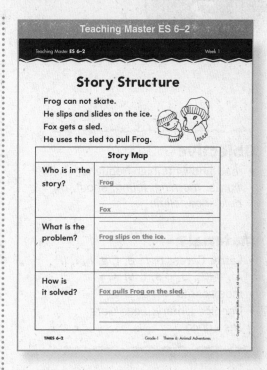

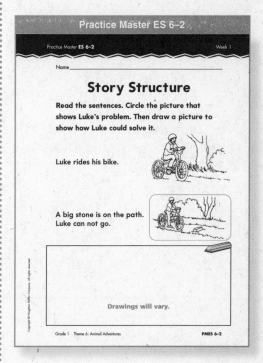

Day 3

SKILL FOCUS: 25–30 MINUTES

High-Frequency Words

Teach

Write the words *morning, found, shout, by, out, show,* and *climb* on the board. Point to each word as you read it aloud. Invite children to help you read the words aloud a second time.

Display the Letter Cards on the chalk tray. Ask children, *How many letters are in the word* found?

Draw five squares on the board.

Ask children to help spell the word *found.* Point to the word on the board and ask, *What letter comes first?* Instruct children to say the letter and draw it in the air. Ask a volunteer to find the letter, write the letter in the first box on the board, and face the group holding the card. Repeat the procedure for the remaining letters, asking, *What letter comes next?* Have volunteers stand side-by-side with the Letter Cards to spell the word *found.* Ask the group to read the word aloud together. Repeat the procedure for the remaining words.

Practice

Instruct children to write each high-frequency word on a large index card. Write the following sentences on the board:

In the morning, I do not climb out of bed.

I like to sleep as long as I can.

Mom and Dad come by with a shout.

"Show us you are up! We found you!
It is time to go out!"

Read the sentences aloud and point to the words as you read. Next, read without pointing, and instruct children to raise their word cards when they hear those words in the sentences.

Check each child's ability to pronounce *morning, found, shout, by, out, show,* and *climb* as the child reads each sentence.

Objective

- read and write high-frequency words: *morning, found, shout, by, out, show, climb*

Materials

- Letter Cards: *b, c, d, f, g, h, i, l, m, n (2), o, r, s, t, u, w, y*
- index cards
- Phonics Library: *Legs Gets His Lunch*

Apply

Have children write the sentences from the previous activity on sentence strips. Then have them cut up the sentence strips and then rebuild the sentences.

LITERATURE FOCUS: 10–15 MINUTES

Review *Legs Gets His Lunch*

Reread the story together with children. Have children take turns reading aloud.

Have children look through *Legs Gets His Lunch* to find the following high-frequency words: *out, climb*. Have them read the sentences that contain these words.

SKILL FOCUS: PHONICS 10–15 MINUTES

Long o (CV, CVCe) and Long u (CVCe)

Teach

Say *no* and ask children to repeat it after you. Tell them that the sound at the end of *no* is the long sound for *o*, the same as the letter's name. Then have them say the long *o* sound after you, /ō/.

Display Picture Card *note* and have children identify the picture. Ask them which *o* sound they hear in note, the long *o* sound, /ō/, or the short *o* sound, /ŏ/. Follow the same procedure with Picture Cards *fox*, *hose*, and *lock*.

Say *cute* and ask children to repeat it after you. Remind children that the long sound for *u* is /yo͞o/, and it can also sound like *u*, /o͞o/. Then have them say the long *u* sound after you, /yo͞o/.

Display Picture Card *mule* and have children identify the picture. Ask them which *u* sound they hear in *mule*, the long *u* sound /yo͞o/, or the short *u* sound /ŭ/. Repeat with Picture Cards *bus*, *cube*, *tube*, and *hug*.

Write *no* on the board. Remind children that many two-letter words that end with *o* have the long *o* sound. Point to each letter and help children blend, /nnnō ō ō/. Then write *note* and *mule*, pointing to the vowel-consonant-*e* pattern. Remind children that the *e* in this pattern is silent. Explain that words with this pattern often have a long vowel sound. Help children use Blending Routine 2 to blend each word. Have them say the sounds for *n*, /n/, and long *o*, /ō/, and blend /nnnō ō ō/. Finally, have them say the sound for *t*, /t/, blend /nnnō ō ōt/, and say *note*. Follow a similar procedure for *mule*.

Practice

Point to *no* on the board. Display Letter Cards *g* and *s*. Have children choose Letter Cards to place in front of *o* and read the new words. If they need help reading, have them blend continuously. Repeat with *note* and Letter Cards *t* and *v*, and *mule* and Letter Card *r*.

Apply

Have partners look for words with long *o* and long *u* in *Duke's Gift*. Have them read aloud each word and the sentence that contains it.

Objectives

- blend phonemes
- associate the long *o* sound with the letter *o* and the long *u* sound with the letter *u*
- independently read words with long *o* and long *u*

Materials

- Letter Cards: *g, r, s, t, v*
- Picture Cards: *bus, cube, fox, hose, hug, lock, mule, note, tube*
- Phonics Library: *Duke's Gift*

Final Clusters *ft, lk, nt*

Teach

Display Letter Card *f* and have children repeat the sound *f* makes after you, /f/. Repeat for the letter *t*. Use the Letter Cards *f* and *t* to model how to blend /f/ and /t/. Hold the Letter Cards apart, and, as you say /f/-/t/, move them together until they touch. Have children repeat /f/-/t/. Repeat for the clusters *lk* and *nt*.

Hold up Picture Card *raft* and ask children to identify the picture. Ask them what they hear at the end of *raft*, /f/ or /ft/. Follow the same procedure with the Picture Card *scarf*. Repeat for the final clusters *lk* and *nt*, using Picture Cards *bell* and *milk* for *lk* and *ant* and *run* for *nt*.

Write *raft* on the board. Underline the *ft* as you explain that when we see the consonants *f* and *t* together, they are always found at the end of a word. Use Blending Routine 2 to help children blend *raft*. Have them say the sounds for *r*, /r/ and *a*, /ă/, and then blend /rrrăăă/. Have them say the sounds for *f*, /f/ and blend /rrrăăă fff/. Finally, have them say the sound for *t*, /t/ and blend the whole word, /rrrăăăffft/, *raft*. Then write *left* and *gift* on the board, underline the *ft*, and have children blend the words with you. Repeat with *milk*, *elk*, and *silk* for *lk* and *ant*, *tent*, and *hunt* for *nt*.

Practice

Distribute the Picture Cards and Word Cards *raft*, *milk*, and *ant* to children. Have the children with the Word Cards find and stand next to the child with the matching Picture Card. Have each pair of children point to the final cluster, say its sound, and read the word.

Apply

Have partners work together to find words with *ft*, *lk*, and *nt* in *Duke's Gift*. Each time a child finds a word, the child should read it aloud and have his or her partner read the sentence that contains it.

Review *The Sleeping Pig*

Reread the story together with children. Ask children to make a list of long *o* and long *u* words that they find in the story.

Objectives

- associate /ft/ with the letters *ft*, /lk/ with the letters *lk*, /nt/ with the letters *nt*
- independently read words ending with -*ft*, -*lk*, and -*nt*

Materials

- Letter Cards: *f, k, l, n, t*
- Picture Cards: *ant, bell, milk, raft, run, scarf*
- Word Cards: *ant, milk, raft*
- Phonics Library: *Duke's Gift*
- Anthology: *The Sleeping Pig*

Objectives

- identify elements of a story
- use a story map to show story structure

Materials

- Phonics Library: *Duke's Gift, Legs Gets His Lunch*
- Anthology: *The Sleeping Pig*

Story Structure

Teach

Have children help plan a story about their class. Ask,

- *Who is in the story?*
- *Where and when does the story take place?*
- *What happens in the story?*
- *Is there a problem to solve?*

Explain to children that every story tells who is in the story, where and when the story takes place, and what happens. Explain that these parts of a story are called the *characters*, the *setting*, and the *plot*. Tell children that the plot often contains a problem to solve.

Practice

Begin a story map for *The Sleeping Pig*. Read aloud the first page of the story. Ask children to identify the setting and the characters. Ask them to tell what they know about the plot so far. Ask, *Is there a problem to solve?* Elicit further information about the plot, new characters, and new information about the setting and complete the story map.

STORY MAP
Place: Watermelon Patch
Setting/Time: Morning
Characters: Celia, Mrs. Pig, Coyote
Problem: A pig is sleeping in the watermelon patch and won't wake up.
What happens: 1. Coyote howls to try to wake pig up. 2.? 3.?
Solution: ?

Apply

Have children use the story map to summarize the story. Record their ideas in a paragraph.

Help children to see how developing a story map and summarizing the story can help them to remember and understand what they read.

Revisit *Duke's Gift, Legs Gets His Lunch,* and *The Sleeping Pig*

Page through the stories with children. Then ask them to find words that end with *ft*, *lk*, and *nt*.

Have children name the different characters and discuss the problems in each story.

Tell children to look through *The Sleeping Pig* to find the following high-frequency words: *morning, found, shout, by, out, show, climb*.

Have them read aloud their favorite sentences or pages from the stories.

Day 1

Objectives

- associate the /ē/ sound with the letter *e*
- blend and read long *e* words

Materials

- Teaching Master ES6-3
- Letter Cards: *b, e* (2), *h, P, s, t*

Technology

Get Set for Reading
CD-ROM

EEK! There's a Mouse in the House

Education Place

www.eduplace.com
EEK! There's a Mouse in the House

Audio CD

EEK! There's a Mouse in the House
Audio CD for **Animal Adventures**

Lexia Phonics
CD-ROM

Primary Intervention

SKILL FOCUS: PHONICS   10–15 MINUTES

Long *e* (CV, CVCe)

Teach

Recite and repeat the chant shown. Ask children to join in.

> **CHANT**
>
> "We need to eat," Steve said to Pete.
>
> "Yes," said Pete, "but let's be neat."

Say *we*. Then have children repeat it several times. Isolate and stretch the long *e* vowel sound. Have children repeat the /ē/ sound. Say: *This is called the long* e *vowel sound.*

Have children listen as you say the chant again. Tell them to raise their hand each time they hear a word with the long *e* vowel sound.

Blend

Use Letter Cards to display *be*. Point to the word and say /bēēē/, *be*. Say that just the one letter *e* can stand for the long *e* sound in some words.

Use Blending Routine 1 to model for children how to blend the word, stretching the long *e* sound. Then have them blend and say the word with you before asking them to try blending it on their own.

Use Letter Cards to display *these*. Say the word for children, and point out that in this word the long *e* sound is made with the vowel-consonant-*e* pattern. Model how to blend *these*, again stretching out the long *e* sound. Have children blend and say the word with you. Repeat the process with the words *she, he,* and *Pete*.

Guided Practice

Display or **distribute** Teaching Master ES6-3, and discuss the illustrations with children. Tell them to use what they know about the long *e* sound as they read the sentences with you. Point to long *e* words in the sentences, and have children read them.

Monitor children to be sure they are blending the words correctly.

SKILL FOCUS: PHONICS   10–15 MINUTES

Vowel Pair *ee*

Teach

Recite and repeat the chant shown. Encourage children to join in.

> CHANT
>
> Beep, jeep, beep!
>
> Through the busy street.

Say *beep* stretching the long *e* vowel sound and have children repeat the word with you. Identify the sound as the long *e* vowel sound. Print *beep* on the board and underline the *ee*. Tell children that the long *e* sound is sometimes spelled *ee*. Repeat the chant asking children to listen for other words that have the long *e* sound.

Blend

Print *keep* on the board. Point to the word as you use Blending Routine 1 to blend the sounds, stretching the /ē/, and then saying the word.

Have children blend *keep* with you, saying /k ē ē ē p/, *keep*. Then have them blend it on their own. Repeat with *deep*, *feel*, *seed*, and *greet*.

Practice/Apply

Distribute Practice Master ES6-3, and discuss the picture with children. Read the directions, explaining to children what they need to do.

Have children read the sentences independently, and then aloud. Ask them to share their responses.

Check that they are blending long *e* words correctly.

LITERATURE FOCUS: 10–15 MINUTES

Preview *Seal Beach*

Preview *Seal Beach* with children. Walk them through the story, discussing the illustrations, naming the characters, and using words from the story such as *we*, *she*, *see*, *steep*, *keeps*, and *feed*.

Objectives

- associate /ē/ with *ee*
- blend and read words with *ee*

Materials

- Practice Master ES6-3
- Phonics Library: *Seal Beach*

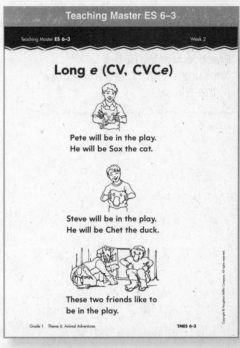

Teaching Master ES 6–3

Long e (CV, CVCe)

Pete will be in the play.
He will be Sox the cat.

Steve will be in the play.
He will be Chet the duck.

These two friends like to be in the play.

Grade 1 • Theme 6: Animal Adventures   TMES 6-3

Practice Master ES 6–3

Name _____

Vowel Pair *ee*

Use sounds you know to read the story. Write the number word that tells how many sheep you see.

Take a peek.
How many sheep do you see?
One sheep? Two sheep? Three sheep?
Thinking of sheep makes Steve sleep.

How many sheep do you see? ____ three

Grade 1 • Theme 6: Animal Adventures   PMES 6-3

Day 2

Objective
- identify details in a story

Materials
- Teaching Master ES6-4
- Practice Master ES6-4
- Anthology: *EEK! There's a Mouse in the House*

Noting Details

Teach

Draw an outline of a house on the board, and tell children that you are going to tell them a story and you want them to think about the details in the story.

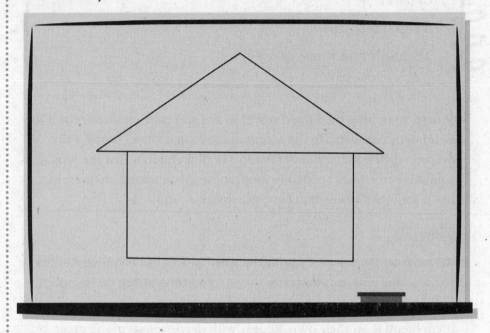

Say: *There was a house sitting at the top of a hill. The front of the house had two windows and a big door. A little boy lived in the house. One day, when the sun was shining brightly, the boy went outside to play under a big tree. He watched a bird flying by and a squirrel climbing up the tree. The boy loved watching all the wildlife around him.*

Ask children to come to the board and add details from the story to the drawing of the house. (Children should draw two windows and a door on the house; the house should be sitting on a hill; the sun is shining; a boy is playing under a large tree; a bird is flying by; a squirrel is running up the tree) **Repeat the story if necessary.**

Explain to children that paying attention to details in a story will help them better remember what the story is about.

Guided Practice

Display or **distribute** Teaching Master ES6-4, and discuss the illustration with children.

Tell them they will read a story with you. Remind children to pay close attention to the details in the story.

Read the story with children.

Ask children which detail in the illustration does not match the story. (Frog is wearing shorts in the picture, but the story says he is wearing long pants.)

Practice/Apply

Distribute Practice Master ES6-4. Discuss the illustrations with children and read the directions with them.

Have children read the sentences independently. Then have them circle the picture that reflects the details mentioned in the text.

Check children's responses to be sure that they are reading carefully and noting the important details.

LITERATURE FOCUS: 10–15 MINUTES

Preview *EEK! There's a Mouse in the House*

Walk children through *EEK! There's a Mouse in the House* on pages 164–182 in their Anthology.

Discuss the illustrations and use words from the story such as *EEK*, *me*, *eating*, *sheep*, and *squeezed*.

Note the suggestions in the Extra Support boxes on Teacher's Edition pages T129, T130, T131, and T137.

Teaching Master ES 6–4

Week 2

Noting Details

Fox has a big hat.
Fox looks sad.
Frog has on long pants.
Frog smiles a lot.

TMES 6–4   Grade 1 Theme 6: Animal Adventures

Practice Master ES 6–4

Week 2

Name

Noting Details

Use what you know about sounds to read the story. Circle the picture that matches the story.

The cat likes the garden.
She sits by the flowers.
She looks at the bees that fly by.

Grade 1 Theme 6: Animal Adventures   PMES 6–4

Day 3

SKILL FOCUS: 25–30 MINUTES

High-Frequency Words

Teach

Write the words *cow, table, now, door, there, through, horse,* and *wall* on the board. Point to each word as you read it aloud. Invite children to help you read the words aloud a second time.

Display the Letter Cards on the chalk tray. Ask children, *How many letters are in the word* cow?

Draw three squares on the board.

Ask children to help spell *cow*. Point to the word on the board and ask, *What letter comes first?* Instruct children to say the letter and draw it in the air. Ask a volunteer to find the letter among the letter cards, write the letter in the first box on the board, and face the group holding the card. Repeat the procedure for the remaining letters, asking, *What letter comes next?* Have volunteers stand side-by-side with the Letter Cards to spell the word *cow*. Ask the group to read the word aloud together.

Repeat the procedure for the remaining words.

Practice

Instruct children to write each high-frequency word on a large index card. Write the following sentences on the board:

> There is a cow on the table.
> A horse has come through the door.
> Now two cats climb up the wall.

Read the sentences aloud, and point to the words. Next, read without pointing, and instruct children to raise their word cards when they hear the corresponding words in the sentences.

Check each child's ability to pronounce *cow, table, now, door, there, through, horse,* and *wall* as the child reads each sentence.

Objective
• read and write high-frequency words: *cow, table, now, door, there, through, horse, wall*

Materials
• Letter Cards: *a, b, c, d, e* (2), *g, h* (2), *l* (2), *n, o* (2), *r, s, t, u, w*
• index cards
• Phonics Library: *Pete and Peach*

Apply

Have children write the sentences on sentence strips. Then direct children to cut up the sentence strips and rebuild the sentences.

Review *Pete and Peach*

Reread the story together with children.

Ask children to look through *Pete and Peach* for the following high-frequency words: *cow, horse, wall*. Have them read the sentences that contain these words.

Day 4

SKILL FOCUS: PHONICS   25–30 MINUTES

Long *e* and Vowel Pairs *ee*, *ea*

Teach

Point to yourself and ask children to guess the word you are demonstrating. When someone has called out *me*, say the word and have children repeat it after you. Remind children that the long *e* sound is the same as the letter name. Then have them say the long /ē/ sound after you, /ē/-/ē/-/ē/.

Hold up the Picture Card *jeep* and ask children to identify the picture. Ask them which *e* sound they hear in *jeep*, the long *e* sound, /ē/ or the short *e* sound, /ĕ/. Follow the same procedure with the Picture Cards *bed*, *queen*, *jeans*, *jet*, *leash*, *web*, *peach*, *leg*, and *seal*.

Hold up the Sound/Spelling Card *eagle*, and point out that *e*, *ea*, and *ee* are three ways that the long *e* sound can be spelled. Have children say /ē/ as you point to each of the different sound/spellings again.

Write *me* on the board. Point out that the single *e* at the end of the word stands for the long *e* sound.

Use Blending Routine 2 to help children blend the sounds in *me*. Have children say the sound for *m*, /m/, then have them say the sound for long *e*, /ē/, and blend /mmmēēē/, *me*.

Display the Word Cards for *feet* and *leaf*. Remind children that the vowel pairs *ee* and *ea* usually stand for the long *e* sound. Run your finger under the *ee* in *feet* and the *ea* in *leaf* and have children say the long *e* sound in both words. Then use Blending Routine 2 to help them blend each word.

Objectives

- associate the long *e* sound with the letter *e* and the vowel pairs *ee*, *ea*
- independently read words with the letter *e* and vowel pairs *ee*, *ea*

Materials

- Picture Cards: *bed, jeans, jeep, jet, leash, leg, peach, queen, seal, web*
- Sound/Spelling Card: *eagle*
- Word Cards: *feet, leaf*
- Phonics Library: *Seal Beach*
- Anthology: *EEK! There's a Mouse in the House*

Practice

Distribute three self-stick notes with the letters *b*, *h*, and *w* written on them. Have children place the notes over the *m* in *me* and read each new word. If they need help reading, have them blend continuously. Example: /wwwēēē/.

Display the Word Card for *feet*. Distribute four self-stick notes with the letters *b*, *m*, *d*, and *l* written on them. Have children place the notes over the *f* or *t* in *feet* and read each new word. (beet, meet, feed, feel)

Follow the same procedure with the Word Card for *seal* and four self-stick notes with the letters *r*, *h*, *m*, and *t* written on them. (real, heal, meal, seat, seam)

Apply

Have partners look for words with long *e* and vowel pairs *ee* and *ea* in *Seal Beach*. Record the words and have volunteers underline the *e*, *ee*, and *ea* in each word, and read the word aloud.

LITERATURE FOCUS: 10–15 MINUTES

Review *EEK! There's a Mouse in the House*

Reread the story together with children.

Ask children to make a list of long *e* words that they find in the story.

Have children take turns reading aloud.

Day 5

Objectives

- note details that help in understanding the story
- record details in a word web

Materials

- Phonics Library: *Seal Beach, Pete and Peach*
- Anthology: *EEK! There's a Mouse in the House*

SKILL FOCUS: COMPREHENSION   25–30 MINUTES

Noting Details

Teach

Tell children to look out a classroom window and describe an object that they see. It could be another building, a playground, or a tree. As they describe the object, draw their attention to small details. Children may say that a building is tall or that there are a lot of swings. Ask, *How many floors does the building have? How many swings are there? What shape are the leaves on the tree?* Ask children to tell what they learned about the object that they didn't know before. Explain that looking carefully at objects and noting details help us understand what we see, and also what we read.

Practice

Reread aloud *EEK! There's a Mouse in the House.* Elicit details from children about characters and what they do. Ask, *Why is the animal brought into the house?* and *What does the animal do in the house?* Record children's suggestions in a word web.

Point out that the child in the story invites animals into the house to solve a problem. Walk through the story with children and work together to complete a word web. Ask them if they think the animals are helping. Remind children that noting details helps us understand what we read.

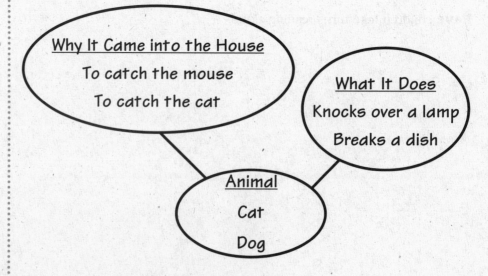

Apply

Have children reread the story, noting details that tell about time and place. Instruct children to look carefully at the pictures. When they are finished, have them draw and label a picture that describes the time and place of the story.

LITERATURE FOCUS: 10–15 MINUTES

Revisit *Seal Beach, Pete and Peach,* and *EEK! There's a Mouse in the House*

Page through the stories with children. Then ask them to find long *e* words.

Have children look through *EEK! There's a Mouse in the House* and discuss the details provided in the pictures.

Tell them to look through *EEK! There's a Mouse in the House* to find the following high-frequency words: *cow, table, now, door, there, through, horse, wall.*

Have children read aloud their favorite sentences or pages from the stories.

Day 1

Objectives

- associate the /ā/ sound with the vowel pairs *ai* and *ay*
- blend and read words with *ai* and *ay*

Materials

- Teaching Master ES6-5
- Practice Master ES6-5
- Phonics Library: *Rain Day*

Technology

Get Set for Reading CD-ROM

Red-Eyed Tree Frog

Education Place

www.eduplace.com
Red-Eyed Tree Frog

Audio CD

Red-Eyed Tree Frog
Audio CD for **Animal Adventures**

Lexia Phonics CD-ROM

Primary Intervention

Vowel Pairs *ai, ay*

Teach

Use the chant shown to introduce the /ā/ vowel sound. Recite the chant and repeat it, encouraging children to join in as they are able.

> **CHANT**
>
> Rain, rain go away.
>
> Come again some other day.

Say the word *rain*, isolating and stretching the long *a* vowel sound. Then have children repeat the /ā/ sound. Say: *This sound is called the long a vowel sound.*

Repeat the chant again asking children to listen for other words with the long *a* sound. (away, day)

Blend

Write *rain* on the board. Point to the word and use Blending Routine 1 to blend the sounds, stretching out the long *a*. Call attention to the two vowel letters that together stand for the sound.

Have children blend and say the word *rain* with you. Then have them blend and say it on their own. Finally, ask children to use *rain* in a sentence.

Use the same blending steps to introduce the vowel pair *ay*. Blend *day* and *play* with children.

Have children blend the following words on their own: *gray, bay, sail, stray, maid, say, pail,* and *trail.*

Check that children are blending the sounds correctly.

Guided Practice

Display or **distribute** Teaching Master ES6-5, and discuss the illustration with children. Tell them to use what they know about the long *a* sound as they read the sentences with you.

Help children identify long *a* words in the sentences and write them on the board.

Ask children to use each of the long *a* words in a new sentence.

Practice/Apply

Distribute Practice Master ES6-5 to children, discuss the illustrations, and read the directions with them.

Have children read the sentences and complete the Practice Master independently.

Check children's responses to be sure they are able to identify the long *a* words.

LITERATURE FOCUS: 10–15 MINUTES

Preview *Rain Day*

Preview *Rain Day* by walking children through the story. Discuss the illustrations, naming the characters and using words from the story such as *rain, day, play,* and *tail.*

Ask children if they think the dog likes to be out in the rain.

Tell children they will read this story with the rest of the class.

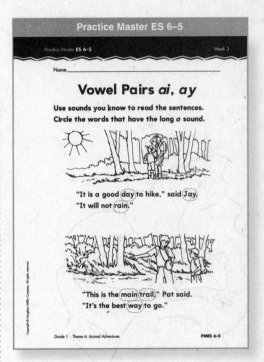

Day 2

Objectives

- use text and picture clues to make predictions
- use previous knowledge to make predictions

Materials

- Teaching Master ES6-6
- Practice Master ES6-6
- Anthology: *Red-Eyed Tree Frog*

SKILL FOCUS: COMPREHENSION   25–30 MINUTES

Making Predictions

Teach

Show children a stack of drawing paper and a supply of crayons or markers. Then say that the paper and crayons or markers are clues to an activity they might do next.

Have children predict what they will do next. (draw and color pictures)

Tell children there are clues in stories, too, that can help them predict what may happen next.

Guided Practice

Display or **distribute** Teaching Master ES6-6. Discuss the illustration with children.

Tell them they will read a story with you. Then read the story, calling on children to help you.

Point to the two sentences below the story. Read them with children. Help children circle the sentence that tells what may happen next.

Have children identify clues in the story that helped them decide. (It rained for days, the street was wet, the van was going fast.)

Practice/Apply

Distribute Practice Master ES6-6 to children. Have them look at the illustration at the middle of the page. Identify the children as Ken and Jack. Then read aloud the directions for the activity.

Ask children to read the sentences independently and circle the picture that shows what will happen next.

Have children identify clues that helped them make their choice.

Check children's responses to be sure they understand the concept of making predictions.

LITERATURE FOCUS: 10–15 MINUTES

Preview *Red-Eyed Tree Frog*

Walk children through *Red-Eyed Tree Frog* on pages 192–214 in their Anthology.

Discuss the photographs and use words from the story such as *rain, day, wait,* and *away*.

Note the suggestions in the Extra Support boxes on Teacher's Edition pages T199, T202, T204, and T209.

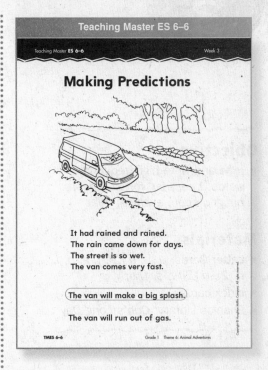

Day 3

Objective

- read and write high-frequency words: *been, far, forest, goes, hungry, soon, evening, near*

Materials

- Letter Cards: *a, b, e (2), f, g, h, i, n (2), o (2), r, s, t, u, v, y*
- index cards
- Phonics Library: *Cub's Long Day*

SKILL FOCUS: 25–30 MINUTES

High-Frequency Words

Teach

Write the words *been, far, forest, goes, hungry, soon, evening*, and *near* on the board. Point to each word as you read it aloud. Invite children to help you read the words aloud a second time.

Display the Letter Cards on the chalk tray. Ask children, *How many letters are in the word* far?

Draw three squares on the board.

Ask children to help spell the word *far*. Point to the word on the board and ask, *What letter comes first?* Instruct children to say the letter and draw it in the air. Ask a volunteer to find the letter, write the letter in the first box on the board, and face the group holding the card. Repeat the procedure for the remaining letters asking, *What letter comes next?* Have volunteers stand side-by-side with the letter cards to spell the word far. Ask the group to read the word aloud together.

Repeat the procedure for the remaining words.

Practice

Instruct children to write each high-frequency word on a large index card. Write the following sentences on the board:

> Soon it will be evening.
>
> The family is hungry.
>
> They have been far in the forest all day.
>
> Will they be near home when the sun goes down?

Read the sentences aloud and point to the words as you read. Next, read without pointing, and instruct children to raise their word cards when they hear those words in the sentences.

Check each child's ability to pronounce *been, far, forest, goes, hungry, soon, evening*, and *near* as the child reads each sentence.

Apply

Have children write the sentences from the previous activity on sentence strips. Then have children cut up the sentence strips so that they can rebuild the sentences.

Review *Cub's Long Day*

Reread the story together with children. Have children take turns reading aloud.

Have children to find and read the following high-frequency words in *Cub's Long Day: forest, hungry, evening.* Have them read the sentences that contain these words.

Day 4

SKILL FOCUS: PHONICS   25–30 MINUTES

Vowel Pairs *ai, ay*

Teach

Hold up the Sound/Spelling Card *acorn*, and ask children to identify the picture. Remind them that the long *a* sound is the same as the letter name. Have children say the long *a* sound after you, /ā/-/ā/-/ā/.

Display the Picture Card for *braid*, and ask children to identify it. Say *braid*, and ask children to repeat it after you. Ask them which *a* sound they hear in *braid*, the long *a* sound, /ā/, or the short *a* sound, /ă/. Follow the same procedure with the Picture Cards for *hay, cab, gray, train, bat, chain, cat, tray,* and *mat*.

Display the Word Cards for *braid* and *hay* next to the Picture Cards for *braid* and *hay*. Then hold up the Sound/Spelling Card *acorn*. Point to the *ai* on the acorn card and the *ai* in the word braid as you say /ā/ and have children repeat after you. Repeat this for the *ay* in *hay*. Tell children that *ai* and *ay* are two ways that the /ā/ sound can be spelled. Then help children to blend *hay* and *braid* using Blending Routine 2. Example: Have children say the sound for *h*, /h/, then the sound for *ay*, /ā/, and blend /hhhāāā/, *hay*.

Practice

Draw two boxes on the board as shown in the first row. In the last box, print *ay*. Tell children that you are putting two letters in one box to show that two letters stand for one sound.

Display Letter Cards *d, h, m, p, r,* and *s*. Have a volunteer choose a letter to place in the first box and blend it continuously with *ay* to make a new word. Continue with the other Letter Cards. Follow the same procedure with *ai* and three boxes. Write *ai* in the middle box and *n* in the last box; display the Letter Cards *m, p, r,* and *v*.

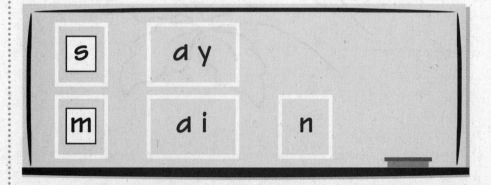

Objectives

- associate the long *a* sound with the vowel pairs *ai, ay*
- independently read words with vowel pairs *ai, ay*

Materials

- Letter Cards: *d, h, m, p, r, s, v*
- Picture Cards: *bat, braid, cab, cat, chain, gray, hay, mat, train, tray*
- Sound/Spelling Card: *acorn*
- Word Cards: *braid, hay*
- Phonics Library: *Rain Day*
- Anthology: *Red-Eyed Tree Frog*

Apply

Have children look for words with vowel pairs *ai* and *ay* in *Rain Day*.
Each time they find a word, ask them to say it aloud so you can write it
in one column on a chart. When the search is complete, have volunteers read the chart.

LITERATURE FOCUS: 10–15 MINUTES

Review *Red-Eyed Tree Frog*

Reread the story together with children.

Ask children to make a list of long *a* words that they find in the story.

Have children take turns reading aloud.

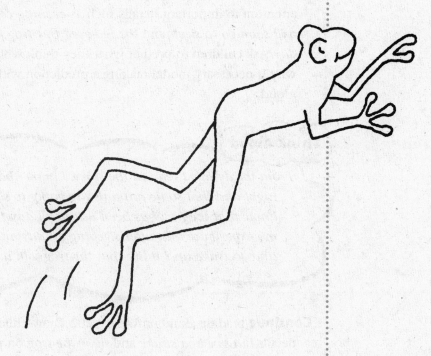

RETEACH

SKILL FOCUS: COMPREHENSION
25–30 MINUTES

Making Predictions

Teach

Have several children dramatize the following action. Tell the children, *Put your jackets on and pack your bags.* Ask their classmates to tell what they think will happen next. Correct responses include they will leave the room and they will go home. Discuss why children think those events will follow.

Explain that we use what we already know from our experiences and clues from our environment to figure out what will happen next. When we tell what we think will happen next, we are making a prediction.

Practice

Read aloud the first three pages of *Red-Eyed Tree Frog.* Draw children's attention to important details such as *evening comes, some animals will soon go to sleep*, and *the red-eyed tree frog has been asleep all day.* Ask children to predict what they think will happen next, and why. If necessary, model making a prediction with the following Think Aloud.

Think Aloud

From the details I read in the story, I know that it is almost night and that some animals are going to sleep. I also know that the frog has been asleep all day. I know from my experience that after sleeping all day or all night it is time to wake up. I think that the frog will wake up soon.

Continue reading aloud until page 202. Draw children's attention to the details *hungry boa snake* and *near the frog* on page 203. Ask children what they know about a hungry snake and what they can tell about it from the picture. Ask them to predict what will happen next. Explain to children that they used details from the story, and what they already know from their experience about hungry snakes.

Objective
- use story details and personal knowledge to make predictions

Materials
- Phonics Library: *Rain Day, Cub's Long Day*
- Anthology: *Red-Eyed Tree Frog*

Apply

Have children make predictions with a partner for the following parts of the story. Instruct children to explain how they make their predictions.

pages 208 and 209: The frog sees a moth on a leaf. What will the frog do? (It will eat the moth.)

page 211: The tree frog is no longer hungry. What will it do next? (It will go to sleep.)

LITERATURE FOCUS: 10–15 MINUTES

Revisit *Rain Day, Cub's Long Day,* and *Red-Eyed Tree Frog*

Page through the stories with children. Then ask them to find long *a* words.

Have children look through *Rain Day* and predict whether the little girl and the dog will stay out and continue to play in the rain.

Tell children to look through *Red-Eyed Tree Frog* to find the following high-frequency words: *been, far, forest, goes, hungry, soon, evening, near.*

Have children read aloud their favorite sentences or pages from the stories.

Theme 7

We Can Work It Out

Day 1

Vowel Pairs *oa, ow*

Objectives
- associate the /ō/ sound with the vowel pairs *oa* and *ow*
- blend and read words with *oa* and *ow*

Materials
- Teaching Master ES7-1
- Practice Master ES7-1
- Phonics Library: *Pet Show*

Get Set for Reading CD-ROM
That Toad Is Mine!

Education Place
www.eduplace.com
That Toad Is Mine!

Audio CD
That Toad Is Mine!
Audio CD for **We Can Work It Out**

Lexia Phonics CD-ROM
Primary Intervention

Teach

Use the chant to introduce /ō/. Recite the chant several times with children, inviting them to join in. Then have children listen for and produce the /ō/ vowel sound.

> **CHANT**
>
> Toad and Crow row the boat.
>
> Row, row, row the boat!

Say *boat*, and have children repeat it. Isolate and stretch out the long *o* sound, and have children repeat it. Identify the sound as the long *o* vowel sound. Remind children they have worked with this sound before.

Have children listen to and repeat more long *o* words: *toad, crow, row, float, soak.*

Demonstrate how to row a boat. Say: *Listen to each word as I say it. If it has the /ō/ sound, pretend to row a boat. If it doesn't have the /ō/ sound, sit still. Here are the words:* hot, moan, grow, cow, coat, mop.

Blend

Write *toad* on the board. Use Blending Routine 1 to model how to blend the sounds, stretching out the long *o* sound and then saying the word. Explain to children that the two vowel letters *o* and *a* together make the long *o* vowel sound.

Have children blend the word with you. Then have children blend the word on their own. Ask a volunteer to use *toad* in a sentence. Repeat the same steps with the word *boat*.

Write the following words on the board and have children blend them: *float, goat, groan, road.*

Use the same blending steps to introduce the vowel pair *ow*. Model blending *row* and *snow* with children. Then have them blend *crow, glow,* and *mow*.

Guided Practice

Display or **distribute** Teaching Master ES7-1. Talk briefly with children about the illustration.

Tell children to use what they know about sounds as they read the sentences with you. Then point to words from the sentences randomly, and have children read them.

Direct attention again to the illustration of the animals in the boat. Ask children to decide which animal or animals should get out of the boat to make it light enough to float.

Practice/Apply

Distribute Practice Master ES7-1 to children. Talk with them about the pictures. Then read the directions.

Have children read and match the sentences independently.

Review the activity. Have volunteers read the sentences aloud. Then have children identify words that have the long *o* vowel sound.

Check children's ability to read words with *oa* and *ow*.

LITERATURE FOCUS: 10–15 MINUTES

Preview *Pet Show*

Familiarize children with *Pet Show* by walking them through the story. Discuss the illustrations, naming the characters and using words from the story such as *goat*, *toad*, *crow*, *show*, and *slow*.

Ask children which animal causes trouble at the pet show. (the goat)

Tell children they will read this story with the rest of the class.

Day 2

Objective
• identify story problem and solution

Materials
• Teaching Master ES7-2
• Practice Master ES7-2
• Anthology: *That Toad is Mine!*

Problem Solving

Teach

Tell children that you hoped they could draw some pictures for you, but that you don't have enough sheets of drawing paper for everyone. Show just a few sheets. Ask how you could solve the problem.

Discuss children's ideas, which may include borrowing paper from another teacher, cutting the sheets into halves, and so on.

Say: *In stories there are often problems the characters have to solve. It's fun to read to find out what they do. Sometimes you can think of other ways the characters could have tried to solve their problems, too.*

Guided Practice

Display or **distribute** Teaching Master ES7-2 to children, and discuss the illustration at the top.

Have children read the story with you. Tell them to think about the problem.

Have them look at the illustrations and sentences that suggest solutions. Read the solution sentences with children, and have them decide which solution is better. Encourage them to say why.

Help children choose the sentence that is the better solution and underline it.

Practice/Apply

Distribute Practice Master ES7-2 to children, and discuss the illustration at the top of the page. Then read aloud the directions for the page.

Ask children to read the page independently. Have them circle the sentence that tells what the story problem is and circle the picture that shows the solution.

Check children's responses to make sure they can use problem solving in their reading.

LITERATURE FOCUS: 10–15 MINUTES

Preview *That Toad is Mine!*

Walk children through *That Toad Is Mine!* on pages 17–37 in their Anthology.

Discuss the illustrations and use words from the story such as *share, lemonade, agree, mad, turn, hoptoad, toad, know,* and *road*.

Note the suggestions in the Extra Support boxes on Teacher's Edition pages T47, T49, T50 and T55.

Teaching Master ES 7–2

Teaching Master **ES 7-2**   Week 1

Problem Solving

Ken eats a snack.
He spills jam on his jeans.
There is a big stain.
What can Ken do to fix his jeans?

Ken can cut out the stain.

Ken can clean his jeans.

TMES 7-2   Grade 1   Theme 7: We Can Work It Out

Practice Master ES 7–2

Practice Master **ES 7-2**   Week 1

Name _____

Problem Solving

Read the story. Circle the sentence that tells the problem.

It is lunch time.
Pam would like to sit with her friends.
She cannot.
Why?

Pam has no meal.   Pam has no seat.

Circle the picture that shows the solution.

Grade 1   Theme 7: We Can Work It Out   PMES 7-2

Day 3

Objective

• read and write high-frequency words *again*, *both*, *gone*, *or*, *want*, *turn*, *hard*

Materials

• Phonics Library: *Nick Is Sick*

SKILL FOCUS: 25–30 MINUTES

High-Frequency Words

Teach

Write *again*, *both*, *gone*, *or*, *want*, *turn*, and *hard* on the board. Read each word aloud while pointing to it, and then have children say it with you. Remind children that they should use what they know about letters and sounds to read the new words.

Draw word boxes on the chalkboard for two-, four-, and five-letter words.

Begin a game in which you give clues about each new word and ask children to identify which word it is. For example, begin by saying, *I am thinking of a word that has four letters.* (Children can eliminate only two of the words.) *This word usually refers to "two"—two people, two animals, two holidays.* As children identify the word *both*, have them point to it on the chalkboard.

Have volunteers work with you to copy the letters into the boxes. As they write, all children can say the letters together and write the letters in the air.

Follow this same procedure with the remaining words.

Write on the board the following sentences, and read them together with children:

Turn to look both ways.

Are they gone?

Look again!

Check each child's ability to pronounce *again*, *both*, *gone*, and *turn* as the child reads each sentence.

Practice

Write the following rhyme frame on the chalkboard.

My friend and I
Both want to share
But it is hard for him and me.
We share our ________ or ________
again and again,
But not our ________ you see.

Have children read it together. Then have them copy the rhyme, completing the blanks with things they like and don't like to share with a friend. Children can draw pictures to match what they have written.

Apply

Have children show and read their completed poems to the group. Then ask children to exchange and read one another's poems.

LITERATURE FOCUS: 10–15 MINUTES

Review *Nick Is Sick*

Reread the story together with children.

Tell children to look through *Nick Is Sick* for the following high-frequency words: *both, gone, want*. Have them read the sentences that contain these words.

Day 4

SKILL FOCUS: PHONICS 25–30 MINUTES

Vowel Pairs *oa*, *ow*

Teach

Display the Picture Card for *boat*, and ask children to identify the picture. Remind them that the long *o* sound they hear in *boat* is the same as the letter name. Have children say the long *o* sound after you, /ō//ō//ō/.

Display the Picture Card for *snow*, and ask children to identify the picture. Then ask them which *o* sound they hear in *snow*, the long *o* sound, /ō/, or the short *o* sound, /ŏ/.

Follow the same procedure with the Picture Cards for *box*, *boat*, *crow*, *cot*, *dot*, *goat*, *lock*, and *bow*.

Display the Sound/Spelling Card *ocean* and point out the vowel pairs *oa* and *ow*. Remind children that the vowel pairs *oa* and *ow* usually stand for the long *o* sound.

Display the Word Cards for *boat* and *snow* next to the Picture Cards for *boat* and *snow*. Point to the *oa* in *boat* and the *ow* in *snow*, and remind children that both *oa* and *ow* stand for the long *o* sound.

Help children blend *boat* and *snow* using Blending Routine 2. Example: Have children say the sound for *b* /b/, then the long *o* sound for vowel pair *oa* /ō/, and blend /bōō/; then have them say the sound for *t* /t/ and have them blend /bōōt/ and say *boat*.

Objectives

- associate the long *o* sound with the vowel pairs *oa*, *ow*
- independently read words with vowel pairs *oa*, *ow*

Materials

- Letter Cards: *b, c, g, l, m, r, s, t*
- Picture Cards: *boat, bow, box, cot, crow, dot, goat, lock, snow*
- Word Cards: *boat, snow*
- Sound/Spelling Card: *ocean*
- Anthology: *That Toad Is Mine!*

Practice

Make a horizontal box that is divided into two squares. In the last square, print *ow*. Tell children that you are putting two letters in one square to show that two letters stand for one sound.

Display the Letter Cards *b, l, m, r, s*, and *t*. Have a volunteer choose a letter to place in the square in front of *ow* to make a new word. Follow the same procedure with *oa*. Create a horizontal box with three squares and put *oa* in the middle box; display the Letter Cards *b, c, t*, and *g*.

Have children choose letters to place in both boxes to make new words. If any children have trouble reading one of the new words, help them to blend it continuously.

Apply

Have children look for words with vowel pairs *oa* and *ow* in *Pet Show*. Each time they find a word, ask them to take turns saying the word aloud as you write it on the board. Have volunteers come to the board to underline the *oa* or *ow* in each word.

LITERATURE FOCUS: 10–15 MINUTES

Review *That Toad Is Mine!*

Reread the story together with children.

Ask children to make a list of *oa* and *ow* words that they find in the story.

Day 5

Objectives
- use strategies to problem solve in a story
- identify other possible ways to problem solve

Materials
- Phonics Library: *Pet Show, Nick Is Sick*
- Anthology: *That Toad Is Mine!*

RETEACH

SKILL FOCUS: COMPREHENSION   25–30 MINUTES

Problem Solving

Teach

Show children a pile of math counters—the same number as are in the group plus half that amount extra. Tell children, *I have a pile of counters for you all. I want to divide the counters in a way that is fair. What can I do?* Call on volunteers to answer. (possible answers: give one to each person and keep any extra for another day; divide them evenly) Then count the children and count the counters and ask children what can be done. (possible answers: give some children two and half the group only one; divide them evenly) Evaluate each of the possibilities and work with children to determine which solution is the fairest for all.

Explain to children that you had a problem, and together you found a way to solve it. Help them to see that together you were able to: 1) define the problem; 2) think of several solutions; 3) evaluate possible solutions; and 4) decide on the best solution. Tell children that characters in books often have problems, and the story is about how the problem gets solved. Tell children that a problem in a story helps to connect them to the characters and make the story more real.

Practice

Direct children to look back at the story *That Toad is Mine!* Remind them that the boys in the story have a problem. Reread pages 26–30. Ask the following questions while referring to the text and pictures of the story.

page 26 *What problem do John and his friend have?* (They both want the same toad.)

pages 26–28 *What solutions do they think of?* (cut the toad in half; take turns every day with the toad)

page 30 *Do their solutions work?* (No, the toad hops away.) Point out that when the toad hops away, John and his friend have a new problem. Refer back to page 32. Ask, *What is the problem for John and his friend now?* (They are mad at each other.) Read together pages 34–36. Ask, *How do the children solve their problem this time?* (They kick the stone until they aren't mad anymore.)

Apply

Have children identify other ways they might have solved the problems that John and his friend have. Have them: 1) define the problem; 2) think of possible solutions; 3) evaluate possible solutions; and 4) decide on the best solution. Point out that this problem-solving strategy can help them to evaluate the ways in which story characters solve their problems and how they may have done it differently.

LITERATURE FOCUS: 10–15 MINUTES

Revisit *Pet Show*, *Nick Is Sick*, and *That Toad Is Mine!*

Page through the stories with children. Ask them to find *oa* and *ow* words.

Have children look through *That Toad Is Mine!* to decide if the boys have solved their problem.

Tell children to look through *Nick Is Sick* to find the following high-frequency words: *both, gone, want.*

Have children read aloud their favorite sentences or pages from the stories.

Day 1

Objectives
- associate the /o͝o/ sound with *oo*
- blend and read words with *oo*, as in *book*

Materials
- Teaching Master ES7-3

Get Set for Reading
CD-ROM
Lost!

Education Place
www.eduplace.com
Lost!

Audio CD
Lost!
Audio CD for **We Can Work It Out**

Lexia Phonics
CD-ROM
Primary Intervention

SKILL FOCUS: PHONICS   10–15 MINUTES

The /o͝o/ Sound for oo

Teach

Recite and repeat the chant, encouraging children to join in.

> CHANT
>
> Look, oh look,
>
> What he can cook.
>
> Mmm—good! Mmm—good!

Repeat the word *look*. Isolate and stretch the /o͝o/ vowel sound. Then have children repeat *look* and stretch the vowel sound. Have them listen to and repeat more words with the /o͝o/ sound: *cook, good, shook,* and *wood*.

Tell children to clap each time they hear a word with the /o͝o/ sound. Say: *moon, box, hood, book, stood.*

Blend

Display *look.* Use Blending Routine 1 to model how to blend the sounds, stretching the vowel sound and then saying the word. Explain to children that the two vowel letters together produce the vowel sound.

Have children blend the word and say it with you, before blending it on their own. Repeat the same steps with the words *good, took,* and *wood*.

Guided Practice

Display or **distribute** Teaching Master ES7-3, and have children identify the picture at the top. Tell them to use what they know about sounds as they read the story with you.

Ask children to identify words with the /o͝o/ sound. Help them write the words on the cook's hat. Have children read the words on the list.

SKILL FOCUS: PHONICS 10–15 MINUTES

Compound Words

Teach

Recite and repeat the chant, encouraging children to join in.

> CHANT
>
> Time for a bath,
>
> so into the tub.
>
> Rub-a-dub-dub
>
> in the BATHTUB.

Say *bathtub* and tell children that it is made up of two words put together. Print *bath*, *tub*, and *bathtub*, one word below the other on the chalkboard. Have children observe how *bath* and *tub* have been combined to form the compound word *bathtub*.

Blend

Print *sun* and *shine* on the chalkboard. Use Blending Routine 1 to model how to blend the sounds in each word. Then blend the two words together and say *sunshine*.

Repeat with *cupcake*, *cookbook*, *Sunday*, and *railroad*.

Practice/Apply

Distribute copies of Practice Master ES7-3, and discuss the picture with children. Read the directions, reminding children to use what they know about sounds and letters to help them read the sentences.

Check children's responses to be sure that they can name the two small words that make up a compound word.

LITERATURE FOCUS: 10–15 MINUTES

Preview *Chan's Gift*

Preview *Chan's Gift* by walking children through the story. Discuss the illustrations, naming the characters and using words from the story.

Objectives

- recognize compound words
- blend and read words that are compounds

Materials

- Practice Master ES7-3
- Phonics Library: *Chan's Gift*

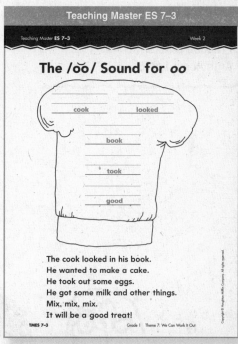

Day 2

SKILL FOCUS: COMPREHENSION   25–30 MINUTES

Sequence of Events

Teach

Talk with children about the order of events in a typical classroom routine, such as what happens at the end of the day when it is time to leave school. Say, for example: *First, we put away our books and papers. Next, we get and put on our coats. Last, we line up and leave the classroom.*

Ask: *Would it make sense for us to line up and leave the classroom before we got and put on our coats?* Make the point that the order in which things happen is important.

Tell children that things happen in order in stories, too. Explain that paying attention to the order of events makes it easier to understand and remember a story.

Objective
• order story events

Materials
• Teaching Master ES7-4
• Practice Master ES7-4
• Anthology: *Lost!*

Guided Practice

Display or **distribute** Teaching Master ES7-4. Encourage children to talk about the illustration at the top.

Have children read the story with you. Ask them what happens first in the story. Help them write *First* before the first sentence of the story. Then ask what happens next, and help them write *Next* before the second sentence. Repeat for what happens last.

Reread the story with children, including the sequence words *first*, *next*, and *last*.

Practice/Apply

Distribute Practice Master ES7-4 to children, and tell them they will put the pictures in the correct order to match the story. Talk about each picture briefly. Read aloud the directions for the page.

Have children read the story independently, cut out the pictures, and paste them on the page in correct story order. Have them use their sequence of pictures to retell the story in their own words.

Check children's responses to be sure they can put a set of pictures in the correct story sequence.

LITERATURE FOCUS: 10–15 MINUTES

Preview *Lost!*

Walk children through *Lost!* on pages 47–69 in their Anthology.

Discuss the illustrations and use words from the story such as *afraid, bear, idea, follow, elevator, city, park, books,* and *good-bye.*

Note the suggestions in the Extra Support boxes on Teacher's Edition pages T129, T131, T132, T137, and T138.

Teaching Master ES 7–4

Practice Master ES 7–4

Day 3

Objective

- read and write high-frequency words *afraid, any, bear, follow, most, tall, water, idea*

Materials

- Word Cards: *afraid, any, bear, follow, most, tall, water, idea*
- Phonics Library: *Ann Can't Sleep*

RETEACH

SKILL FOCUS: 25–30 MINUTES

High-Frequency Words

Teach

Write *afraid, any, bear, follow, most, tall, water,* and *idea* on the board. Read each word aloud while pointing to it, and then have children say it with you. Remind children that they should use what they know about letters and sounds to read the new words.

Display the Word Cards on the chalk ledge. Draw word boxes on the chalkboard for three-, four-, five-, and six-letter words.

Begin a game in which you give clues about each new word and ask children to identify which word it is. For example, begin by saying, *I am thinking of a word that has six letters.* (Children can now eliminate several of the words.) *It tells about a feeling someone has when frightened.* As children identify the word *afraid,* have volunteers choose it from the chalk ledge and work with you to copy the letters into the boxes. As they write, all children can say the letters together and write the letters in the air.

Follow this same procedure with the remaining words.

Write on the board the following sentences, and read them together with children:

Is any bear afraid of water?

Watch that tall bear splash!

Check each child's ability to pronounce *afraid, any, bear, tall,* and *water* as the child reads each sentence.

Practice

Write the following sentence starters on the chalkboard and have children read them.

> I am afraid of _____.
>
> Water, _____, and _____ are good for a bear.
>
> _____ is as tall as I am.
>
> Most of the time, it is a good idea to follow _____.

Have children work in pairs to copy and complete the sentences.

Apply

Have children show and read their completed sentences to the group. As they read their sentences, keep a list on the board of their responses. Write their responses under these headings: *What are we afraid of? What is good for a bear? Who is as tall as I am? What should you follow most of the time?*

Have children read each question heading and read along with you as you point to their responses.

LITERATURE FOCUS: 10–15 MINUTES

Review *Ann Can't Sleep*

Reread the story together with children. Have children take turns reading aloud.

Have children look through *Ann Can't Sleep* to find the following high-frequency words: *afraid, bear, idea.* Have them read the sentences that contain these words.

Day 4

Objectives

- associate *oo* with the sound /o͞o/
- independently read words with the sound /o͞o/

Materials

- Letter Cards: *b, d, g, w*
- Picture Cards: *book, box, dot, foot, hood*
- Sound/Spelling Card: *book*
- Word Card: *book*
- Phonics Library: *Chan's Gift*

The /o͞o/ Sound for oo

Teach

Display the Picture Card *book*. Say *book*, and ask children to repeat it. Have children say the vowel sound for *oo* after you, /o͞o/. Hold up Picture Card *foot*, and ask children to identify the picture. Ask them which sound they hear in *foot*, the *oo* sound, /o͞o/, or the short *o* sound, /ŏ/. Repeat with the Picture Cards *box*, *hood*, and *dot*.

Display the Sound/Spelling Card *book*, and remind children that the letters *oo* can stand for the /o͞o/ sound. Have children listen for the /o͞o/ sound as you say *book*, and have them repeat the word after you. Display Word Card *book*. Then use Blending Routine 2 to help children blend *book*. Have them say the sound for *b*, /b/, then the sound for *oo*, /o͞o/ and blend /bo͞o/. Finally have them say the sound for *k*, /k/ and have them blend the whole word, /bo͞ok/, *book*.

Practice

Write *cook* on the board. Read the word aloud and have children repeat it. Display the Letter Cards *b, g, d, l,* and *w*. Then have a volunteer come to the board, choose one of the letters, erase the *c* or *k* and write the new letter in front of or after *oo* to make a new word. Have the volunteer continuously blend the new letter sounds with *oo*. Repeat the procedure to make the new words: *book, look, good, wood.*

Apply

Have partners look for words with the /o͞o/ sound in *Chan's Gift*. Each time they find a word, ask them to say the word aloud so you can write it on the board. When the search is complete, have each partner choose an *oo* word, and use it in a sentence.

Compound Words

Teach

Write *bedtime* on the chalkboard, and read it aloud. Draw a slash between *bed* and *time*, and explain that *bedtime* is a compound word made up of two smaller words. Say *bed* and *time*, and have children repeat the words separately and then together as a compound word.

Write *bathtub* on the board. Explain that one way to read a compound word is to find the first small word. Underline *bath*. Then draw a slash between *bath* and *tub*. Point out that the second small word is *tub*. Circle *tub*. Then say *bathtub* and have children repeat it after you.

Write *homesick* on the chalkboard. Read the word aloud and have children repeat it after you. Then say the words *home* and *sick* separately as you run your finger under each word. Ask a volunteer to come to the board and draw a slash between the two smaller words. Repeat with *classmate*, *seashells*, and *sunshine*. If children have difficulty identifying the smaller words, help them to use Blending Routine 2 to blend each of the smaller words.

Practice

Write the words *snap*, *note*, *back*, and *cup* in a column on the board. Write *cake*, *pack*, *book*, *time*, and *shut* in a second column. Have children read the words aloud. Then have volunteers match a word in the left column with a word in the right column to make a compound word. Write each compound word. Then have volunteers draw a slash between the two smaller words in each compound word.

Apply

Have pairs of children find compound words in *Chan's Gift*. Write the words on the board. Have volunteers come to the board and draw a slash between the two smaller words that make up each compound word.

Review *Lost!*

Reread the story together with children. Ask children to make a list of /o͞o/ words and compound words that they find in the story.

Objectives

- recognize that compound words are made up of two smaller words
- independently read compound words

Materials

- Phonics Library: *Chan's Gift*
- Anthology: *Lost!*

RETEACH

SKILL FOCUS: COMPREHENSION 25–30 MINUTES

Sequence of Events

Teach

Ask children if they have ever lost something in their house. Call on volunteers to explain how they found the missing items. Repeat their stories, using the words *first, next, then, last*, and *finally*.

Use the following Think Aloud to detail a sequence of events.

> **Think Aloud**
>
> *When I tell about something that I have done, I put the events in order in my mind. I remind myself what happened first and what came next. I use words like* first, next, then, last, *and* finally *to tell my story. These words help me connect the events in my story.*

Explain that authors often use clue words like *first, next, then, last*, and *finally* to tell their stories in sequential order.

Practice

Direct children back to the story *Lost!* Remind them that in this story, a bear gets lost and a little boy helps him find his way home. Tell children that there are many sequences of events in this story, and you are going to retell the events of the story using sequence words.

Tell children to turn to page 48. Ask, *How did the bear get lost?* Guide children to use sequence words and details from the text and picture, such as: *First, the bear climbed on the truck, and then he fell asleep. Next, the truck driver drove away. Finally, the truck stopped in the city.*

Objectives

- retell the sequence of events in a story
- use strategies to determine sequence of events

Materials

- Phonics Library: *Chan's Gift, Ann Can't Sleep*
- Anthology: *Lost!*

Have children continue to retell other events in the story, using the clue words *first*, *next*, *then*, *last*, and *finally* by asking these questions:

pages 49–50 *How does the boy find the bear?* (first he hears crying, then he looks in the truck)

pages 60–62 *What do the bear and the boy do in the park?* (first they take a boat ride, then they have lunch, finally they go to the play-ground)

pages 64–65 *What do the boy and the bear do in the library?* (first they get some books, next they look at pictures, then they find a map)

Apply

Have children act out events that happen in the story *Lost!* in the order in which they happen.

Bear: *climbs into truck and falls asleep* (next: wakes up and cries)

Boy: *walks down street and hears a noise* (next event: finds bear crying)

Both: *go up an elevator in a tall building and look around* (next: go down the elevator and walk across three streets)

Both: *eat lunch* (next: go to playground and swing)

LITERATURE FOCUS: 10–15 MINUTES

Revisit *Chan's Gift, Ann Can't Sleep,* and *Lost!*

Page through the stories with children. Then ask them to find /o͞o/ words and compound words.

Have children look through the stories and compare their sequence of events.

Tell children to look through *Lost!* to find the following high-frequency words: *afraid, any, bear, follow, idea, most, tall, water.*

Have children read aloud their favorite sentences or pages from the stories.

Day 1

Objectives

- associate the /o͞o/ sound with the vowel pairs *ew* and *oo*
- blend and read words with *ew* and *oo*

Materials

- Teaching Master ES7-5
- Practice Master ES7-5
- Phonics Library: *Clues from Boots*

Get Set for Reading CD-ROM

If You Give a Pig a Pancake

Education Place

www.eduplace.com
If You Give a Pig a Pancake

Audio CD

If You Give a Pig a Pancake
Audio CD for **We Can Work It Out**

Lexia Phonics CD-ROM

Primary Intervention

PRETEACH

SKILL FOCUS: PHONICS　　　25–30 MINUTES

Vowel Pairs *ew, oo,* (/o͞o/)

Teach

Use the chant shown to introduce the /o͞o/ sound. Recite and repeat the chant, encouraging children to join in. Then have children practice producing the vowel sound.

> **CHANT**
>
> The wind blew and blew.
>
> The leaves flew and flew.
>
> Snow will come soon.

Say the word *blew* and have children repeat it. Isolate and stretch the vowel sound. Then have children repeat the vowel sound. Have children listen to and repeat more words with the vowel sound /o͞o/. Say, *few, new, boot,* and *tooth.*

Say, *Listen to each word as I say it. If it has the /o͞o/ sound, moo like a cow.* Demonstrate a cow moo, stretching the vowel sound. Here are words to use: *hot, shoot, grew, now, new, bath,* and *booth.*

Blend

Display *blew.* Use Blending Routine 1 to model how to blend the sounds, stretching the vowel sound and then saying the word. Explain to children that the two vowel letters together produce the /o͞o/ vowel sound. Have children blend the word and say it with you. Then have children blend the word on their own. Ask a volunteer to use *blew* in a sentence. Repeat with the words *flew, crew, chew, stew,* and *drew.*

Use the same blending steps to introduce the vowel pair *oo.* Model blending *soon* and *tooth* with children. Have children blend *boot, spoon,* and *troop* on their own.

Guided Practice

Display or **distribute** Teaching Master ES7-5, and talk briefly with children about the illustration. Then tell them to use what they know about sounds as they read the sentences with you.

Point to words from the sentences randomly and have children read them.

Direct attention again to the illustration. Have children identify words in the sentences that have the /o͞o/ sound. Help them write the words on the side of the pot.

Practice/Apply

Distribute Practice Master ES7-5 to children. Talk with them about the pairs of pictures. Then read the directions.

Have children read the sentences independently and mark the correct pictures.

Review the activity. Have volunteers read the sentences aloud.

Check children's ability to identify words that have the /o͞o/ vowel sound.

LITERATURE FOCUS:
10–15 MINUTES

Preview *Clues from Boots*

Familiarize children with *Clues from Boots*. Walk children through the story. Discuss the illustrations, naming the characters and using words from the story such as *threw*, *food*, and *clues*.

Ask children how the dog lets the girl know what he wants.

Tell them they will read this story with the rest of the class.

Teaching Master ES 7–5

Teaching Master **ES 7-5** — Week 3

Vowel Pairs *ew*, *oo*, (/o͞o/)

spoon   stew
grew   soon
scoop

Mara dips a spoon in the pot.
She will mix the stew.
It has meat in it and beans she grew.
Soon it will be just right.
Then Mara will scoop up some to eat.

TMES 7–5   Grade 1   Theme 7: We Can Work It Out

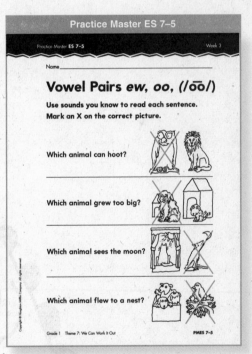

Practice Master ES 7–5

Practice Master **ES 7–5** — Week 3

Name_____

Vowel Pairs *ew*, *oo*, (/o͞o/)

Use sounds you know to read each sentence.
Mark an X on the correct picture.

Which animal can hoot?

Which animal grew too big?

Which animal sees the moon?

Which animal flew to a nest?

Grade 1   Theme 7: We Can Work It Out   PMES 7–5

Day 2

PRETEACH

SKILL FOCUS: COMPREHENSION   25–30 MINUTES

Fantasy and Realism

Teach

Objective
- distinguish between what is real and what is make-believe

Materials
- Teaching Master ES7-6
- Practice Master ES7-6
- Anthology: *If You Give a Pig a Pancake*

Tell children about something you did the previous evening, such as cooking dinner. Weave some fantastic details into your description, such as *My cat and I decided to practice flying around the living room while the dinner cooked. We got as close to the ceiling as possible.* When children react with giggles and object to the fantastic elements of your story, have them tell you what things could really happen and what things are just make-believe.

Say, *Sometimes stories can tell about real things and also tell about make-believe things. Good readers read carefully to know what could really happen and what could never happen in real life.*

Guided Practice

Display or **distribute** Teaching Master ES7-6. Have children read the story with you. Tell them to think about what is real and what is make-believe.

Reread the story with children, sentence by sentence, and ask volunteers to say if each detail describes something that is real or make-believe.

Help children write each detail in the correct portion of the chart.

Practice/Apply

Distribute Practice Master ES7-6 to children. Read aloud the directions.

Ask children to read the sentences independently and to look at the pictures. Have children circle each sentence that tells about something that is make-believe.

Check children's responses to be sure they can distinguish fantasy from realism in their reading.

LITERATURE FOCUS: 10–15 MINUTES

Preview *If You Give a Pig a Pancake*

Walk children through *If You Give a Pig a Pancake* on pages 79–103 in their Anthology.

Discuss the illustrations and use words from the story such as *syrup, bubbles, under, build,* and *glue.*

Note the suggestions in the Extra Support boxes on Teacher's Edition pages T201, T204, T205, T210, and T211.

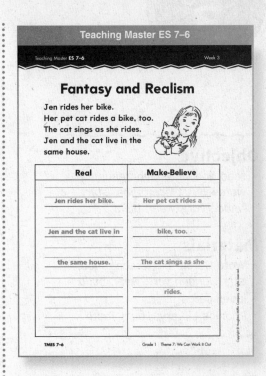

Day 3

SKILL FOCUS: 25–30 MINUTES

High-Frequency Words

Objective

- read and write high-frequency words *old, piece, shoe, start, under, very, wear, build*

Materials

- Word Cards: *old, piece, shoe, start, under, very, wear, build*
- index cards
- Phonics Library: *Lou's Tooth*

Teach

Place the Word Cards in the chalk tray. Draw word boxes on the board for three-, four-, and five-letter words.

Begin a game in which you give clues about each new word and ask children to identify the word. For example, begin by saying, *I am thinking of a word that has five letters.* (Children can now eliminate several of the words.) *It is something you can do with a hammer and nails.* As children identify the word *build*, have volunteers choose it from the chalk ledge and work with you to copy the letters into the boxes. As they write, all children can say the letters together and write the letters in the air.

Follow this same procedure with the remaining words.

Write on the board the following sentences, and read them together with children:

What is under that old shoe?

It is a piece of a very flat pancake!

Check each child's ability to pronounce *old, piece, shoe, under,* and *very* as the child reads each sentence.

Practice

Write the following sentences on sentence strips:

I will start to build a new toy plane.

I will use a piece of paper to start.

I will wear these very old shoes.

Read aloud each sentence. Ask children to draw a picture on a large index card to match the meaning of each sentence.

Apply

Have children read each sentence together while they match the sentence to their picture card. Continue by mixing the cards and sentence strips for children to practice reading and matching. You might want to cut up the sentence strips and have children rebuild the sentences, again matching their pictures to the rebuilt sentences.

Review *Lou's Tooth*

Reread the story together with children.

Tell children to find and read the following high-frequency words in *Lou's Tooth: old, shoe, start.* Have them read the sentences that contain these words.

Day 4

Objectives
- associate the /o͞o/ sound with vowel pairs *oo, ew, ue, ou*
- independently read words with vowel pairs *oo, ew, ue, ou*

Materials
- Picture Cards: *blue, book, hood, hook, soup, spoon, tooth, zoo*
- Sound/Spelling Card: *moon*
- Phonics Library: *Clues from Boots*

RETEACH

SKILL FOCUS: PHONICS   10–15 MINUTES

Vowel Pairs *oo, ew, ue, ou,* (/o͞o/)

Teach

Display the Picture Card *spoon*. Say *spoon*, and ask children to repeat it after you. Have children say the /o͞o/ sound after you, /o͞o//o͞o//o͞o/.

Hold up the Picture Card *tooth*, and ask children to identify the picture. Ask them which sound they hear in *tooth*, /o͞o/ or /o͝o/. Repeat with the Picture Cards *blue, book, hood, hook, soup,* and *zoo.*

Display the Sound/Spelling Card *moon*, and print the vowel pairs *oo, ue, ou,* and *ew* on the board. Remind children that these vowel pairs can stand for the sound /o͞o/. Have children listen for the /o͞o/ sound as you say *spoon, blue, new,* and *soup,* and have them repeat each word.

Write the words *spoon, blue, new,* and *soup*. Call on children to circle the *oo* in *spoon*, the *ue* in *blue*, the *ou* in *soup*, and the *ew* in *new*, and have children say the /o͞o/ sound in all the words.

Use Blending Routine 2 to help children blend each word. For example, have children say the sound for *s, /s/,* then have them say the sound for vowel pair *ou, /o͞o/* and blend /sss o͞o/. Last, have them say the sound for *p, /p/* and blend the whole word, /sss o͞op/, soup.

Practice

Write each of the vowel pairs on self-stick notes. Then write the following on the board: *food, glue, drew, soup*. Hand out the self-stick notes to children. Have each child come up to the board and find the word that matches the letter pair on his or her note, stick the note over the matching letter pair, and read the word. If children have trouble reading a word, help them to blend it continuously.

Apply

Have children look for words with vowel pairs *oo, ew, ue, ou* in *Clues from Boots*. Each time they find a word, ask them to say the word aloud so you can write it in one column on a chart. When the search is complete, have volunteers read the words with *oo, ew, ue, ou*. Have other volunteers underline the vowel pairs in the words.

Long *i* (*igh*, *ie*)

Teach

Ask children this riddle: *What rhymes with* tie *and tastes delicious to eat?* When someone answers *pie*, say *pie* again, and ask children to repeat it. Remind them that the long sound for *i* is the same sound as the letter's name, and have them say the sound after you: /ī/-/ī/-/ī/.

Ask children which *i* sound they hear in *tie*, the long *i* sound, /ī/, or the short *i* sound /ĭ/. Follow the same procedure with the words *lip, kit, right, tight, thigh,* and *fish*.

Hold up the Sound/Spelling Card *ice cream*. Point out that *ie* and *igh* are two ways to spell the long *i* sound. Write *high* and *tie* on the board, and circle the *ie* or *igh* in each word as you have the group say /ī/. Then help children blend each word using Blending Routine 2. For example, have children say the sound for *t*, /t/, then the sound for the letters *ie* /ī/, and blend /t ī ī ī/, *tie*.

Practice

Write *ie* and *igh* on self-stick notes and hand them out to children. Then write the following words on the board: *pie, sigh*. Have each child come up to the board and find the word that matches the letters on his or her note, stick the note over the matching letter pair, and read the word.

Apply

Have partners look for words with the letters *igh* and *ie* in *Clues from Boots*. Each time they find a word, ask them to take turns reading the word aloud as you write it on the board. Have volunteers come to the board to underline the *igh* or *ie* in each word.

Review *If You Give a Pig a Pancake*

Reread the story together with children. Ask children to make a list of *oo, ue, ou* words and *igh* words that they find in the story.

Objectives

- independently read words with the letters *igh* and *ie*
- associate the long *i* sound with the letters *igh* and *ie*

Materials

- Sound/Spelling Card: *ice cream*
- Phonics Library: *Clues From Boots*
- Anthology: *If You Give a Pig a Pancake*

Day 5

SKILL FOCUS: COMPREHENSION   25–30 MINUTES

Fantasy and Realism

Teach

Tell children about a dream with both real and fantasy events, such as the following:

I was driving in my car, when all of a sudden the car floated up into the sky. I drove around in the stars, and then my car landed near a restaurant. I ate a hamburger and fries at the restaurant, and then went back to my car. When I got in my car, it started talking to me. I drove home and parked the car. Then I went into the house and went to bed.

Ask, *What parts of that dream do you think could really happen?* (driving, eating burger and fries, parking the car, going to bed) *What parts of that dream could not really happen?* (car floating, driving in the stars, car talking)

Explain that we use our experiences and what we know about the world to tell the difference between fantasy and reality. Tell children that authors often use a mix of fantasy and reality to tell a story.

Practice

Recall the story *If You Give a Pig a Pancake* with children.

Ask, *Could a real pig do all those things?* (no) *Could a real pig do some of those things?* (yes)

Draw a chart on the board with two columns labeled *Reality* and *Fantasy.* Ask volunteers to name events in the story that could be real, and events that are fantasy. Use examples such as the ones shown.

Reality	Fantasy
Pig eats maple syrup.	Pig talks.
Pig has a bath.	Pig has a bubble bath.
Pig comes from a farm.	Pig wears tap shoes.

Objectives

- identify fantasy characters and real characters
- use prior knowledge to determine fantasy versus real events

Materials

- Phonics Library: *Clues from Boots, Lou's Tooth*
- Anthology: *If You Give a Pig a Pancake*

Point out that *If You Give a Pig a Pancake* has a mix of reality and fantasy in it. Explain that authors often use both elements to make a story seem real and to make it more fun and imaginative than what could really happen.

Apply

Work with children to tell how the story might be different if it included only real events. Help them to see that the pig would not be able to do many of the events in the story. Ask children to retell the story as if it were entirely real. Ask, *How does the fantasy make the story more fun?*

LITERATURE FOCUS: 10–15 MINUTES

Revisit *Clues from Boots, Lou's Tooth,* and *If You Give a Pig a Pancake*

Page through the stories with children. Then ask them to find *oo, ew, ue, ou* and *igh, ie* words.

Have children look through the stories for elements of realism and elements of fantasy.

Tell children to look through *If You Give a Pig a Pancake* to find the following high-frequency words: *build, old, piece, shoes, start, under, very, wear.*

Have children read aloud their favorite sentences or pages from the stories.

Theme 8

Our Earth

Day 1

Base Words and Ending *-ing*

Teach

Recite and repeat the chant shown, having children join in.

> **CHANT**
> Jumping up!
> Jumping down!
> Jumping, jumping
> all around!

Say *jumping*, stretching out the sounds in each syllable. Have children say the word.

Print *jump* and *jumping* on the board. Help children compare the two words, letter by letter so that they see that *-ing* is at the end.

Underline the *-ing* in *jumping*. Tell children that *-ing* is an ending that we sometimes add to words.

Blend

Give the word card *jump* to one child. Use Blending Routine 1 to model how to blend the word. Then have children blend and say the word.

Give the card with the ending *ing* to another child. Model how to blend the ending. Have the child with *ing* stand next to the child with *jump*. Have the children move the two cards together to make *jumping*.

Have children blend the sounds and then say *jumping*.

Repeat the process with other base words written on cards, such as *help*, *rain*, *look*, and *play*.

Objectives
- recognize the ending *-ing*
- read words with the *-ing* ending

Materials
- Teaching Master ES8-1
- Practice Master ES8-1
- word cards: *help, jump, look, play, rain*
- suffix card: *ing*
- Phonics Library: *A Fine Spring Day*

Technology

**Get Set for Reading
CD-ROM**
The Forest

Education Place
www.eduplace.com
The Forest

Audio CD
The Forest
Audio CD for **Our Earth**

**Lexia Phonics
CD-ROM**
Primary Intervention

Guided Practice

Display or **distribute** Teaching Master ES8-1, and discuss the illustration with children.

Tell them to use what they know about words ending with *-ing* as they read the sentences with you.

Ask children to point to and read words with the *-ing* ending. Then have them cover the ending and read the word that is left.

Monitor children as they are reading aloud to be sure they are blending words correctly.

Practice/Apply

Distribute copies of Practice Master ES8-1, read the directions with children, and remind them to use what they know about words ending with *-ing* to read the sentences.

Have children work independently to find each word that ends with *-ing*. Tell them to circle the ending and write the word that is left on the line.

Check children's work to be sure they found the correct words and circled the endings.

LITERATURE FOCUS: 10–15 MINUTES

Preview *A Fine Spring Day*

Walk children through *A Fine Spring Day* and discuss the illustrations. As you talk, name the characters and use words from the story such as *jumping*, *learning*, *building*, *eating*, *climbing*, *looking*, and *going*.

Have each child choose an animal and tell what it is doing. Then ask each child to predict what Cat will do when it begins to rain.

Tell children they will read this story with the rest of the class.

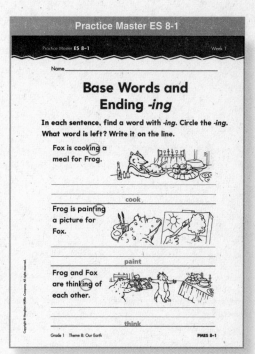

Day 2

Objectives
- categorize and classify objects
- categorize and classify pictures and words

Materials
- Teaching Master ES8-2
- Practice Master ES8-2
- books
- pencils
- Anthology: *The Forest*

SKILL FOCUS: COMPREHENSION   25–30 MINUTES

Categorize and Classify

Teach

Display a few books and pencils, and have children identify the objects.

Ask three volunteers to come forward and face the group. Give books to two of the volunteers and a pencil to the third.

Ask the two volunteers holding books to stand close together, and then ask whether the pencil belongs in the same group with the books. If needed, explain that it does not belong because it is not a book. Have the volunteer with the pencil stand apart from those with the books.

Hold up another pencil. Ask if anyone knows which group this object belongs in. Give the pencil to the child who responds correctly. Have that child join the volunteer with the other pencil.

Continue to hold up books and pencils, and have children group them until you are reasonably sure that everyone is catching on.

Guided Practice

Display or **distribute** Teaching Master ES8-2. Read the names of the pictures with children.

Tell children that we can put pictures of things into groups. Ask which pictures show things to eat, and have children circle them.

Ask which pictures show things to wear and have children cross them out.

Practice/Apply

Distribute Practice Master ES8-2, and name the pictures at the top of the page with children.

Have them work independently to decide whether each thing shown belongs inside or outside a house. Have children write the picture names under the appropriate headings.

Check children's work to be sure they are categorizing correctly.

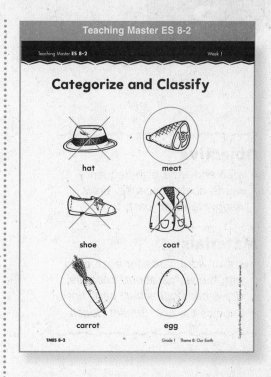

LITERATURE FOCUS: 10–15 MINUTES

Preview *The Forest*

Walk children through *The Forest*, pages 135–149 in their Anthology.

Discuss the photographs and use words from the story such as *tells*, *loves*, *interesting*, *planted*, and *added*.

Note the suggestions in the Extra Support boxes on Teacher's Edition pages T47, T51, and T52.

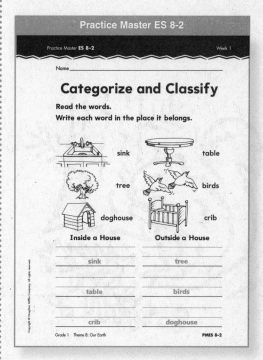

Day 3

Objective

- read and write high-frequency words *about, because, draw, happy, teacher, part, tiny*

Materials

- set of word cards for each child with the words *about, because, draw, happy, teacher, part, tiny*
- Phonics Library: *Sunset Beach*

SKILL FOCUS: 25–30 MINUTES

High-Frequency Words

Teach

Write *about, because, draw, happy, teacher, part,* and *tiny* on the board. Give each child a group of high-frequency word cards. Read each word aloud while pointing to it on the board. Ask children to find the word in their set of word cards.

Pause to give children an opportunity to say each word after you. Invite children to suggest sentences using each word while everyone holds up the word contained within that child's sentence.

Tell children that you will give clues for each of the words and they should look carefully at the words in their card decks to find the word that is being described. When they find it, ask them to hold it up for all to see. Here are some possible clues: *I am thinking of a word that begins with the same sound that you hear at the beginning of* hard. *This word is the opposite of sad.* (happy) *I am thinking of a word that rhymes with* start. (part)

Continue in this way until all of the word cards have been identified.

Write the following sentences on the board, and read them together with children:

We plant tiny seeds in part of our yard.

Our teacher tells us about how they grow.

We are happy because they are growing.

I will draw a picture of them.

Check each child's ability to pronounce *about, because, draw, happy, teacher, part,* and *tiny* as the child reads the sentence.

Practice

Write the sentence starter, *Our teacher is nice to us because* _____. and have children read it. Then have them copy the sentence and write two or three reasons that they believe the teacher is nice to them. Encourage children to use as many of their new words as possible and to repeat the sentence starter each time they add a new idea.

Apply

Have children read their completed sentence to the class. Add each
child's suggested responses to the sentence starter on the chalkboard.

Review *Sunset Beach*

Reread the story together with children. Have children take turns
reading aloud.

Ask children to look through *Sunset Beach* for the following high-
frequency words: *about, draw, happy, tiny.* Have them read the
sentences that contain these words.

Day 4

SKILL FOCUS: PHONICS   25–30 MINUTES

Base Words and Endings
-s, -ed, -ing

Teach

Objectives

- understand that *-s*, *-ed*, and *-ing* are endings that can be added to base words without making spelling changes
- independently read base words with endings *-s*, *-ed*, and *-ing*

Materials

- Picture Card: *smell*
- Word Card: *smell*
- Phonics Library: *A Fine Spring Day*
- Anthology: *The Forest*

Display the Picture Card for *smell*, and ask children to identify the picture.

Display the Word Card for *smell* next to the Picture Card. Read the word aloud and ask children to repeat it. Remind children that *smell* is an action word that tells what a person, animal, or thing does. Then point to the word *smell* and explain that *smell* is a base word to which different endings can be added. Then write *smells*, *smelled*, and *smelling* next to *smell*. Say the word *smell* aloud and have children repeat it after you. Point to the words *smells*, *smelled*, and *smelling*, and circle the base word *smell* in each word. Explain that the simplest part of a word is the base word and the letter or letters that have been added to it is the ending.

Have two volunteers pretend to be smelling flowers. Say,

_____ and _____ *smell the flowers.*

Have another volunteer stand up at his or her desk and mime the same action. Say,

_____ *smells the flowers.*

Repeat each sentence, and ask children to listen carefully for the word *smell* or *smells*. Then, on the board, underline the *s* at the end of *smells*.

Repeat the procedure with the endings *-ed* and *-ing* and the sentences: _____ *smelled the flowers;* _____ *is smelling the flowers.* Remind children that if the ending *-ed* is added to a base word, the new word tells that something happened in the past. Explain that adding *-ing* to a base word tells that something is happening now.

Practice

Write the following base words on the board:

spell   jump   lock   pick   need

Read the base words aloud, and have children repeat them after you. Ask volunteers to use each of them in a sentence. Have children come to the board to add *-s*, *-ed*, and *-ing* to each base word and then use each of the new words in a sentence.

Apply

Have pairs of children find words with *-s*, *-ed*, and *-ing* in *A Fine Spring Day*. Each time children find an *-s*, *-ed*, or *-ing* word, they should read it aloud while you write the word on the board. Have children come to the board and circle the base word and underline the ending in each word.

LITERATURE FOCUS: 10–15 MINUTES

Review *The Forest*

Reread the story together with children. Tell children to make a list of words that end with *-s*, *-ed*, and *-ing*.

Have children take turns reading aloud.

Day 5

RETEACH

SKILL FOCUS: COMPREHENSION 25–30 MINUTES

Categorize and Classify

Teach

Cut out pictures from magazines of plants and animals before beginning the lesson. Ask, *Are plants and animals different? How are they different?* (animals can move, animals make noise, animals have babies, etc.)

Draw a chart similar to the one below.

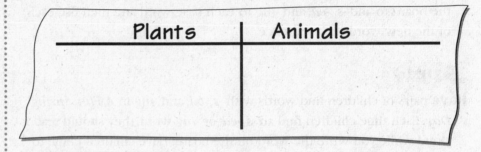

Plants	Animals

Point to the two categories on the chart and name them. Tell the children that you are going to hold up a picture. Direct them to tell you whether to put each picture in the category of plants or animals. Attach each picture to the chart in the appropriate category.

Remind children that when you classify things, you sort them into groups based on characteristics, like you just did with the plant and animal pictures.

Practice

Direct children back to the story *The Forest*. Draw a new plant/animal chart on the board or on chart paper. Tell children that they are going to help you categorize objects from the story. After reading each page, ask, *What plants or plant parts and animals did you read about on this page?* Write children's responses on the chart.

Help children to understand that classifying and categorizing can help them to remember what they read.

Apply

Have students think about what other plants and animals might live in the forest. Direct them to fold a piece of paper into fourths. Have them draw a plant or an animal in each section and label it. Display books or magazines with pictures of forests for children to refer to.

Objectives

• find examples of categorizing in a story
• group objects by attributes

Materials

• Phonics Library: *A Fine Spring Day, Sunset Beach*
• Anthology: *The Forest*

Revisit *A Fine Spring Day, Sunset Beach,* and *The Forest*

Page through the stories with children. Work with them to create a list of the different things they would find in a field, on a beach, and in a forest.

Tell children to find words in the stories with the endings *-s, -ed,* or *-ing*.

Ask children to look through *The Forest* for the following high-frequency words: *about, because, draw, happy, part, teacher, tiny*.

Have children read aloud selected sentences or pages from the stories.

Day 1

Objectives
- associate /ou/ with the letter pairs *ou* and *ow*
- blend and read words with *ou* and *ow*

Materials
- Teaching Master ES8-3
- Letter Cards: *c, h, l, n, o, p, t, u, w*

Get Set for Reading
CD-ROM
Butterfly

Education Place
www.eduplace.com
Butterfly

Audio CD
Butterfly
Audio CD for **Our Earth**

Lexia Phonics
CD-ROM
Primary Intervention

SKILL FOCUS: PHONICS   10–15 MINUTES

Vowel Pairs *ou*, *ow* (/ou/)

Teach

Recite and repeat the chant shown, having children join in.

> CHANT
> Say ow now.
> Ow, ow, ow.
> Be sure to say it loud.
> OW! OW! OW!

Say *now*, stretching out the /ou/ sound. If needed, model for children the /ou/ mouth position. Have children repeat *ow* several times.

Print *ow* on the board, and tell children that these two letters can stand for the /ou/ sound. Print *ou* on the board and explain that the letters *ou* can also stand for the /ou/ sound.

Blend

Give a volunteer the Letter Cards for *o* and *w*. Ask the volunteer to hold the cards next to each other with the letters in the correct sequence. Use Blending Routine 1 to model how to blend the sounds. Have children blend the sounds for *ow* /ou/. Give another volunteer the Letter Card for *c* and have the volunteer say the sound, /k/.

Tell the two volunteers to move their Letter Cards together to form *cow*. As they do so, have children blend the sounds to make the word *cow*. Repeat with *how*, *now*, and *owl*.

Follow the same procedure with the Letter Cards *o*, *u*, and *t* to make the word *out*. Repeat with *pout*.

Guided Practice

Display or **distribute** Teaching Master ES8-3 and discuss the illustration with children. Tell them to use what they know about the /ou/ sound as they read the sentences with you.

Point to *ou* and *ow* words, and have children read them.

Monitor children to be sure they are blending words correctly.

SKILL FOCUS: PHONICS   10–15 MINUTES

Syllabication

Teach

Recite and repeat the chant shown, having children join in.

> CHANT
> Football, soccer, tennis too!
> Outside games are fun for you!

Say *football*, emphasizing the two syllables. Ask, *How many parts are in the word* football? (2) Tell children that a word part is called a syllable. Have them repeat the first line of the chant as you show them how to clap out the syllables.

Print *football* on the board and draw a slash between the *t* and *b* to show what the two word parts are. Explain that if two consonants appear together in the middle of a word, the word is divided between them into syllables. Repeat with the words *soccer*, *tennis*, and *outside*.

Blend

Print *funny* on the board. Using Blending Routine 1, model how to blend the sounds. Blend and then say the word with children, before having them blend the word on their own. Repeat the process with *hungry* and *happy*.

Practice/Apply

Distribute Practice Master ES8-3 and read the directions with children. Have them complete the Practice Master independently. Tell them to explain their drawings and read the words with two syllables aloud.

Check that children are reading the words correctly.

LITERATURE FOCUS: 10–15 MINUTES

Preview *Hound Dog and Round Dog*

Walk children through *Hound Dog* and *Round Dog*. Discuss the illustrations, naming the characters and using words from the story.

Objective
- independently read two-syllable words

Materials
- Practice Master ES8-3
- Phonics Library: *Hound Dog and Round Dog*

Teaching Master ES 8-3

Teaching Master **ES 8-3**   Week 2

Vowel Pairs ou, ow (/ou/)

My dog is a hound.
He does not growl.
But he does like to howl!

TMES 8-3   Grade 1 Theme 8: Our Earth

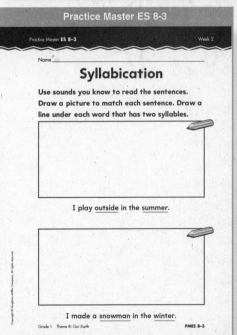

Practice Master ES 8-3

Practice Master **ES 8-3**   Week 2

Name_____

Syllabication

Use sounds you know to read the sentences. Draw a picture to match each sentence. Draw a line under each word that has two syllables.

I play outside in the summer.

I made a snowman in the winter.

Grade 1 Theme 8: Our Earth   PMES 8-3

Day 2

Objectives

- identify topic, main idea, and details of a story
- summarize a story

Materials

- Teaching Master ES8-4
- Practice Master ES8-4
- Anthology: *Butterfly*

Topic, Main Idea, Details/Summarizing

Teach

Ask children to listen as you tell a story about yourself. Say:

I am (your name), your teacher.

I can teach you how to read.

I can show you how to count.

I can help you write stories.

Ask whom the story tells about. Write your name or the word *teacher* on the board. Explain that this is the topic of the story and would be a good title for it.

Say the first sentence again. Tell children that it tells the main idea of the story. You may want to explain that the main idea is the biggest idea of the story.

Say the second sentence again. Explain that this is a detail that tells more about the main idea. Repeat for the remaining detail sentences.

Guided Practice

Display or **distribute** Teaching Master ES8-4. Read the story with children.

Point to the title. Explain that a title usually tells the topic of a story or what the story is about. Ask what this story is about. (Dan's Pets)

Read the first sentence with children. Explain that this is the main idea of the story.

Read the remaining sentences with children. Point out that they tell details about the main idea; they tell what kinds of pets Dan has.

Direct children's attention to the story web. Have a child point out the part that tells the title of the story. Remind them that this is called the topic. Have another child point out the main idea sentence.

Help children write the details that tell more about the main idea. Model for children how to use the story web to retell the story.

Practice/Apply

Distribute Practice Master ES8-4 and read the directions with children. You may want to remind children that they can look back at the Teaching Master if they need help.

Have children independently read the story and then complete the story web. Ask them to work with partners to compare their responses and retell the story to each other.

Check children's story webs to be sure they understand the concepts of topic, main idea, and details.

LITERATURE FOCUS: 10–15 MINUTES

Preview *Butterfly*

Walk children through *Butterfly*, pages 161–177 in their Anthology.

Discuss the illustrations and use words from the story such as *about*, *out*, *now*, *how*, *pouch* and *flowers*.

Note the suggestions in the Extra Support boxes on Teacher's Edition pages T127, T128, and T132.

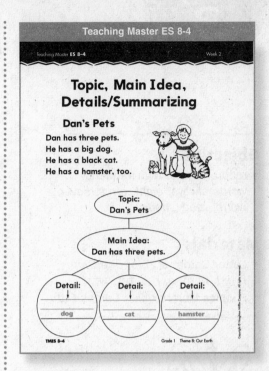

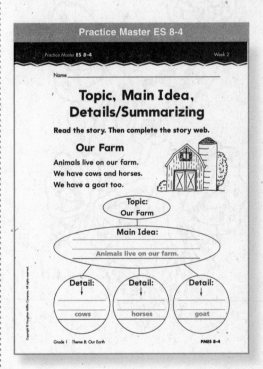

Day 3

High-Frequency Words

Teach

Write *always, eight, arms, seven, warm, ready,* and *body* on the board. Read the words aloud, pointing to each as you go.

Display the Letter Cards on the chalk ledge. Ask the group, *How many letters are in the word* always? Draw six squares on the board. Have six children come up to the board. Ask them to find each letter in the word *always* and help you spell *always.* Say, *Show me the letter I should write in the first box.* Repeat for the second through sixth boxes. Then ask, *How many different letters did I write?*

Tell children to put the letters back on the chalk tray. Have them stay in front to help lead the cheer. Tell children to tap their left foot for each letter and then clap for each syllable as you spell and say the word: *a-l-w-a-y-s, always.* Repeat the procedure with the other words on the list.

Write the following sentences on the board, and read them together with children:

I put my arms around my dog.

His body is warm and furry.

He is seven or eight years old.

He is always ready to play!

Check each child's ability to pronounce *always, eight, arms, seven, warm, ready,* and *body* as the child reads each sentence.

Practice

Write a sentence from the story that contains the word *always.* Ask the children to help you read the sentence. Tell them to read the word *always* all together as a chorus when it occurs in the sentence. Point to each word in the sentence as you read. Pause before the word *always* and resume reading after the group has supplied the word. Repeat this activity for each high-frequency word.

Objective
- read and write high-frequency words *always, eight, arms, seven, warm, ready, body*

Materials
- Letter Cards: *a(2), b, d, e(2), g, h, i, l, m, n, o, r, s, t, v, w, y*
- Phonics Library: *Allen Camps Out*

Apply

Have children work in small groups. Give each group two sentence starters on sentence strips. Ask children to complete the sentence by drawing a picture or writing a word. Invite children to share what they have written or drawn.

I have _____ body.

I have _____ arms.

I have seven _____.

I have eight _____.

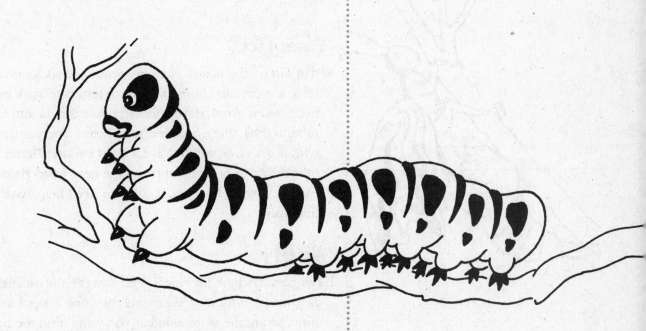

Review *Allen Camps Out*

Reread the story together with children. Have children take turns reading aloud.

Ask children to look through *Allen Camps Out* to find the following high-frequency words: *always, arms, ready, warm*. Have them read the sentences that contain these words.

Day 4

Objectives

- associate the /ow/ sound with the vowel pairs *ou*, *ow*
- independently read words with vowel pairs *ou*, *ow*

Materials

- Sound/Spelling Card: *owl*
- Picture Cards: *box, brown, cow, cot, cloud, clown, dot, house, mouth*
- Word Cards: *mouth, cow*
- Phonics Library: *Hound Dog and Round Dog*

SKILL FOCUS: PHONICS   10–15 MINUTES

Vowel Pairs *ou*, *ow* (/ou/)

Teach

Display the Picture Card for *cow*. Say *cow*, and ask children to repeat it. Then have children repeat the /ow/ sound after you, /ow/.

Hold up the Picture Card for *house* and ask children to identify the picture. Ask them which *o* sound they hear in *house*, the /ow/ sound, or the short *o* sound, /ŏ/. Follow the same procedure with the Picture Cards for *box, brown, cot, clown, dot, cloud,* and *mouth*.

Write the following vowel pairs on the board: *ou, ow*. Then hold up the *owl* Sound/Spelling Card and remind children that the vowel pairs *ou* and *ow* can stand for the /ow/ sound. Have children listen for the /ow/ sound as you say *mouth* and *cow*. Have them repeat each word.

Display the Word Cards for *cow* and *mouth* next to the picture cards for those words. Remind children that the vowel pairs *ou* and *ow* can stand for the /ow/ sound. Point out the *ou* in *mouth* and the *ow* in *cow*, and have children say the /ow/ sound in both words. Then have children blend *cow* using Blending Routine 2. Have them say the sound for *c*, /k/, then the sound for *ow*, /ow/, blend continuously /kow/, and say *cow*.

Practice

Write *out* on the board. Then distribute self-stick notes with *tr* and *sp*. Have a volunteer choose a letter or letters to stick in front of *out* to make a new word. Have children circle the *ou* and use the new words in sentences. Write *brown* on the board. Then distribute self-stick notes with *d, g, t, cl, cr,* and *fr*. Have a child choose a letter or letters to stick over the *br* in *brown* and blend the new word. Have children repeat each new word together. If children need help, have them blend continuously.

Apply

Have partners look for words with vowel pairs *ou* and *ow* in *Hound Dog and Round Dog*. Each time they find a word, ask them to take turns saying the word aloud as you write it on the board. Have children come to the board to underline the *ou* or *ow* in each word.

Syllabication

Teach

Display Picture Cards *snow* and *man*, and have children identify them. Write *snowman* on the chalkboard, read it emphasizing the two syllables, and have children repeat it. Draw a slash between *snow* and *man*.

Write *sunshine* on the board, say it, and have children repeat it. Explain that one way to read a word with more than one syllable is to find out if it is a compound word. Remind children that a compound word is made up of two smaller words. Point out that *sunshine* starts with the word part *sun*, and underline it. Then draw a slash between *sun* and *shine*. Ask children how many syllables are in *sunshine*.

Draw a mitten on the board, and have children identify it. Write *mitten* below the picture. Then say *mitten*, emphasizing the two syllables. Explain that one way to read a new word is to figure it out one syllable at a time. Point out that the word on the board has two consonants in the middle, *t* and *t*. Remind children that if two consonants appear in the middle of a word, the word is divided between them into syllables. Draw a slash between *mit* and *ten*.

Practice

Write the following words in on the board:

sand/box	rain/coat	sud/den	zig/zag	rab/bit

Read each word aloud, and have children repeat it. Have children clap out the word parts and draw slashes between the two syllables.

Apply

Have children find two-syllable words in *Hound Dog and Round Dog*, write them on the board, and draw a slash between the syllables.

Review *Butterfly*

Reread the story together with children. Have children make a list of words with vowel pairs *ou* and *ow*.

Objectives

- recognize that words can be divided into syllables
- independently read two-syllable words

Materials

- Picture Cards: *snow, man*
- Phonics Library: *Hound Dog and Round Dog*
- Anthology: *Butterfly*

Objectives
- identify the topic and main ideas within a story
- identify supporting details within a story

Materials
- Phonics Library: *Hound Dog and Round Dog, Allen Camps Out*
- Anthology: *Butterfly*

Topic, Main Idea, Details/Summarizing

Teach

Direct children to listen while you read the following to them:

The dragonfly is a very interesting insect. The dragonfly can fly at very fast speeds — up to 30 miles per hour. When it flies, it is able to twist and turn and hover and dart; it can even fly backwards. The eyes of a dragonfly are very powerful. Dragonflies have over 20,000 lenses in their eyes that allow them to see in many directions at once. The dragonfly was probably the first flying insect. It lived over 300 million years ago, even before the dinosaur.

Ask children to tell you the topic that most of the paragraph is about. (dragonflies) Ask what they think the main idea of the paragraph is. (The dragonfly is a very interesting insect.) Help children to see that each of the sentences that follows the first one supports the main idea *the dragonfly is a very interesting insect.*

Practice

Direct children back to the story *Butterfly*. Ask them what the topic of the book is. (butterflies) Read each main idea sentence, stated in the left-hand page headings. Then ask, *What sentences or pictures on these two pages support this main idea?* You might want to record children's responses on a Main Idea/Supporting Detail graphic organizer. After children identify the supporting details successfully on several pages, you might have them begin to identify both the main idea sentences and the supporting details. Help children to see how identifying main idea and supporting details can help them better understand what they have read.

Apply

Have children work together with partners to choose one of the main idea sentences in the story *Butterfly*. Then have them write two sentences that support the main idea with new details, drawing from both the text and the illustration. Invite children to share what they have written.

Revisit *Hound Dog and Round Dog, Allen Camps Out,* and *Butterfly*

Page through the stories with children. Work with children to find the main idea of the stories. Then make a list of the details supporting the main idea.

Tell children to find words in each of the stories that have the /ou/ sound.

Ask children to look through *Butterfly* for the following high-frequency words: *always, arms, body, eight, ready, seven, warm.*

Have children read aloud selected sentences or pages from the stories.

Day 1

SKILL FOCUS: PHONICS
25–30 MINUTES

Base Words and Ending -ing

Teach

Recite and repeat the chant shown, having children join in.

> **CHANT**
>
> Hop
> First add p,
> Then add i-n-g.
> What do you get?
> Hopping!
>
> Hope
> First take away the e,
> Then add i-n-g.
> What do you get?
> Hoping!

Say the first part of the chant with children. Remind them that *-ing* is an ending we sometimes add to words. Say *hopping*, stretching out the sounds in each syllable. Have children say the word.

Print *hop* and *hopping* on the board. Help children compare the two words, letter by letter. Point out that another *p* is added to *hop* before the *-ing* ending is added.

Say the second part of the chant with children. Say *hoping*, stretching out the sounds in each syllable. Have children say the word.

Print *hope* and *hoping* on the board. Help children compare the two words, letter by letter. Point out that the final *e* of *hope* is taken away before the *-ing* ending is added.

Objectives
- build words by adding the *-ing* ending
- read words with the *-ing* ending

Materials
- Teaching Master ES8-5
- Practice Master ES8-5
- word cards: *hop, hope*
- suffix card: *ing*
- Letter Card: *p*
- Phonics Library: *Hen's Big Show*

Technology

Get Set for Reading
CD-ROM

Johnny Appleseed

Education Place
www.eduplace.com
Johnny Appleseed

Audio CD
Johnny Appleseed
Audio CD for **Our Earth**

Lexia Phonics
CD-ROM
Primary Intervention

Blend

Give the word card *hop* to one child. Use Blending Routine 1 to model how to blend the word. Then have children blend and say the word.

Give a card with the ending *ing* to another child. Model how to blend the ending. Tell children that before they can add the ending, they must add another *p* to *hop*. Give the letter card for *p* to a volunteer. Tell the child with the card for *p* to stand between the other two. Then have the children move the cards together to form the word *hopping*.

Follow a similar procedure, using two volunteers, for *hoping*. Ask the child holding the card with *ing* to overlap it so that it covers the *e* in *hope* to form *hoping*. Explain to children that if a word ends with *e*, they must take away the *e* before adding *-ing*.

Guided Practice

Display or **distribute** Teaching Master ES8-5. Tell children to use what they know about words ending with *-ing* as they read the sentences with you.

Tell children to point to words with the *-ing* ending. Have them read the words. Ask children to tell you what happened to *dig* and *make* before *-ing* was added.

Practice/Apply

Distribute Practice Master ES8-5. Read the directions and discuss the pictures with children.

Tell children to complete the Practice Master independently. Then have children share their illustrations and read the story aloud.

Check children's responses to be sure they understand base words and the *-ing* ending.

LITERATURE FOCUS: 10–15 MINUTES

Preview *Hen's Big Show*

Walk children through *Hen's Big Show* and discuss the illustrations. As you talk, be sure to name the characters and use words from the story such as *begging*, *flapping*, *hopping*, *skipping*, and *joking*. Ask children to tell what each animal in the story is doing in the show. Tell them they will read this story with the rest of the class.

Day 2

SKILL FOCUS: COMPREHENSION   25–30 MINUTES

Drawing Conclusions

Teach

Tell children to listen as you ask the following riddle. Say:

I ride in a big red truck.

I wear a black coat, boots, and a hat.

I help put out fires.

Who am I?

Ask what clues helped children identify the worker as a firefighter. If needed, display a picture of a firefighter, and reread the riddle.

Objective
- draw conclusions

Materials
- Teaching Master ES8-6
- Practice Master ES8-6
- Anthology: *Johnny Appleseed*

Guided Practice

Display or **distribute** Teaching Master ES8-6. Read the story aloud with children.

Ask if children can figure out who Tuck is. If needed, point out the first clue: *I hold onto Tuck's leash.* Ask what a leash is usually used for. (to walk a dog)

Ask if children can find another clue. If needed, point out the word *treat* in the last sentence.

Tell children that sometimes readers need to figure things out for themselves. When that happens, they should look for clues that the author gives.

Practice/Apply

Distribute Practice Master ES8-6, and read the directions with children. Explain that the riddles have clues to help the children solve them.

Have children solve the riddles and complete the Practice Master independently.

Check children's responses to be sure they understand how to draw conclusions.

LITERATURE FOCUS: 10–15 MINUTES

Preview *Johnny Appleseed*

Walk children through *Johnny Appleseed*, pages 184–206 in their Anthology.

Discuss the illustrations and use words from the story such as *moving*, *stopped*, *liked*, and *going*.

Note the suggestions in the Extra Support boxes on Teacher's Edition pages T195, T196, and T204.

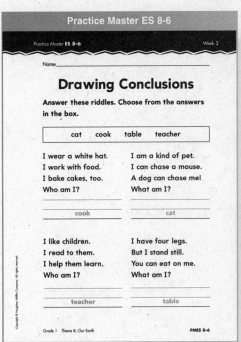

Day 3

SKILL FOCUS: 25–30 MINUTES

High-Frequency Words

Teach

Write *carry*, *kind*, *put*, *saw*, *butter*, *were*, *work*, and *person* on the board. Read each word aloud while pointing to it. Say the word again, and then have children say it with you. Remind children that as they look at each word, they should use what they know about letters and sounds to read the new words.

Display the Letter Cards on the chalk ledge. Draw word boxes on the chalkboard for three-, four-, five-, and six-letter words.

Begin a game in which you give clues about each new word and ask children to identify which word it is. For example, begin by saying, *I am thinking of a word that has four letters. It describes a person who does nice things for others.* As children identify the word *kind*, have volunteers choose the letters from the chalk ledge and help you copy the letters into the boxes. As they write, all children can say the letters together. Follow this same procedure with the remaining words.

Write the following sentences on the board, and read them together with children:

> *Were you the person I saw?*
> *You were kind to help carry my bag.*
> *Please put it here.*
> *Have some butter cookies for your hard work.*

Check each child's ability to pronounce *carry*, *kind*, *put*, *saw*, *butter*, *were*, *work*, and *person* as the child reads each sentence.

Practice

Write the following sentence starters on the chalkboard and have children read them together.

> Put the butter _____.
>
> Help! Can you carry my work _____?
>
> _____ is a very kind person.
>
> Were you kind _____?

Objective

- read and write high-frequency words *carry*, *kind*, *put*, *saw*, *butter*, *were*, *work*, *person*

Materials

- Letter Cards: *a, b, c, d, e(2), i, k, n, o, p, r(2), s, t(2), u, w, y*
- Phonics Library: *Writing Home*

Have children work in pairs to complete the sentences with drawings or words.

Apply

Have children show and read their completed sentences to the class. Then have children cut them into sentence strips, cut apart and mix up the words, and rebuild the sentences, using their drawings or text to complete each one.

LITERATURE FOCUS: 10–15 MINUTES

Review *Writing Home*

Reread the story together with children.

Tell children to look through *Writing Home* for the following high-frequency words: *put, saw, butter*. Have them read the sentences that contain these words.

Day 4

Objectives

- understand that *-ed* and *-ing* are endings that can be added after making spelling changes to some base words
- independently read base words with endings *-ed* and *-ing*

Materials

- Picture Cards: *hop, wave*
- Word Cards: *hop, wave*
- Phonics Library: *Hen's Big Show*
- Anthology: *Johnny Appleseed*

RETEACH

SKILL FOCUS: PHONICS   25–30 MINUTES

Base Words and Endings
-ed, -ing

Teach

Display the Picture Card for *hop* and ask children to identify the picture. Then display the Word Card for *hop* next to the Picture Card. Read the word aloud and ask children to repeat it. Point to the word *hop* and explain that *hop* is a base word to which different endings can be added. Then write *hopped* and *hopping* and circle the base word *hop* in each word. Explain that the simplest part of a word is the base word and the letter or letters that have been added to it is the ending.

Remind children that sometimes spelling changes are made to base words before endings are added. Explain that in base words that have the CVC pattern, the last consonant is often doubled before an ending is added. Point to the words *hopped* and *hopping*, and underline the *pp* in each word. Then write the words *digging, zipped, grinned*, and *grabbed*. Circle the base words in each word and then underline the double consonants in each word.

Repeat the procedure with the Picture and Word Cards for *wave*, explaining that in base words ending in *e*, the *e* is often dropped before an ending is added. Write the words *waved* and *waving* on the board and remind children that the final *e* was dropped before the endings *-ed* and *-ing* were added to the base word *wave*.

Practice

Write base words on the board. Then have children add the endings and write the new words next to the base words.

bake	(add *-ed*)	dig	(add *-ing*)
hop	(add *-ed*)	step	(add *-ing*)
shop	(add *-ing*)	move	(add *-ed*)
skate	(add *-ed*)	dance	(add *-ing*)

Apply

Have pairs of children find words with *-ed* and *-ing* in *Hen's Big Show*. Each time a child finds an *-ed* or *-ing* word, he or she should read it aloud while you write the word on the board. Have volunteers come to the board, and circle the base word and underline the ending in each word.

Review *Johnny Appleseed*

Reread the story together with children. Ask them to make a list of words with the endings *-ed* and *-ing*.

Have children take turns reading aloud.

Day 5

Objectives
- use prior knowledge to form conclusions
- draw conclusions about events in a story

Materials
- Phonics Library: *Hen's Big Show, Writing Home*
- Anthology: *Johnny Appleseed*

Drawing Conclusions

Teach

Display a photograph or illustration that clearly depicts one season, for example, winter. As you display the picture for students, ask, *What do you think the season is in this picture?* (winter) Ask, *What details helped you to form your answer?* (Possible answers might be: snow, bare trees, children in warm clothes)

Say, *You used the details in the picture and facts you know to form a conclusion about the season in this picture.* You might want to repeat the process with pictures of spring, summer, and fall.

Explain that authors don't always explain everything in a story. Tell children that often authors give some facts and details, and they rely on the reader to use those clues to form their own understanding.

Practice

Have children look at the illustrations on pages 186 and 187. Read page 187 aloud. Ask, *Does this story take place in the past or in the present?* (past) Ask, *What did you see and hear that helped you draw that conclusion?* (covered wagon and horse and the text says "when our country was young") Ask, *Does the author tell you that this story happened in the past?* (no)

Point out to students that they used facts and details to help them draw a conclusion. Return to the story and identify other details that can be used to draw conclusions not stated in the story. Here are some examples you might want to use:

Page 188 Johnny wanted to plant apple trees to make the West a nicer place to live. Ask, *How would apple trees provide a nicer place to live?* (shade, apples for food, trees to play in)

Pages 190–191 Ask, *Why did Johnny wear rags and have bare feet?* (He had worn out his clothes and shoes.) *What details help you draw this conclusion?* (The text says, "He walked for days and weeks.")

Apply

Summarize by asking, *Do you think Johnny Appleseed was happy?* Ask children to find evidence in the story that helps them to conclude that Johnny Appleseed was or was not happy. Have children work together to find details and facts from the story to support their opinion.

LITERATURE FOCUS: 10–15 MINUTES

Revisit *Hen's Big Show, Writing Home,* and *Johnny Appleseed*

Page through the stories with children. Have children draw conclusions about whether or not the stories could have really happened.

Tell children to look for words that have an *-ed* or an *-ing* ending. Discuss with children what letters needed to be dropped or added before the ending was added to the base word.

Have children read aloud selected sentences or pages from the stories.

Theme 9

Special Friends

Day 1

SKILL FOCUS: PHONICS
25–30 MINUTES

Sounds for *y*

Teach

Recite and repeat the chant. Tell children to join in as they are able.

> CHANT
>
> "My, my, my!"
>
> Laughed the fly.
>
> "What's so funny?"
>
> Asked the bunny.

Say the first two lines with children. Then say *my*, stretching out the /ī/ sound. Have children repeat *my* several times. Print *my* on the board, and tell children that the letter *y* can stand for the long *i* sound.

Follow a similar procedure for *bunny*, explaining that the letter *y* can also stand for the long *e* sound. Have children say *my bunny* several times. Ask them to listen for the vowel sound at the end of each word as they say it.

Blend

Give three volunteers the letters *f, l,* and *y*. Point to *f*, and have children say its sound. Repeat for *l*. Then point to *y*, and tell children to say the long *i* sound. Have the volunteers move the cards together to form *fly*.

Use Blending Routine 1 to model for children how to blend the sounds, emphasizing the long *i*. Then have children blend the sounds and say the word. Repeat with *dry* and *sky*.

Follow the same procedure with the word *messy*. Explain to children that this time, they should use the long *e* sound for *y*. Repeat with *sandy* and *daddy*.

Objectives
- associate the /ī/ and the /ē/ sounds with the letter *y*
- blend and read words with the /ī/ and /ē/ sounds for *y*

Materials
- Teaching Master ES9-1
- Practice Master ES9-1
- Letter Cards: *a, d (3), e, f, k, l, m, n, r, s (2), y*
- Phonics Library: *Fussy Gail*

Technology

Get Set for Reading CD-ROM
When I Am Old with You

Education Place
www.eduplace.com
When I Am Old with You

Audio CD
When I Am Old with You
Audio CD for **Special Friends**

Lexia Phonics CD-ROM
Primary Intervention

Guided Practice

Display or **distribute** Teaching Master ES9-1, and discuss the illustrations with children. Tell them to use what they know about sounds as they read the sentences with you.

Help children draw a line to match each picture with the correct sentence.

Point to words from the sentences and have children read them.

Practice/Apply

Distribute copies of Practice Master ES9-1 to children, discuss the pictures, and read the directions with them.

Have children read the story independently and draw a picture to show how the story ends.

Ask them to read the story aloud and share their illustrations.

Check that children are correctly blending words that end in *y*.

LITERATURE FOCUS: 10–15 MINUTES

Preview *Fussy Gail*

Walk children through *Fussy Gail*. Discuss the illustrations, naming the characters and using words from the story such as *shy, yucky, fussy,* and *yummy*.

Ask children to name different foods that Mama Bear serves. Ask which foods children think are yummy and which are yucky.

Tell children they will read this story with the rest of the class.

Day 2

Objectives
- recall details that help with understanding the story
- draw a picture that includes important story details

Materials
- Teaching Master ES9-2
- Practice Master ES9-2
- Anthology: *When I Am Old with You*

Noting Details

Teach

Explain to children that details are small pieces or bits of information telling more about a big idea.

Write the following sentence on the board: *We play games outside*. Read the sentence aloud and tell children that this is the big idea. Explain that you want to make a list of the details.

Ask children to name different games that are played outside. List them on the board. Point out that the games listed are details that tell more about playing games outside.

Guided Practice

Display or **distribute** Teaching Master ES9-2, and discuss the illustration with children. Point out that it is important to look for details as we read.

Read the sentences with children. Then ask them to use the information to answer the question: *What does the plant need in order to grow?* (soil, sunlight, and water) Help children underline the words *soil*, *sunlight*, and *water* in the sentences.

Tell them that they can get information from details in the pictures, too.

Have children look at the picture of the plant. Ask questions about it such as: *Where is this plant kept?* (on a windowsill) *Why do you think it is kept there?* (so it gets lots of light)

Practice/Apply

Distribute Practice Master ES9-2, and read the directions with children. Be sure they understand that they need to include details from the story in their pictures. If needed, read aloud the second sentence. Ask children what they will draw in the sky to show this detail. (sun)

Have children share their pictures. Ask the group to note which details have been included. Ask if any have been left out.

Check children's drawings to be sure they included the details from the story.

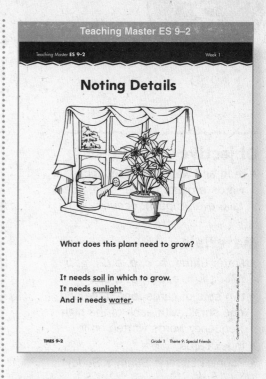

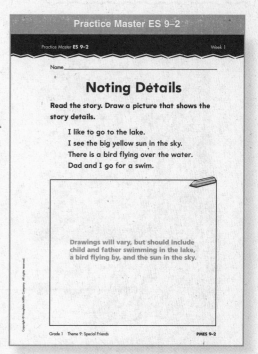

LITERATURE FOCUS: 10–15 MINUTES

Preview *When I Am Old with You*

Walk children through *When I Am Old with You* on pages 16–40 in their Anthology.

Discuss the illustrations and use words from the story such as *Grandaddy*, *by*, *my*, *any*, *try*, and *cry*.

Note the suggestions in the Extra Support boxes on Teacher's Edition pages T47, T48, T51, T55, and T56.

Day 3

Objective

- read and write high-frequency words *around, dance, else, open, talk, ever, though, ocean*

Materials

- Letter Cards: *a, c, d, e (2), g, h (2), k, l, n, o, p, r, s, t, u, v*
- two sets of cards, one large and one small, with each of the high-frequency words written on it
- index cards
- Phonics Library: *Sunny's Buddy*

High-Frequency Words

Teach

Write *around, dance, else, open, talk, ever, though,* and *ocean* on the board. Read each word aloud while pointing to it.

Place the Letter Cards on the chalk ledge below the words. Ask, *How many letters do we need to spell the word* around? Assign one letter to each of six children, and tell them to come up and hold their letters. When each of them has a letter, ask them to hold onto the letter and turn all the other letters over, so the blank sides show. Ask them to arrange their letters in the chalk tray to spell *around*.

Have all children pick a partner. Have each pair look through *When I Am Old with You* and locate the word *around*. When they find it, have them "slap five" and then read a sentence from the story that contains the word *around*.

Repeat this procedure for the remaining words.

Write the following sentences on the board, and read them together with children:

We dance around on the beach by the ocean.

Then we sit by the open door and talk.

I do not ever want to go anywhere else.

Soon we should go home, though.

Check each child's ability to pronounce *around, dance, else, open, talk, ever, though,* and *ocean* as the child reads each sentence.

Practice

Write each of the high-frequency words on a set of large cards and a set of small cards. Put the large cards in one pile, face up, and the small cards in another, face down. Then ask a child to choose a word from the small card pile and act out the word so that others can guess what it is. If the word is difficult to act out (*else, ever, though*), have children make up a sentence, saying "blank" for the chosen word. When a child guesses the word correctly, have him or her find it in the large card pile and show it to others. If a child guesses the wrong word, children keep playing.

Apply

Have children work with partners to draw a picture for each high-frequency word on the front of an index card and write the word on the back. Then have them work in groups of four, having one pair display their pictures while the other pair guesses the word. Rather than saying the word, children can use their own set of word cards to demonstrate which word they think it is.

LITERATURE FOCUS: 10–15 MINUTES

Review *Sunny's Buddy*

Reread the story together with children. Have children take turns reading aloud.

Have children look through *Sunny's Buddy* to find the following high-frequency words: *dance, around, open, ocean, talk, though, ever*.

Day 4

SKILL FOCUS: PHONICS 25–30 MINUTES

Sounds for *y*

Objectives

- associate *y* with the sounds /ī/ and /ē/
- independently read words with the /ī/ and /ē/ sound for *y*

Materials

- Picture Cards: *fly, penny*
- Sound/Spelling Cards: *eagle, ice cream*
- word cards: *fly, penny*
- Phonics Library: *Fussy Gail*
- Anthology: *When I Am Old with You*

Teach

Write the letter *y* on the board. Then display Sound/Spelling Card *eagle*. Ask children to repeat the sound they hear at the beginning of *eagle*, /ē/. Then point to the spelling _*y* on the card. Explain that when the letter *y* is at the end of a word it sometimes has the /ē/ sound. Point to the *y* on the board, and have children repeat /ē/.

Display the Sound/Spelling Card *ice cream*. Ask children to repeat the sound they hear at the beginning of *ice cream*, /ī/. Then point to the spelling _*y* on the card. Explain that the letter *y* can also have the /ī/ sound when it is at the end of the word. Point to the *y* on the board and have children repeat /ī/.

Display the Picture Cards *penny* and *fly*. Have children say the name of each card and identify the sound they hear at the end of each word, /ē/ or /ī/. Then place the word cards *penny* and *fly* next to their Picture Cards. Help children to blend each word using Blending Routine 2.

Practice

Write the headings "long *i* in *fly*" and "long *e* in *penny*" on a Word Pattern Board. Then read the following list: *dry, by, chilly, sticky, shy, lucky, try, dusty*. Ask children to tell you the correct column in which to write each word with a sound for *y*.

Apply

Have partners look for words with the long *i* and long *e* sounds for *y* in *Fussy Gail*. Each time they find a word, ask them to say it aloud so you can write it in the long *i* or long *e* column on the Word Pattern Board. The words from the story are: *shy, yucky, crunchy, jelly, sticky, fussy, dry, sly, yummy*. When the search is complete, have one partner choose a long *i* word and the other partner choose a long *e* word to illustrate on one half of a folded piece of paper. They may share their "partner pictures" with the group.

LITERATURE FOCUS: 10–15 MINUTES

Review *When I Am Old with You*

Reread the story together with children.

Ask children to make a list of words that end in *y* with the long *i* sound or the long *e* sound that they find in the story. Ask children to use each word in a sentence.

Have children take turns reading aloud.

Day 5

Objectives

- listen for details in a story
- use details in a description

Materials

- Phonics Library: *Fussy Gail, Sunny's Buddy*
- Anthology: *When I Am Old with You*

Noting Details

Teach

Play a game of "Who Am I?" with children. Tell them to listen while you describe a person with a specific job, and see if they can guess what the person's job is. Ask them to not speak their answer until you give them the cue, "Who Am I?"

Say: *I wear a uniform to work. It is my job to lead you to your seat and to welcome you. I give you a menu and ask what you would like to order. I bring you your food and take your plate when you are finished. Who am I?* (food server, waiter)

Ask the students what information helped them to identify the answer. (uniform, menu, order, food) Tell them that small pieces of information often are called details. Explain that authors use details in stories to help you picture or visualize the characters or the events that are happening.

Have children provide clues for another occupation, encouraging them to use as many details as they can. Point out to children the details used that helped solve the riddle.

Practice

Direct children to look back at the story *When I Am Old with You*. Say, *There are many details in this story, both in the words and in the pictures*. Read the story together with children. Pause after every few pages and ask the children for details about what the grandfather is like. Tell them to use both the pictures and the story. Ask questions such as the following:

- *What activities does the grandfather like to do? How do you know?*

- *What does the grandfather like to eat?*

- *How does the little girl feel about her grandfather? What makes you think so?*

Apply

Have children use what they have learned from the story details to write a character sketch of Grandaddy. When finished, have children share what they write. Identify the words children used to describe him, for example, *kind, loving, caring,* and *interesting.* Help children to see how the author, Angela Johnson, helps the reader understand the character of Grandaddy.

LITERATURE FOCUS: 10–15 MINUTES

Revisit *Fussy Gail, Sunny's Buddy,* and *When I Am Old with You*

Page through the stories with children. Then ask them to find words that end with *y* in each story.

Have children look at page 16 of *Sunny's Buddy.* Ask children to talk about the details shown in the illustration. Ask, *What are the different characters doing? What are they wearing?*

Tell children to look through *When I Am Old with You* to find the following high-frequency words: *around, dance, else, open, talk, ever, though, ocean.*

Have children read aloud their favorite sentences or pages from the stories.

Day 1

Objectives

- build words by adding the ending *-es*
- read words ending with *-es*

Materials

- Teaching Master ES9-3
- Practice Master ES9-3
- Word Cards: *fox, peach*
- suffix card: *es*
- Phonics Library: *Bo's Bunnies*

Technology

Get Set for Reading CD-ROM
The New Friend

Education Place
www.eduplace.com
The New Friend

Audio CD
The New Friend
Audio CD for **Special Friends**

Lexia Phonics CD-ROM
Primary Intervention

Base Words and Ending *-es*

Teach

Recite and repeat the chant. Tell children to join in as they are able.

> CHANT
>
> Make a wish.
>
> Get one kiss.
>
> Make two wishes.
>
> Get two kisses!

Have children say the words *wish* and *wishes*. Remind them that *wishes* means "more than one wish."

Say *wishes* slowly, stretching out the sounds in the last syllable. Have children say the word.

Print *wish* and *wishes* on the board. Help children compare the words, letter by letter. Point out that when a word ends with *ch, tch, x, s,* or *ss* we add the ending *-es* to make the word mean "more than one."

Follow a similar procedure for *kiss/kisses*.

Blend

Give the Word Card *fox* to one child. Use Blending Routine 1 to model how to blend the word. Then have children blend and say the word. Give a card with the ending *es* to another child. Model how to blend the ending. Have the two children move their cards together to make *foxes*. Blend *foxes* with children, before having them blend and say the word on their own. Follow a similar procedure for *peach/peaches*.

Guided Practice

Display or **distribute** Teaching Master ES9-3, and discuss the illustration with children. Tell them to use what they know about words ending with *-es* as they read the sentences with you.

Help children find words with the *-es* ending, circle the *-es* ending, and say what the base word is. Then have children blend the sounds to read the words.

Check that children are reading words with the *-es* ending correctly.

Practice/Apply

Distribute copies of Practice Master ES9-3, discuss the pictures, and read the directions with children. Remind them to use what they know about word endings as they read the sentences.

Have children find each word that has an ending, circle the ending, and draw a line under the base word.

Ask children to read the words they have marked and tell what they mean.

Check children's responses to be sure they can identify the *-es* ending.

LITERATURE FOCUS: 10–15 MINUTES

Preview *Bo's Bunnies*

Walk children through *Bo's Bunnies*. Discuss the illustrations, naming the characters.

Use words from the story such as *brushes, splashes, dresses, fixes, dishes,* and *glasses.*

Tell children they will read this story with the rest of the class.

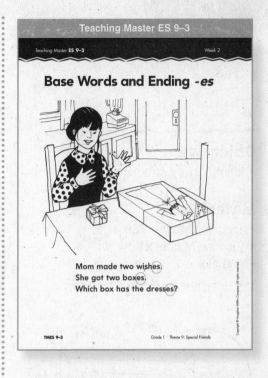

Day 2

PRETEACH

SKILL FOCUS: COMPREHENSION   25–30 MINUTES

Story Structure

Teach

Remind children that stories have characters, a setting, and story events including a problem and solution.

Have children listen as you read the following story:

Read Aloud

> One day at school, a girl named Ana was playing outside at recess. As she was hanging up her coat after recess, Ana noticed that her bracelet had fallen off and she started to cry. The teacher asked her what was wrong, and Ana told her about the bracelet. The teacher took the class back outside to look for the bracelet, but nobody was able to find it. As the class was going back inside, Ana reached into her coat pocket and she felt something. She pulled it out, and called to her teacher, "I found it, I found it!"

Ask: *Who is the story about?* (Ana) Say, *Yes, Ana is the character in the story.*

Ask: *Where does the story take place?* (at Ana's school) Say, *Yes, Ana's school is the setting for the story.*

Ask: *What happened first?* (Ana was playing outside)

Ask: *What is the problem in the story, and how is it solved?* (Ana loses her bracelet at recess, and then she finds it in her coat pocket.) Say, *Yes, those are the events of the story.*

Guided Practice

Draw a story map like the one below on the board.

Characters Who?	Nan
Setting Where?	a fair
Story Events Beginning Middle (problem) End (solution)	Nan gets a balloon. Nan lets go of the balloon. A clown catches the balloon.

Objective

• identify story structure

Materials

• Teaching Master ES9-4
• Practice Master ES9-4
• Anthology: *The New Friend*

Display or **distribute** Teaching Master ES9-4, discuss the illustrations, and read the story with children.

Direct attention to the first frame. Ask who the character is and what they think the setting of the story is. (a girl named Nan; a fair)

Ask what happens at the beginning of this story. (Nan gets a balloon.)

Ask what the problem is in the story. (Nan lets go of the balloon.)

Direct attention to the last frame. Ask, *How is Nan's problem solved?* (A clown catches the balloon.)

Complete the story map with children's responses.

Practice/Apply

Distribute Practice Master ES9-4 to children.

Read the directions with children. Be sure they understand that they need to tell who is in the story and where it takes place. They also need to tell what happens at the beginning, in the middle, and at the end of the story.

Check children's story maps to be sure they understand the concepts of story structure.

LITERATURE FOCUS: 10–15 MINUTES

Preview *The New Friend*

Walk children through *The New Friend* on pages 53-71 in their Anthology.

Discuss the illustrations and use words from the story such as *brushes*, *boxes*, *wishes*, *cookies*, and *families*.

Note the suggestions in the Extra Support boxes on Teacher's Edition pages T131, T133, and T139.

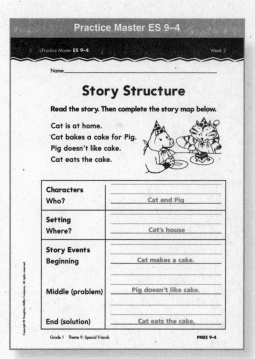

Day 3

SKILL FOCUS: 25–30 MINUTES

High-Frequency Words

Teach

Write *after, before, buy, pretty, school, done, off,* and *wash* on the board. Read each word aloud while pointing to it. Say the word again, then ask children to say it with you. Remind children that as they look at each word, they should use what they know about letters and sounds to read the new words.

Display the Letter Cards on the chalk ledge. Draw word boxes on the chalkboard for three-, four-, five-, and six-letter words.

Begin a game in which you give clues about each new word and ask children to identify which word it is. For example, begin by saying, *I am the opposite of* before. *I have five letters. What word am I?* As children identify the word *after,* have five volunteers locate the letters that make up the word, hold up the letters as they are spelled, and help you write the word in the boxes. The others can say the letters together and write the letters in the air. Follow this same procedure with the remaining words.

Practice

Write the incomplete sentences below on sentence strips. Have children read the words along with you. Help them to understand that they should complete the sentences with words or pictures.

> It was the day before _____.

> Mom said, "_____ will do the wash."

> _____ will clean off the _____.

> We will buy _____ when we are done.

> After they were done, the school looked pretty and _____.

Objective

- read and write high-frequency words *after, before, buy, pretty, school, done, off, wash*

Materials

- Letter Cards: *a, b, c, d, e (2), f (2), h, l, n, o (2), p, r, s, t (2), u, w, y*
- Phonics Library: *The Fleet Street Club*

Check each child's ability to pronouce *after, before, buy, pretty, school, done, off,* and *wash* as the child reads each sentence.

Apply

Have children show and read their completed sentences to the group. When they are finished, you might want to have them cut up the sentence strips, mix up the words, exchange completed sentences with other pairs of children, and then rebuild the sentences.

LITERATURE FOCUS: 10–15 MINUTES

Review *The Fleet Street Club*

Reread the story together with children.

Ask children to look through *The Fleet Street Club* for the following high-frequency words: *after, school, wash.* Have them read the sentences that contain these words.

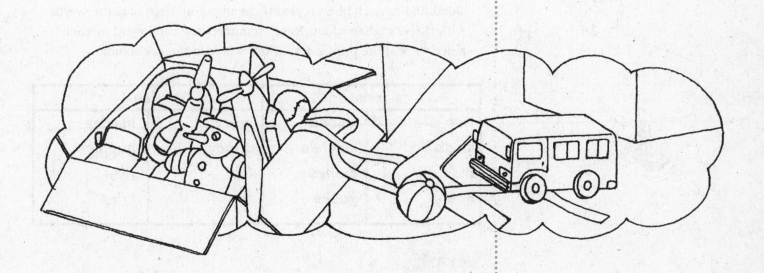

Day 4

Base Words and Endings
-es, -ies

Objectives
- understand that *-es* and *-ies* can be added to base words
- independently read base words with *-es* and *-ies*

Materials
- Phonics Library: *Bo's Bunnies*

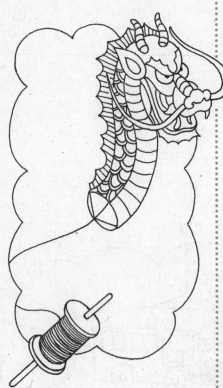

Teach

Write *box* and *boxes* on the board. Remind children that *box* means one box and *boxes* means more than one. Underline the word *box* in *boxes* and circle the ending. Explain that some base words need an *-es* rather than an *-s* to show more than one. Point out that when *-es* is added to a word, it stands for the /ĕz/ sounds.

Write the words *foxes, watches, buses, rashes,* and *fusses.* Remind children that base words that end in *x, ch, s, sh,* and *ss* take *-es* endings. Use Blending Routine 2 to blend the words with children.

Write *baby* and *babies* on the board. Explain that when a base word ends with a consonant followed by *y,* as in *baby,* the *y* must be changed to *i* before *-es* is added. Write *fly* on the board and have children repeat it after you. Ask children to tell you the word for more than one fly. Erase the *y* and have a volunteer add *-ies* to *fly* to make *flies.* Show children how to blend *flies* using Blending Routine 2.

Practice

Write the chart on the board. Read the base words in the first column aloud, and have children repeat them after you. Then read the words with the *-es* ending added. Have volunteers use each word in a sentence. Repeat the procedure for the words in the *-ies* column.

-es		-ies	
kiss	kisses	berry	berries
lunch	lunches	guppy	guppies
dish	dishes	fly	flies
gas	gases	try	tries

Apply

Have pairs of children find words with *-es* and *-ies* in *Bo's Bunnies.* Each time a child finds a word, he or she should read it aloud while you write the word on the board.

Prefixes *un-*, *re-*

Teach

Write the prefixes *un-* and *re-* on the chalkboard. Remind children that a prefix is a letter or letters added to the beginning of a word that changes the meaning of the word.

Remind children that when the prefix *un-* is added to a word and means *not,* it changes the meaning of that word to its opposite. Say pairs of words such as *tie/untie; happy/unhappy; fold/unfold; lock/unlock,* and have children repeat them after you. Repeat the procedure with the words *read/reread; use/reuse; start/restart; build/rebuild,* reminding children that the prefix *re-* means *again.*

Write *pack, unpack,* and *repack* on the board. Then place a box at the front of the classroom. Begin to fill the box with books as you say: *I pack books into the box.* Point to *pack,* and have children repeat it after you. Then take the books out of the box while you say: *I unpack the books from the box.* Point to *unpack* and have children say it after you. Then put the books back into the box and say: *I repack books into the box.* Point to *repack* and have children repeat it after you. Help children to blend *unpack* and *repack* using Blending Routine 2.

Practice

Write *read, tell, happy, snap, lock,* and *safe* on the board. Read the words aloud and have children repeat them. Then have volunteers add *un-* or *re-* to each word and use each of the new words in a sentence.

Apply

Have pairs of children find words with the prefixes *un-* and *re-* in *Bo's Bunnies.* Have children read the words aloud while you write them on the board. Have volunteers come to the board, circle the base word, underline the prefix, and say the meaning of each word.

Objectives
- understand that prefixes *un-* and *re-* can be added to the beginning of words to change the meaning of the words
- understand that *un-* means *not* and *re-* means *again*
- independently read base words with prefixes *un-, re-*

Materials
- Phonics Library: *Bo's Bunnies*
- Anthology: *The New Friend*

Review *The New Friend*

Reread the story together with children. Ask children to make a list of words that have the suffixes *-es* and *-ies* or the prefixes *re-* and *un-*.

SKILL FOCUS: COMPREHENSION 25–30 MINUTES

Story Structure

Objectives
- identify setting, characters, and plot in a story
- use a story map to show the structure of a story

Materials
- Phonics Library: *Bo's Bunnies, The Fleet Street Club*
- Anthology: *The New Friend*

Teach

Ask children to suggest the name of a familiar fairy tale. Ask the following questions:

Who are the characters in the story?

Where does the story take place?

What are the events of the story? What happens at the beginning? In the middle? At the end of the story?

Use the words *character*, *setting*, and *plot*, as you talk with children about the story. Remind children that the characters are the people or animals in the story, the setting is the time and place the story occurs, and the plot is what happens.

Practice

Ask children to look at the story, *The New Friend*. Ask, *Who is this story about?* (Makoto, his mother, his father, Martin, Luis, and the boy telling the story)

Turn to the beginning of the story *The New Friend* on page 54. Say, *Where does this story take place? What is the time of the story?* Have children listen while you read page 54 of the story aloud. Ask, *What clues tell you where this story takes place?* (city, old house) *Does this story take place in the present time or long ago?* (present)

Ask questions such as these: *What happens at the beginning of the story?* (People move into a vacant house.) *What happens in the middle of the story?* (The children play together.) *What happens at the end of the story?* (The children realize they have a new friend.)

Apply

Have children fill in a story map and summarize the story.

In the story, there are two boys whose names are _____ and _____. The story takes place _____. Makoto has just moved next door. The children _____. They learn things about each other. They learn _____. At the end of the story, _____.

Revisit *Bo's Bunnies, The Fleet Street Club*, and *The New Friend*

Page through the stories with children. Then ask them to find words that have the suffixes *-es* and *-ies*.

Have children reread *The Fleet Street Club* and make a story map of the story.

Tell children to look through *The New Friend* to find the following high-frequency words: *after, before, buy, pretty, school, done, off, wash.*

Have children read aloud their favorite sentences or pages from the stories.

Day 1

SKILL FOCUS: PHONICS
25–30 MINUTES

Vowel Pairs *oi, oy, aw, au*

Teach

Recite and repeat the chant shown, asking children to join in.

> CHANT
>
> Baby Roy is
>
> A quiet boy.
>
> Little Paul,
>
> Likes to crawl!

Say the first two lines with children. Then say *boy*, stretching out the /oi/ sound. Have children repeat *boy* several times.

Print *boy* on the board, and tell children that the letters *oy* can stand for the /oi/ sound. Follow a similar procedure for *boil*. Explain that the letters *oi* can also stand for the /oi/ sound.

Say *Paul*, stretching out the /ô/ sound. Have children repeat *Paul* several times.

Print *Paul* on the board, and tell children that the letters *au* can stand for the /ô/ sound. Follow a similar procedure for *crawl*, explaining that the letters *aw* can also stand for the /ô/ sound.

Blend

Give a volunteer the Letter Card for *t*. Have the volunteer say the sound for *t*. Give two other volunteers Letter Cards for *o* and *y*. Ask them to hold their cards so they are touching. Have them say the sound for *o* and *y* together: /oi/.

Have the three volunteers move the cards together to form *toy*. As they do so, use Blending Routine 1 to model how to blend the word. Have children blend the sounds to make the word *toy*. Repeat with the words *yawn*, *oil*, and *haul*.

Objectives

- associate /oi/ with the letters *oi* and *oy*
- associate /ô/ with the letters *aw* and *au*
- blend and read words with *oi, oy, aw,* and *au*

Materials

- Teaching Master ES9-5
- Practice Master ES9-5
- Letter Cards: *a, h, i, l, n, o, t, u, w, y*
- Phonics Library: *Jenny's Big Voice*

Technology

**Get Set for Reading
CD-ROM**

The Surprise Family

Education Place

www.eduplace.com
The Surprise Family

Audio CD

The Surprise Family
Audio CD for **Special Friends**

**Lexia Phonics
CD-ROM**

Primary Intervention

Guided Practice

Display or **distribute** Teaching Master ES9-5 and discuss the illustrations with children.

Tell children to use what they know about sounds as they read the sentences with you. Then help children match the pictures with the corresponding sentences. Point to words from the sentences, and have children read them.

Practice/Apply

Distribute copies of Practice Master ES9-5, and discuss the illustrations with children.

Read the directions, and be sure children understand that they are to draw lines to match the sentences with the pictures.

Check children's responses to be sure they are reading *oi, oy, aw*, and *au* words correctly.

LITERATURE FOCUS: 10–15 MINUTES

Preview *Jenny's Big Voice*

Walk children through *Jenny's Big Voice*. Discuss the illustrations, naming the characters and using words from the story such as *noise*, *voice*, *bawled*, and *shawl*.

Ask children how they think Jenny sounded when she bawled in her big voice. Then ask how they think she sounded when she spoke with a soft voice.

Tell children they will read this story with the rest of the class.

Teaching Master ES 9–5

Teaching Master **ES 9–5**   Week 3

Vowel Pairs *oi, oy, aw, au*

Too many toys may spoil the boy.

There is a lot of noise when Paul cuts the lawn.

TM ES 9–5   Grade 1 Theme 9: Special Friends

Practice Master ES 9–5

Practice Master **ES 9–5**   Week 3

Name _____

Vowel Pairs *oi, oy, aw, au*

Use sounds you know to read the sentences. Draw lines to match the sentences with the pictures.

1. Paul has some coins.

2. Roy is yawning now.

3. This boy can draw.

Grade 1 Theme 9: Special Friends   PM ES 9–5

Day 2

Objectives

- identify likenesses and differences
- use a Venn diagram to compare and contrast

Materials

- Teaching Master ES9-6
- Practice Master ES9-6
- Anthology: *The Surprise Family*

SKILL FOCUS: COMPREHENSION   25–30 MINUTES

Compare and Contrast

Teach

Hold up two different types of balls. For example, hold up a tennis ball and a baseball.

Ask children to think about how they are alike and different. Discuss with children the different ways the two balls are alike and different. (Possible answers: Alike: round, used for games; Different: colors, size, texture)

Remind children that when you find ways two objects are alike you are comparing them and when you find ways they are different you are contrasting them.

Guided Practice

Display or **distribute** Teaching Master ES9-6. Have children look at the pictures of the cat and the dog at the top of the page.

Tell children they will discuss how the cat and the dog are alike and different. Remind them that a Venn diagram can be used to help organize likenesses and differences.

Ask children if a dog can be a pet. Ask if a cat can be a pet, too. Explain that being a pet is one way that a dog and a cat are alike. Print *pet* in the middle of the Venn diagram, where the circles overlap.

Point to the picture of the cat. Ask: *How many legs does a cat have?* Point to the picture of the dog. Ask: *How many legs does a dog have?* Print *four legs* in the middle, under *pet*.

Ask: *Which animal has stripes?* (the cat) *Which animal has spots?* (the dog) Explain that the two animals have different markings, so this is a way in which they are different.

Print *stripes* in the part of the diagram labeled *cat*. Ask children where they think you should print *spots*. Then print it in the part of the diagram labeled *dog*.

Ask children if they can think of another way in which the two animals are different. Print their suggestions under the appropriate labels.

Continue until several similarities and differences have been noted.

Practice/Apply

Distribute Practice Master ES9-6 to children, and read the directions with them.

Have children choose partners and spend a few minutes talking with them about how they are alike and how they are different.

Have partners complete their Venn diagram and share it with the group.

Check children's responses to be sure they understand how to use a Venn diagram to compare and contrast.

LITERATURE FOCUS: 10–15 MINUTES

Preview *The Surprise Family*

Walk children through *The Surprise Family* on pages 78–108 in their Anthology.

Discuss the illustrations and use words from the story such as *taught, hawk, saw, pointed, fuzzy, fluffy,* and *carefully.*

Note the suggestions in the Extra Support boxes on Teacher's Edition pages T201, T204, and T212.

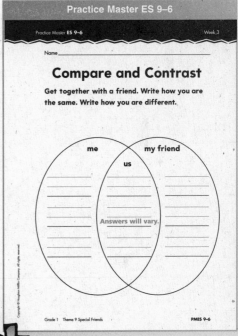

Day 3

Objective
• read and write high-frequency words *only, together, watched, baby, edge, enough, garden, sharp*

Materials
• Letter Cards: *a, b (2), c, d, e (2), g, h, l, n, o, p, r, s, t (2), u, w, y*
• flower petal-shaped cards
• Phonics Library: *Joy Boy*

High-Frequency Words

Teach

Write *only, together, watched, baby, edge, enough, garden,* and *sharp* on the board. Read each word aloud while pointing to it. Say the word again, and then have children say it with you. Remind them that they should use what they know about letters and sounds to read the new words.

Display the Letter Cards on the chalk ledge. Draw word boxes on the chalkboard for four-, five-, six-, seven-, and eight-letter words.

Begin a game in which you give clues about each new word and ask children to identify which word it is. For example, begin by saying, *I have just four letters. I rhyme with* lonely. *Who am I?* As children identify the word *only,* have four volunteers locate the letters that make up the word, lead classmates in spelling the word as they hold up the letters, and then write the word in the boxes. As children write the word *only,* the others can say the letters together while writing the letters in the air. Follow this same procedure with the remaining words.

Write the following sentences on the board, and read them together with children:

I watched the cats play together in the garden.

Does that kitten have sharp claws?

No, it is only a baby.

Make sure they stay far enough from the edge of the road.

Check each child's ability to pronounce *only, together, watched, baby, edge, enough, garden,* and *sharp* as the child reads each sentence.

Practice

Have children write each of the high-frequency words on cards in the shape of a flower petal. Then have them go back into the story and match the words on the word cards with the words in the text. Finally, have children read the sentence that contains the word on the word card.

Apply

Compile children's flower word cards. Assemble them on chart paper or on a bulletin board. Tell children that you will point to the words and that they should say them as quickly as they can. Point to the same words several times until children are able to say them instantly. Continue to have children add words on flower shapes and display them on a bulletin board called "Our Flower Word Garden."

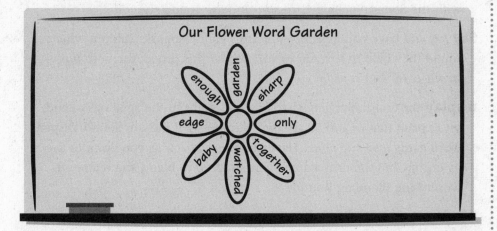

Our Flower Word Garden

enough · garden · sharp · edge · only · baby · watched · together

---

LITERATURE FOCUS: 10–15 MINUTES

Review *Joy Boy*

Reread the story together with children. Have children take turns reading aloud.

Tell children to look through *Joy Boy* for the following high-frequency words: *watched, together, garden, sharp, baby, edge, enough.*

Day 4

SKILL FOCUS: PHONICS   10–15 MINUTES

Vowel Pairs *oi, oy, aw, au*

Teach

Display the Sound/Spelling Card *boy* and ask children to repeat the sound they hear at the end of the word, /oi/. Repeat the procedure with the Sound/Spelling Card *saw* and the sound /ô/.

Say *toy* and have children repeat it after you. Then ask children which sound they hear in *toy*, /oi/ or /ô/. Repeat this procedure with *boy*, *straw*, *coin*, and *caught*.

Display the Sound/Spelling Card *boy* and point to the spellings *oi* and *oy*. Explain that *oi* and *oy* are two ways to spell the /oi/ sound. Display word cards *toys* and *coins*. Have children say /oi/ as you point to the *oy* in *toys* and the *oi* in *coins*. Help children to blend and read each word using Blending Routine 2.

Display the Sound/Spelling Card *saw* and point to the spellings *aw* and *au*. Explain that *aw* and *au* are two ways to spell the /ô/ sound. Display word cards *paw* and *cause*. Have children say /ô/ as you point to the *aw* in *paw* and the *au* in *cause*. Then help children to blend and read each word using Blending Routine 2.

Practice

Write *yawn*, *pause*, and *straw* on the board. Give a volunteer two self-stick notes with the letters *aw* on one, and *au* on the other. Have the child match the correct note to the *aw* in *yawn* and read the word. Have other volunteers do the same for the words *pause* and *straw*. Repeat this procedure with *boy*, *joy*, *join*, and *moist*.

Apply

Have children look for words with vowel pairs *oi, oy, aw, au* in *Jenny's Big Voice*. Each time they find a word, ask them to say the word aloud so you can write it on a Word Pattern Board. When the search is complete, have volunteers read the words with *oi, oy, aw, au* on the Word Pattern Board and circle the letters that stand for the /oi/ and /ô/ sounds.

Objectives

- associate the /oi/ sound with vowel pairs *oi, oy* and the /ô/ sound with vowel pairs *aw, au*
- independently read words with vowel pairs *oi, oy, aw, au*

Materials

- Sound/Spelling Cards: *boy, saw*
- word cards: *cause, coins, paw, toys*
- Phonics Library: *Jenny's Big Voice*

Suffixes -ful, -ly, -y

Teach

Write *helpful* on the board. Say *helpful* aloud and have children repeat it after you. Then circle *help* in *helpful* and explain that it is a base word to which the ending *-ful* has been added. Underline the *-ful* in *helpful*, and tell children that *-ful* is a suffix. Remind them that a suffix is a word part added to the end of a base word that adds to the meaning of the base word. Ask children to think about the meanings of *help* and *helpful* as you say: *Sara can <u>help</u> me carry my books. She is <u>helpful</u>.*

Follow a similar procedure for the suffix *-ly*, using the words *sad* and *sadly* and the following sentences: *Jon is <u>sad</u>. "I lost my ball," he said <u>sadly</u>.*

Repeat the procedure again with the suffix *-y*, using the words *luck* and *lucky* and the following sentences: *It's good <u>luck</u> to find a four-leaf clover. I feel so <u>lucky</u> when I find one.*

Help children blend *helpful*, *lucky*, and *sadly* using Blending Routine 2.

Practice

Write *playful*, *gladly*, and *sleepy* on the board. Ask children to identify and circle the base word in each word. Have other children identify and underline the suffixes in the three words.

Apply

Have partners find words with the suffixes *-ful*, *-ly*, and *-y* in *Jenny's Big Voice*. Each time a partner finds a word, he or she should read it aloud while you write the word on the board. Have volunteers underline the suffix in each word. Then have partners take turns reading aloud the sentences in which they found the words.

Review *The Surprise Family*

Reread the story with children. Ask them to make a list of words with the vowel pairs *oi, oy, aw,* and *au* that they find in the story.

Objectives

- understand that suffixes can be added to base words
- recognize that when suffixes are added to words, the new words have different meanings
- independently read base words with suffixes

Materials

- Phonics Library: *Jenny's Big Voice*
- Anthology: *The Surprise Family*

Day 5

Compare and Contrast

Teach

Hold up two different feathers (or other available items that can be compared and contrasted). Tell the children that the feathers are alike in some ways and different in others. Ask: *How are the feathers alike? How are the feathers different?* Call on volunteers to answer the questions.

Repeat the ways in which the feathers are alike and different. Tell children when they discover ways in which objects are alike or different, they are *comparing* (ways objects are the same) and *contrasting* (ways objects are different).

Practice

Direct children back to the story *The Surprise Family*. Remind children that in this story, there is an unusual family. Ask: *Who are the members of the Surprise Family?* (boy, chicken, ducks) *Are the characters in the Surprise family the same as your family or different from your family?* (different)

Draw a Venn diagram like the one below. Label the two circles *Surprise Family* and *Our Families*, and label the overlap *Both*.

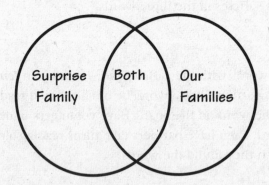

Continue to have children compare and contrast the characters from *The Surprise Family* with their own families. Begin by identifying the characters in both families, e.g., there is a boy, a chicken, and some ducks in *The Surprise Family*, and a father, mother, brothers, sisters, stepparents, grandparents, or pets in theirs.

Objectives
- compare and contrast characters in a story
- use a Venn diagram to compare story characters to children's families

Materials
- Phonics Library: *Jenny's Big Voice, Joy Boy*
- Anthology: *The Surprise Family*

Ask: *How are our families like the Surprise Family?* Call on volunteers and write answers in the overlap on the diagram. If children are having trouble thinking of ways, ask questions, such as *How did the chicken feel about her babies?* (She loved them.) *How did the boy treat the chicken?* (He took care of her.) *Do your families take care of you? In what ways do your families show they love you?*

Apply

Have children summarize by completing the following statements:
*Our families are the same as the Surprise Family because
_____. Our families are different from the Surprise Family
because _____.*

Ask children to share their responses.

LITERATURE FOCUS: 10–15 MINUTES

Revisit *Jenny's Big Voice, Joy Boy,* and *The Surprise Family*

Page through the stories with children, asking them to find words with the vowel pairs *oi, oy, aw,* and *au.*

Have children reread pages 102–105 of *The Surprise Family.* Discuss the ways in which the ducklings are different from the hen. Then talk about the ways they are the same.

Ask children to look through *The Surprise Family* to find the following high-frequency words: *only, together, watched, baby, edge, enough, garden, sharp.*

Have children read aloud their favorite sentences or pages from the stories.

Theme 10

We Can Do It!

Day 1

r-Controlled Vowels: *or, ore*

Teach

Recite and repeat the chant, having children join in as they are able.

> **CHANT**
>
> In the north, there is a storm.
>
> Rain and hail begin to form.
>
> Waves pound upon the shore,
>
> As the man begins to snore.

Say *north*, stretching out /ôr/. Have children repeat *north* several times. Print *north* on the board. Explain that the letters *or* can stand for /ôr/. Repeat with *storm* and *form*.

Write *shore* on the board, and explain that *ore* can also stand for /ôr/. Have children say *shore* several times. Repeat with *snore*.

Blend

Give volunteers Letter Cards *h, o, r,* and *n*. Have the volunteers with *o* and *r* hold their cards side by side, and say the sound for *or*: /ôr/.

Have all volunteers move their cards together to form *horn*. As they do so, use Blending Routine 1 to model how to blend the sounds. Then have the whole group blend the sounds and say *horn*. Repeat with the words *fork*, *more*, and *store*.

Guided Practice

Display or **distribute** Teaching Master ES10-1, and discuss the pictures with children. Tell them to use what they know about the /ôr/ sound as they read the story with you.

Help children underline and read the /ôr/ words.

Check that children are correctly blending and reading /ôr/ words.

Objectives

- associate /ôr/ with the letters *or, ore*
- blend and read words with *or, ore*

Materials

- Teaching Master ES10-1
- Letter Cards: *e, f, h, k, m, n, o, r, s, t*

Technology

**Get Set for Reading
CD-ROM**

Two Greedy Bears

Education Place

www.eduplace.com

Two Greedy Bears

Audio CD

Two Greedy Bears
Audio CD for **We Can Do It!**

**Lexia Phonics
CD-ROM**

Primary Intervention

SKILL FOCUS: PHONICS   10–15 MINUTES

r-Controlled Vowels: er, ir, ur

Teach

Recite and repeat the chant shown, asking children to join in.

> **CHANT**
>
> Chirp, chirp, chirp.
>
> A bird sings to a fern.
>
> Chirp, chirp, chirp.
>
> Now you take a turn.

Display the Sound/Spelling Card *bird*. Say *bird*, stretching out the /ûr/ sound. Have children repeat *bird* several times. Print *bird*, *fern*, and *turn* on the board, and tell children that the letters *ir*, *er*, and *ur* can stand for the /ûr/ sound.

Blend

Give four volunteers Letter Cards *b, i, r,* and *d*. Ask the two volunteers with *i* and *r* to hold their cards so they are touching. Have them say the sound for *i* and *r* together: /ûr/. Have all four volunteers move the cards together to form *bird*. Use Blending Routine 1 to model how to blend the sounds. Then have the whole group blend the sounds and say *bird*. Repeat with *fern* and *turn*.

Practice/Apply

Distribute copies of Practice Master ES10-1, discuss the pictures, and read the directions with children. Have them read the story independently, and draw lines to match each sentence with a picture.

Check that children are blending /ûr/ words correctly.

LITERATURE FOCUS: 10–15 MINUTES

Preview *Sport Gets a Bath*

Walk children through *Sport Gets a Bath*. Discuss the illustrations, naming the characters and using story words.

Objectives

- associate /ûr/ with *er, ir, ur*
- read words with *er, ir, ur*

Materials

- Practice Master ES10-1
- Letter Cards: *b, d, e, f, i, n, r, t, u*
- Sound/Spelling Card: *bird*
- Phonics Library: *Sport Gets a Bath*

Teaching Master ES 10–1

Practice Master ES 10–1

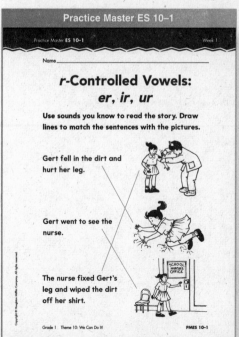

SKILL FOCUS: COMPREHENSION 25–30 MINUTES

Making Predictions

Teach

Remind children that when they make a prediction, they use what they know to help them guess what might happen next.

Read aloud the following situations and have children predict what will happen.

Read Aloud

Ana is outside playing soccer. She gets really hot and takes off her coat. After a while, the sun goes in and the wind picks up. It starts to get cold. What will Ana do? (Ana will put on her coat.)

John washed his face and hands. Then he brushed his teeth and put on his pajamas. What is John getting ready to do? (John is getting ready for bed.)

Guided Practice

Display or **distribute** Teaching Master ES10-2, discuss the illustration, and read aloud the sentences with children. Point out that the last sentence is not finished.

Help children jot down what they think Joy and Jan are going to do. Have them share their ideas.

Ask children how they were able to figure out what the girls are going to do. If needed, point out these clues: the picture shows them with skates; the words say that they are on their way to the lake and that they like to try new sports.

Explain that children made a prediction when they told what the girls would do.

Objective
• use previous knowledge to make predictions

Materials
• Teaching Master ES10-2
• Practice Master ES10-2
• Anthology: *Two Greedy Bears*

Practice/Apply

Distribute Practice Master ES10-2, and read the directions with children. Tell them that they will write where they think Fred and his family went on their trip.

Check children's ability to make predictions as they share their predictions and tell what they were thinking when they made them.

Preview *Two Greedy Bears*

Walk children through *Two Greedy Bears* on pages 143–165 in their Anthology.

Discuss the illustrations and use words from the story such as *thirsty, water, more, burst, morning,* and *turning.*

Note the suggestions in the Extra Support boxes on Teacher's Edition pages T49, T53, and T59.

SKILL FOCUS: 25–30 MINUTES

High-Frequency Words

Teach

Write *began, laugh, sure, head, divide, second,* and *break* on large index cards. Read each word aloud while displaying it. Say the word again, then have children say it with you. Remind children to use what they know about letters and sounds to read the new words.

Display the Letter Cards on the chalk ledge. Draw word boxes on the chalkboard for four-, five-, and six-letter words.

Begin a game in which you give clues about each new word and ask children to identify which word it is. For example, begin by saying, *I have five letters. I happen after a funny joke. I am fun to do. Who am I?* As children identify the word *laugh*, have five volunteers locate the letters that spell the word, lead classmates in spelling the word as they hold up the letters, and then write the word in the boxes. As children write the word *laugh*, the others can say the letters together while writing the letters in the air. Follow this same procedure with the remaining words.

Practice

Write the sentence starters below on the board and have children read them. Then have them copy the sentences and complete the endings.

> I began to laugh _____.
>
> I was sure the glass would break when_____.
>
> My head hurt_____.
>
> I can divide my paper into _____.
>
> When I am in second grade _____.

Check each child's ability to pronounce *began, laugh, sure, head, divide, second,* and *break* as the child reads each sentence.

Objective

- read and write new high-frequency words *began, laugh, sure, head, divide, second, break*

Materials

- Letter Cards: *a, b, c, d (2), e, g, h, i (2), k, l, n, o, r, s, t, u, v*
- index cards
- Phonics Library: *Home Run*

Apply

Ask children to help compose new sentences. Use chart paper to write a new sentence (or new sentences) for each word. You may want to put these sentences on sentence strips, cut apart the words, and ask children to rebuild the sentences.

Review *Home Run*

Reread the story together with children. Have children take turns reading aloud.

Tell children to find and read the following high-frequency words in *Home Run: began, head, second.* Have them read the sentences that contain these words.

Day 4

SKILL FOCUS: PHONICS | 10–15 MINUTES

r-Controlled Vowels: *or, ore*

Teach

Display the Sound/Spelling Card *orange*. Ask children to identify the picture. Say *orange* and ask children to repeat it. Then have children listen for and repeat the *r*-controlled vowel sound after you, /ôr/.

Hold up the Picture Card *horse* and ask children to identify the picture. Ask them which vowel sound they hear in *horse*, the short *o* vowel sound, /ŏ/ or the vowel sound *or*, /ôr/. Follow the same procedure with the Picture Cards for *mop, fork, ox, store,* and *cot.*

Point to the spellings *or* and *ore* on the *orange* Sound/Spelling Card and write them on the board. Remind children that when *o* is followed by *r* or *re*, the letters together stand for the sound they hear in *orange*. Display word cards *fork* and *store* next to their Picture Cards. Point out that words with /ôr/ can be spelled *or* or *ore* with a silent *e*. Help children blend the words *fork* and *store* using Blending Routine 2.

Practice

Display the Letter Cards *o* and *r* on the chalk ledge. Write the following words on the board, leaving blank placeholder spaces for the letters *or*: *storm, corn, short.* For each word, have a child come to the board and write the letters *or* in the blanks. Then have the child blend the word continuously and use it in a sentence. Repeat this procedure with Letter Cards *o, r,* and *e*, and the words *snore, more,* and *score.*

Apply

Have partners look for words with *or* and *ore* in *Sport Gets a Bath*. Each time they find a word, ask them to take turns reading the word aloud as you write it on the board. Have volunteers come to the board to underline the *or* or *ore* in each word.

Objectives

- associate the /ôr/ sound with the letters *or* and *ore*
- independently read words with *or* and *ore*

Materials

- Letter Cards: *e, o, r*
- Picture Cards: *cot, fork, horse, mop, ox, store*
- Sound/Spelling Card: *orange*
- word cards: *fork, store*
- Phonics Library: *Sport Gets a Bath*

r-Controlled Vowels: *er, ir, ur*

Teach

Display Picture Cards *fern, girl,* and *purse.* Ask children to identify each picture. Say the words and ask children to repeat them. Then have them listen for and repeat the *r*-controlled vowel sound after you, /ûr/.

Hold up Picture Card *nurse* and ask children to identify the picture. Ask them which vowel sound they hear in *nurse,* /ûr/ or /ôr/. Repeat with Picture Cards *horse, herd,* and *store.*

Display Sound/Spelling Card *bird.* Point to the *er, ir,* and *ur* spellings on the card. Explain that when the letter *e, i,* or *u* is followed by an *r,* the letter pair is pronounced /ûr/.

Display the word cards for *fern, girl,* and *purse* next to the matching Picture Cards. Run your finger under the *er* in *fern,* the *ir* in *girl,* and the *ur* in *purse* and have children say the /ûr/ sound in each word. When you get to the word *purse,* explain that the *e* at the end of many *r*-controlled *u* words is silent. Help children blend and read each word using Blending Routine 2.

Practice

Display the Letter Cards *e* and *r.* Then write the following words on the board, leaving blank placeholder spaces for the letters *er: clerk, germ.* For each word, have a child come to the board and write the letters *er* in the blanks. Then have the child blend the word continuously and use it in a sentence. Repeat with Letter Cards *i, r* and the words *dirt, shirt;* and Letter Cards *u, r* and the words *turn, nurse.*

Apply

Have partners look for words with *er, ir,* and *ur* in *Home Run.* Ask them to read each word aloud as you write it on the board.

Review *Two Greedy Bears*

Reread the story together with children. Ask children to make a list of /ôr/ and /ûr/ words that they find in the story.

Objectives

- associate the /ûr/ sound with the letters *er, ir,* and *ur*
- independently read words with *er, ir,* and *ur*

Materials

- Letter Cards: *e, i, r, u*
- Picture Cards: *fern, girl, herd, horse, nurse, purse, store*
- Sound/Spelling Card: *bird*
- word cards: *fern, girl, purse*
- Phonics Library: *Home Run*
- Anthology: *Two Greedy Bears*

SKILL FOCUS: COMPREHENSION   25–30 MINUTES

Making Predictions

Teach

Read the following situation aloud:

Read Aloud

> It was recess time. Three students were playing on the slide. One of the children was at the top of the slide when the whistle blew to go inside.

Ask children to make a prediction about what might happen next. As children are responding to this question, ask them to tell you how they made their predictions. Ask, *What information did you use?* Help children to see that when they make predictions, they use details, their experience, and thinking to predict what might happen.

Practice

Reread the story of *Two Greedy Bears*. Stop several times and ask children to describe what they think might happen next. You might want to use the following places to pause the reading:

Page 145 After the bears drink water for the second time.

Page 148 After the bears look at their very full stomachs.

Page 150 When the bears decide they were hungry.

Page 153 When the fox offers to help.

After children make each prediction, ask, *Why do you think that?* Help them to see that by using clues from the story and the illustrations and using what they know from their experience and thinking, they can sometimes predict what will happen next.

Objectives

- make predictions based on personal experiences and information from the story
- apply what children have learned to make new predictions

Materials

- Phonics Library: *Sport Gets a Bath, Home Run*
- Anthology: *Two Greedy Bears*

Apply

Ask children to think about what the greedy bears might have learned from their experience of dividing the cheese. Have children work together to brainstorm ways the bears might solve the problem of dividing the cheese the next time they are in that situation. Remind children to use what they know from the story and from their experience and thinking to figure out what might happen. Some children might want to record their predictions on audiocassette tape.

Ask children to share their predictions with the class. Allow classmates to ask questions for understanding, for example, *Do the predictions make sense?*

LITERATURE FOCUS: 10–15 MINUTES

Revisit *Sport Gets a Bath,* *Home Run,* and *Two Greedy Bears*

Page through the stories with children. Then ask them to find words with *er, ir, or, ore,* and *ur.*

Have children reread *Home Run.* Ask them to predict whether they think Jane will come back to finish the game or not.

Tell children to look through *Two Greedy Bears* to find the following high-frequency words: *began, laugh, sure, head, divide, second, break.*

Have children read aloud their favorite sentences or pages from the stories.

Day 1

PRETEACH

SKILL FOCUS: PHONICS
25–30 MINUTES

r-Controlled Vowels: *ar*

Teach

Recite and repeat the chant, asking children to join in as they are able.

> CHANT
>
> Arf, arf, arf!
>
> My dog Spark
>
> Likes to bark.
>
> Arf, arf, arf!

Objectives

- associate /är/ with the letters *ar*
- blend and read words with *ar*

Materials

- Teaching Master ES10-3
- Practice Master ES10-3
- Letter Cards: *a, f, m, r, s, t*
- Phonics Library: *Big Star's Gifts*

Say *bark*, stretching out the /är/ sounds. Then say: *Get ready to say* bark. *Then go* arf, arf! *Are you ready? Let's go*. Have children repeat *bark* and *arf, arf* several times. If necessary, point out that a dog's bark sometimes sounds like *arf, arf!*

Print *bark* on the board. Explain that the letters *ar* stand for /är/. Follow the same procedure for the dog's name, *Spark*.

Blend

Give four volunteers Letter Cards for *f, a, r,* and *m*. Ask the two volunteers with *a* and *r* to hold their cards so they are touching. Have the volunteers say the sounds for *a* and *r* together: /är/.

Get Set for Reading
CD-ROM

Fireflies for Nathan

Education Place

www.eduplace.com
Fireflies for Nathan

Audio CD

Fireflies for Nathan
Audio CD for **We Can Do It!**

Lexia Phonics
CD-ROM

Primary Intervention

Have all four volunteers move together to form *farm*. As they do so, model for children how to blend the sounds, using Blending Routine 1. Then have the whole group blend the sounds and say the word *farm*. Repeat with the word *star*.

Guided Practice

Display or **distribute** Teaching Master ES10-3, and discuss the picture with children. Tell them to use what they know about sounds as they read the sentences with you.

Help children underline the *ar* words in the sentences. Then have them read the words aloud.

Practice/Apply

Distribute Practice Master ES10-3, discuss the pictures, and read the directions with children. Explain that they need to use what they know about the /är/ sound as they read the sentences.

Tell children to draw a line to match each sentence with a picture.

Have children read the sentences aloud.

Check that they are blending /är/ words correctly.

LITERATURE FOCUS: 10–15 MINUTES

Preview *Big Star's Gifts*

Walk children through *Big Star's Gifts*. Discuss the illustrations, naming the characters and using story words such as *yard, hard, dark, sharp, arms,* and *scarf*.

Ask children to use the pictures to tell the order in which Barb did things as she built her snowman.

Tell children they will read this story with the rest of the class.

Teaching Master ES 10–3

r-Controlled Vowels: *ar*

The car won't start.
But I can see a barn.
Let's walk to the farm.
It's not too far!

TMES 10-3   Grade 1 • Theme 10: We Can Do It!

Practice Master ES 10–3

Name _____

r-Controlled Vowels: *ar*

Use sounds you know to read the sentences.
Draw lines to match each sentence with a picture.

Mark made a card for me.

They'll start to march soon.

Art's scarf has stars on it.

Grade 1 • Theme 10: We Can Do It!   PMES 10-3

Day 2

Objectives
- identify sequence of events
- recognize *first, next,* and *last* as clues to sequence

Materials
- Teaching Master ES10-4
- Practice Master ES10-4
- Anthology: *Fireflies for Nathan*

Sequence of Events

Teach

Tell children to watch as you do the following silently:

Pick up a piece of chalk.

Write a word on the board.

Erase the word.

Discuss what you did with children, pointing out that there was an order to the things you did. Ask children what you did *first, next,* and *last.* Ask if it would make sense for you to have erased the board before you wrote on it.

Explain to children that you will now tell them three things to do. Mention that they should do the things in the order in which you say them. Say the following, pausing so that children can complete each step.

Pick up a pencil.

Write the word cat.

Draw a line under one letter in the word.

Ask children if they could have written *cat* before picking up the pencil. Ask if they could have underlined a letter in *cat* before writing the word.

Elicit from children that doing things in order makes sense.

Guided Practice

Display or **distribute** Teaching Master ES10-4, and discuss the illustrations with children.

Point out that the pictures are in an order that tells a story. Ask if the girl and her mom could have skied down the hill before going up it.

Read the sentences below the pictures with children. Help children underline the words *First, Next,* and *Last.*

Have children use the words *First, Next,* and *Last* as they retell the story, using the pictures.

Practice/Apply

Distribute Practice Master ES10-4 to children. Read the directions with them. Be sure children understand that they are to cut out the pictures at the bottom of the page and put them in order to match the story. Once children have ordered the pictures, they can paste them, in the correct order, in the empty boxes.

Have partners compare the order in which they have pasted the pictures. Partners can then read the story to each other and then to the group.

Check children's responses to be sure they can sequence events in a story.

Preview *Fireflies for Nathan*

Walk children through *Fireflies for Nathan* on pages 176–199 in their Anthology.

Discuss the illustrations and use words from the story such as *star, jar, monarch butterfly, arm,* and *dark.*

Note the suggestions in the Extra Support boxes on Teacher's Edition pages T133, T136, T138, and T141.

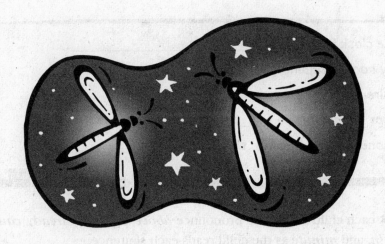

Teaching Master ES 10–4

Sequence of Events

First, we put on our skis.

Next, we ride to the top of the hill.

Last, we ski down the hill!

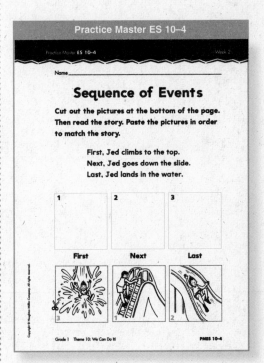

Practice Master ES 10–4

Name _____

Sequence of Events

Cut out the pictures at the bottom of the page. Then read the story. Paste the pictures in order to match the story.

First, Jed climbs to the top.
Next, Jed goes down the slide.
Last, Jed lands in the water.

1	2	3
First	Next	Last

Day 3

Objective

• read and write new high-frequency words *above, against, already, caught, begin, minute*

Materials

• Letter Cards: *a (2), b, c, d, e, g, h, i, l, m, n, o, r, s, t, u, v, y*
• index cards
• Phonics Library: *Car Trip*

SKILL FOCUS: 25–30 MINUTES

High-Frequency Words

Teach

Write *above, against, already, caught, begin,* and *minute* on large index cards. Read each word aloud while displaying it. Say the word again, then have children say it with you. Remind children to use what they know about letters and sounds to read the new words.

Display the Letter Cards on the chalk ledge. Draw word boxes on the chalkboard for four-, five-, six-, and seven-letter words.

Begin a game in which you give clues about each new word and ask children to identify which word it is. For example, begin by saying, *I have five letters. A synonym for me is* start. *Who am I?* As children identify the word *begin,* have five volunteers locate the letters that spell the word, lead classmates in spelling the word as they hold up the letters, and then write the word in the boxes. As children write the word *begin,* the others can say the letters together while writing the letters in the air. Follow this same procedure with the remaining words.

Practice

Write the sentence starters below on the board and have the children read them. Then have them copy the sentences and complete the endings.

> The clock is above _____.
>
> My book is against _____.
>
> I already begin to _____.
>
> I got caught in the _____.
>
> In one minute, it will be time for _____.

Check each child's ability to pronounce *above, against, already, caught, begin,* and *minute* as the child reads each sentence.

Apply

Have children write their sentences on sentence strips or construction paper. Ask them to share their sentences with the group. Then have them cut the sentence into individual words, trade with another student, and rebuild each sentence.

LITERATURE FOCUS: 10–15 MINUTES

Review *Car Trip*

Reread the story together with children.

Tell children to look through *Car Trip* for the following high-frequency words: *already, above, caught*. Have them read the sentences that contain these words.

Day 4

SKILL FOCUS: PHONICS   25–30 MINUTES

r-Controlled Vowels: *ar*

Teach

Display the Sound/Spelling Card *artist*, and have children identify the picture. Say *artist* and have children repeat the word. Then have children listen for and repeat the *r*-controlled vowel sound after you, /är/. Point to the spelling *ar* on the card and write it on the board. Remind children that when *a* is followed by *r*, the two letters together stand for the sound they hear in *artist*.

Hold up the Picture Card for *yard*, and ask children to identify the picture. Ask them which vowel sound they hear in *yard*, the *r*-controlled vowel sound /är/, the *r*-controlled vowel sound /ûr/, or the *r*-controlled vowel sound /ôr/. Follow the same procedure with the Picture Cards for *thorn, yarn, herd, scarf, car,* and *girl.*

Display the word card *car* next to its Picture Card. Run your finger under the *ar* in *car* and have children repeat the /är/ sound with you. Then help children to blend and read the word *car* using Blending Routine 2.

Remind children that they can make more words by adding different sounds to the beginning and end of *ar*. Have children blend the following sounds: /f/ - /är/, /y/ - /är/ - /d/, /sm/ - /är/ - /t/, /b/ - /är/ - /n/.

Practice

Write *ar* on the board. Then distribute Letter Cards for *b, c, d, f, h, k, m, n, p, t,* and *y.* Have a volunteer choose a letter or letters to blend with *r*-controlled vowel sound *ar* to make the following new words: *bark, farm, yarn, card, harp, part.* Have children repeat each new word.

Objectives

- associate the /är/ sound with the letters *ar*
- independently read words with *ar*

Materials

- Letter Cards: *b, c, d, f, h, k, m, n, p, t, y*
- Picture Cards: *car, girl, herd, scarf, thorn, yard, yarn*
- Sound/Spelling Card: *artist*
- word card: *car*
- Phonics Library: *Big Star's Gifts*
- Anthology: *Fireflies for Nathan*

Apply

Have children look for words with *ar* in *Big Star's Gifts*. Each time they find a word, ask them to read it aloud as you write it on the board. Have volunteers circle the *ar* in each word. Then have children choose one of the words to illustrate.

Review *Fireflies for Nathan*

Reread the story together with children.

Ask them to make a list of /är/ words that they find in the story. Have them use the words in a sentence.

Have children take turns reading aloud.

Objectives

- identify the order in which events happen in a story
- use words like *first, then, next,* and *last* to give directions

Materials

- Phonics Library: *Big Star's Gifts, Car Trip*
- Anthology: *Fireflies for Nathan*

RETEACH

SKILL FOCUS: COMPREHENSION   25–30 MINUTES

Sequence of Events

Teach

Select a task that children do (or see you do) every day that needs to be done in a particular sequence. For example, tell children that you are going to put on your jacket. Ask children to watch you complete the task to be sure you are doing it correctly. Holding your jacket, button (or zip) the jacket first. Then attempt to put the jacket on. Let children tell you that you buttoned the jacket before putting it on. Then ask children to instruct you on how to correctly complete the same task, using the words *first, next, then,* and *last.* Help children to see why it is important to do some tasks in the correct order.

Have children tell why the sequence of events is important in a task or in a story. Remind them that words like *first, next, then, last, beginning, middle,* and *end* let us know that there is a sequence or order to what we are reading or doing.

Practice

Talk with children about the story *Fireflies for Nathan* by Shulamith Levey Oppenheim. Remind them that Nathan wants to catch fireflies just the way his dad did when he was young. Have children follow along as you reread the story or walk children through the story looking at the illustrations. Tell them that, based on the story, you will all write step-by-step directions for catching fireflies. You might want to use a sequence list, like the following, to record ideas:

<u>How to Catch Fireflies:</u>

> *First, get a jar to hold the fireflies.*
> *Then, wait for the night to come.*
> *Next, watch for the fireflies to begin glowing.*
> *Then, creep across the lawn carefully.*
> *Next, cup your hands around a glow.*
> *Then, keep the firefly in your hands ... don't peek!*
> *Next, drop the firefly in the jar.*
> *Then, catch more fireflies for the jar.*
> *Next, watch your fireflies.*
> *Last, let the fireflies go.*

Ask children what might have happened if Nathan used a different sequence to catch fireflies.

Apply

Have children work together to write and illustrate the step-by-step process for catching fireflies. Tell children that they can change the steps if they think there is another way to catch fireflies. Then have children share their work with others, explaining why they might have changed the sequence or added other steps.

LITERATURE FOCUS: 10–15 MINUTES

Revisit *Big Star's Gifts, Car Trip,* and *Fireflies for Nathan*

Page through the stories with children, asking them to find /är/ words.

Have children reread *Big Star's Gifts.* Ask them to sequence the events in the story.

Tell children to look through *Fireflies for Nathan* to find the following high-frequency words: *above, against, already, caught, begin, minute.*

Have children read aloud their favorite sentences or pages from the stories.

Day 1

Objectives
• read words ending with *-er, -est*
• build words with *-er, -est*

Materials
• Teaching Master ES10-5
• Practice Master ES10-5
• word card: *short*
• suffix cards: *er, est*
• Phonics Library: *Ice-Cold Drinks*

**Get Set for Reading
CD-ROM**
The Hat from *Days with Frog and Toad*

Education Place
www.eduplace.com
The Hat from *Days with Frog and Toad*

Audio CD
The Hat from *Days with Frog and Toad*
Audio CD for **We Can Do It!**

**Lexia Phonics
CD-ROM**
Primary Intervention

PRETEACH

SKILL FOCUS: PHONICS　　　　25–30 MINUTES

Base Words and Endings
-er, -est

Teach

Recite and repeat the chant, asking children to join in as they are able.

> **CHANT**
> Tall, taller
> Who's the taller of the two?
> Tall, taller, tallest
> Who's the tallest of the group?

Draw two trees on the board. Make each tree a different size, with one obviously taller than the other. Repeat the first two lines of the chant. Ask a volunteer to point out the taller tree. Print *taller* below this tree.

Say *taller* stretching out the syllables. Then have children repeat it several times. Underline the *-er* ending and explain that *-er* is an ending that we add to some words when we are comparing two things.

Draw another tree next to the others. Make this one the tallest of the three. Repeat the last two lines of the chant and ask a child to point out the tallest tree. Print *tallest* below this tree.

Say *tallest*, stretching out the sounds in each syllable. Then have children say it several times. Underline the *-est* ending. Tell children that *-est* is an ending we can add to some words when we are comparing more than two things.

Blend

Give the word card *short* to one child. Model how to blend the word, using Blending Routine 1. Then have children blend and say the word.

Give a card with the ending *er* to another child. Model how to blend the ending. Have the child with *er* stand next to the child with *short*. Have the children move the two cards together to make *shorter*. Blend and say *shorter*. Then have children blend and say the word on their own. Follow a similar procedure for *shortest*.

Guided Practice

Display or **distribute** Teaching Master ES10-5, and help children identify the vest, the jacket, and the coat in the picture. Read the first sentence with children. Ask a volunteer to point to the word *warm*. Have another volunteer point to the picture of the vest.

Read the second sentence with children. Have them read the word with the *-er* ending. (warmer). Ask *What two things are being compared?* (the jacket and the vest) Help children circle the picture of the one that is warmer.

Have children read the third sentence with you. Ask which article of clothing is the warmest of the three. (the coat) Help children mark an X on the picture of the coat.

Practice/Apply

Distribute Practice Master ES10-5. Discuss the illustrations and read the directions with children. Remind them to use what they know about words with endings as they read the sentences independently.

Check that children are reading *-er* and *-est* words correctly as they share their answers with the group.

Preview *Ice-Cold Drinks*

Walk children through *Ice-Cold Drinks*. Discuss the illustrations, naming the characters and using story words such as *sweetest, coolest, sweeter, cooler,* and *louder.*

Ask children to tell how the sign that Rose and Bruce made changes throughout the story.

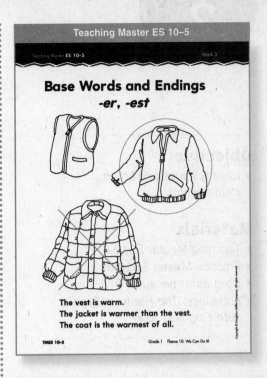

Teaching Master ES 10–5

Base Words and Endings
-er, -est

The vest is warm.
The jacket is warmer than the vest.
The coat is the warmest of all.

TMES 10-5   Grade 1   Theme 10: We Can Do It!

Practice Master ES 10–5

Name

Base Words and Endings
-er, -est

Read each sentence. Circle something in the picture that answers the question.

Is the bag or the box lighter?

Which flower is the longest?

Which bug is smaller?

Grade 1   Theme 10: We Can Do It!   PMES 10-5

Day 2

PRE TEACH

SKILL FOCUS: COMPREHENSION 25–30 MINUTES

Cause and Effect

Teach

Display the word card *because*, and help children to read the word. Tell them that they are going to use the word *because* to tell why things happen.

Model how to use the word *because* for children. You might say: *I am wearing a sweater because I am cold.* After you say the sentence, ask a *why* question about it, for example: *Why am I wearing a sweater?* (because you are cold)

Remind children that a cause is something that makes something else happen. Say: *The cause is that I am cold. The effect is that I put on a sweater.*

Explain that the word *because* often signals what the cause is. Ask a few volunteers to suggest sentences using *because*. After each, ask a *why* question about the sentence, and have children answer it.

Tell children that we can also ask *why* questions about things that happen in stories. The answers will often include the word *because*.

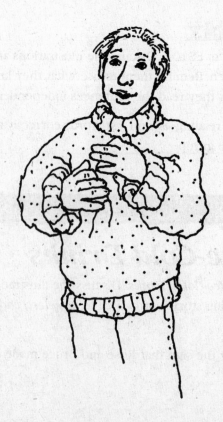

Objective

• identify cause-and-effect relationships

Materials

• Teaching Master ES10-6
• Practice Master ES10-6
• word card: *because*
• Anthology: *The Hat* from *Days with Frog and Toad*

Guided Practice

Display or **distribute** Teaching Master ES10-6, and discuss the pictures with children.

Read the first sentence with children. Ask, *Why does Pam want a kitten?* If necessary, lead children to respond by saying: *She wants a kitten because she thinks kittens are fun to play with.*

Help children underline the part of the sentence that tells what caused Pam to want a kitten.

Follow a similar procedure for the second sentence.

Practice/Apply

Distribute Practice Master ES10-6 to children. Read the directions with them. Be sure children understand that they are to base their choices on the information provided in the story.

Check children's responses to be sure they can identify cause and effect in a story.

LITERATURE FOCUS: 10–15 MINUTES

Preview *The Hat* from *Days with Frog and Toad*

Walk children through *The Hat* on pages 209–219 in their Anthology.

Discuss the illustrations and use words from the story such as *larger*, *biggest*, and *smaller*.

Note the suggestions in the Extra Support box on Teacher's Edition page T205.

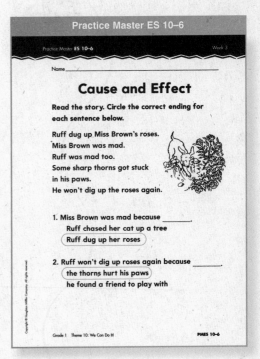

Day 3

Objective
- read and write new high-frequency words *able, eye, present, thoughts*

Materials
- Letter Cards: *a, b, e (2), g, h (2), l, n, o, p, r, s, t (2), u, y*
- index cards
- Phonics Library: *The Best Pie*

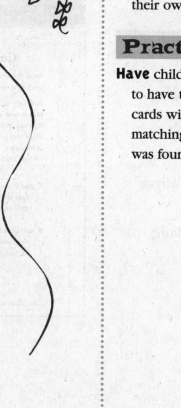

RETEACH

SKILL FOCUS: 25–30 MINUTES

High-Frequency Words

Teach

Write *able, eye, present,* and *thoughts* on large index cards. Read each word aloud while pointing to it. Say the word again, then have children say it with you. Remind children to use what they know about letters and sounds to read the new words.

Display the Letter Cards on the chalk ledge. Draw word boxes on the chalkboard for three-, four-, seven-, and eight-letter words.

Continue in this way until children have said, spelled out, and worked with you to write the words in the boxes. Begin a game in which you give clues about each new word and ask children to identify which word it is. For example, *I have three letters. I am the part of the body you use to see. Who am I?* (eye) As children identify the letters that make up the word, have them write the word in the air and then on their own papers.

Practice

Have children write each of these new words on cards. You may choose to have the cards in the shape of a hat. Ask students to match the word cards with words from the story *The Hat.* When the children find the matching words, have them read aloud the sentence in which the word was found.

Apply

Write the following story on the board. Have children read it together. When finished, reread the story, this time having children underline each new high-frequency word.

> Today, I began to learn to ride my bike. I had to work hard so that I would not fall down. At the end of the day, I was <u>able</u> to stay on the bike. All that work made me tired. My <u>eyes</u> were starting to close. I went home and took a nap. I woke up with <u>thoughts</u> of my bike. Then my grandma was standing there. She had a <u>present</u> for me. A new horn for my bike!

Check each child's ability to pronounce *able*, *eye*, *present*, and *thoughts* as the child reads each sentence.

LITERATURE FOCUS: 10–15 MINUTES

Review *The Best Pie*

Reread the story together with children.

Ask children to look through *The Best Pie* to find the following high-frequency words: *able*, *thought*, *eye*. Have them read the sentences that contain these words.

Day 4

RETEACH

SKILL FOCUS: PHONICS   25–30 MINUTES

Base Words and Endings
-er, -est

Objectives

- understand that *-er* and *-est* can be added to base words
- recognize that when *-er* and *-est* are added to describing words, the new words are used to compare two or more things
- independently read base words with *-er* and *-est* endings

Materials

- index cards
- Phonics Library: *Ice-Cold Drinks*
- Anthology: *The Hat* from *Days with Frog and Toad*

Teach

Write *tall*, *taller*, and *tallest* on the chalkboard. Remind children that a base word is a word to which an ending can be added. Say *tall* and have children repeat it after you. Then point to the word *tall* and explain that it is a base word to which the endings *-er* and *-est* can be added. Point to *taller* and *tallest* and circle the base word *tall* in each word.

Remind children that when the endings *-er* and *-est* are added to describing words, the new words are used to compare things. Explain that a describing word that ends in *-er* compares two things and a describing word that ends in *-est* compares more than two things. Write the words *tall, taller, tallest* on three large index cards. Ask three children of varying heights to come to the front of the class and have each child hold the appropriate word card as you say:

_____ *is tall.*

_____ *is taller than* _____.

_____ *is the tallest of the three children.*

Repeat the procedure with the base words *small* and *long*, using classroom objects for the comparisons.

Practice

Write the following base words on the board:

| fast | high | cold | deep | slow | old |

Read the base words aloud and have children repeat them after you. Then have volunteers add *-er* and *-est* to each base word and use each of the new words in a sentence.

Apply

Have pairs of children find words with *-er* and *-est* in *Ice-Cold Drinks*. Each time a child finds an *-er* or *-est* word, he or she should read it aloud while you write the word on the board. Have volunteers come to the board and circle the base word and underline *-er* or *-est*.

LITERATURE FOCUS: 10–15 MINUTES

Review *The Hat* from *Days with Frog and Toad*

Reread the story together with children.

Ask children to make a list of words with *-er* and *-est* endings that they find in the story. Have them use the words in a sentence.

Have children take turns reading aloud.

Day 5

Objectives

- identify cause-and-effect relationships
- make a chart of causes and effects

Materials

- Phonics Library: *Ice-Cold Drinks, The Best Pie*
- Anthology: *The Hat* from *Days with Frog and Toad*

Cause and Effect

Teach

Recite the nursery rhyme *Humpty Dumpty* to the class. Ask children to brainstorm a list of the many causes for Humpty's fall from the wall. When they run out of ideas, ask them to then brainstorm a list of the effects of his falling. Use leading examples such as the following, if necessary:

Causes: The wind was blowing hard.

Effects: He fell off the wall.

Help children to understand that in the example, *The wind was blowing hard, so Humpty Dumpty fell off the wall*, the cause (The wind was blowing hard.) answers the question, *Why did it happen?* and the effect (Humpty Dumpty fell off the wall.) answers the question, *What happened?*

Practice

Revisit the story *The Hat*. As you are reading, pause to help children identify the main cause-and-effect relationships. Use this chart format to help children organize and understand these relationships:

Cause	Effect
Frog gives Toad a present.	Toad is happy.
The hat is too big.	Toad trips and runs into things on their walk.
Frog takes the hat home and pours water on it.	The hat shrinks.
The hat shrinks.	It fits Toad.

Apply

Have children choose one cause-and-effect relationship between Frog and Toad in the story. Ask children to think about other effects that could have happened in the story. In the sentence, *Frog gave Toad a present*, for example, another effect might be that Toad gave Frog a hug. Help children to see that it is helpful to identify cause-and-effect relationships because they help us to understand how and why things happen in a story.

LITERATURE FOCUS: 10–15 MINUTES

Revisit *Ice-Cold Drinks, The Best Pie,* and *The Hat* from *Days with Frog and Toad*

Page through the stories with children. Ask them to look for words with the endings *-er* and *-est*.

Have children reread *Ice-Cold Drinks*. Ask *What did Rose and Bruce finally do that caused people to buy their drinks?*

Tell children to look through *The Hat* to find the following high-frequency words: *able, eye, present, thoughts.*

Have children read aloud their favorite sentences or pages from the stories.

Consonants *m* and *t*

Short *a*

Blend the sounds. Read the words. Then write the words.

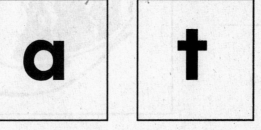

_____

- - - - - - - - - - - - - - - - - -

_____

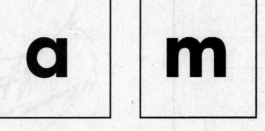

_____

- - - - - - - - - - - - - - - - - -

_____

_____

- - - - - - - - - - - - - - - - - -

Sequence of Events

_____
- - - - - - - - - - - -
_____

_____
- - - - - - - - - - - -
_____

_____
- - - - - - - - - - - -
_____

Name_____

Sequence of Events

Cut out the pictures and put them in story order.

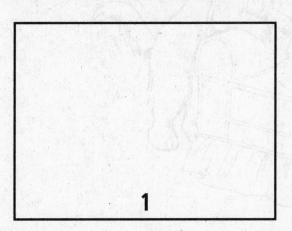

1

2

3

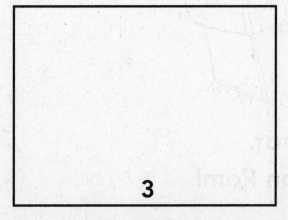

Consonants f and p

Pam sat.

Fat Pat sat.
Pat sat on Pam!

Name_____

Blending Short *a* Words

Use sounds you know to read. Draw lines to match each sentence with a picture.

1. Nan can tap.

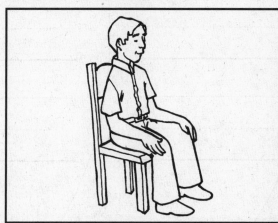

2. The cat can nap.

3. The man sat.

Compare and Contrast

pen   both   pencil

Name_____

Compare and Contrast

Look at both pictures for things that are the same and things that are different. Put an X on the things that are different.

Consonants *b* and *r*

Bear has a big bat.

Bear ran and ran!

Name_____

Blending Short *i* Words

Use sounds you know to read. Draw lines to match each sentence with a picture.

1. Big Pig can sit.

2. Big Pig ran.

3. Big Pig can hit.

Cause and Effect

Nan is glad.

Nan can go here.

Why?

Nat is sad.

Nat can not go here.

Why?

Name_____

Cause and Effect

Look at each picture. Draw a line from the picture on the left to a picture on the right to show why it happened.

Consonants *d* and *l*

Blending Short *o* Words

Use sounds you know to read. Draw lines to match each sentence with a picture.

1. **The fox can hop.**

2. **Bob can mop.**

3. **The ox is hot.**

Noting Details

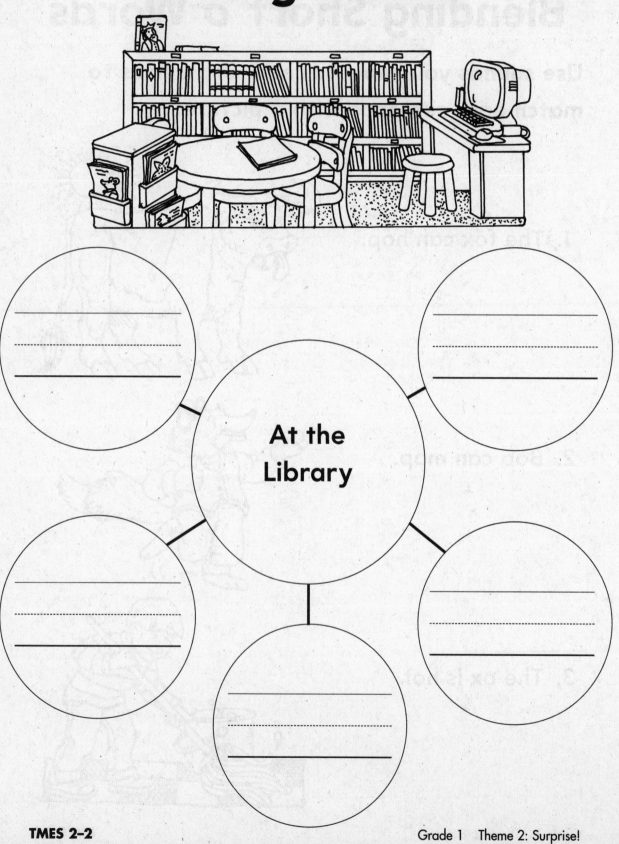

At the
Library

Name_____

Noting Details

Read each sentence. Add the details to the picture.

A hat can go on the big cat.

A wig can go on the pig.

The fox can have a box.

Consonants *y* and *v*

It is time to visit the vet, Vito.

No, no, not yet! You can bring me back next year for a visit.

Name_____

Blending Short e Words

Use sounds you know to read. Draw lines to match each sentence with a picture.

The vet got a box.

The men have a van.

Ben and Ed have a pet.

Fantasy and Realism

Fox said, "Ken, do not go in my den."

Ken said, "I will not go in the fox den."

Name_____

Fantasy and Realism

**Look at each picture and read the sentence.
Circle each picture that shows something that
could really happen.**

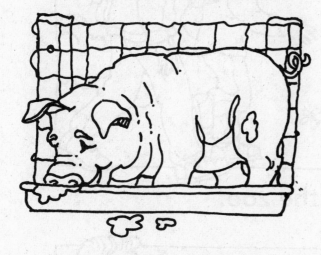

The pig is in the pen.

The pig can fix the van.

The dog can draw
a map.

"My dog can jump to
get the ball," said Jen.

Consonants *j* and *z*

Jan is at the zoo.

Jan sees a zebra.
She jumps for joy.

Name_____

Blending Short *u* Words

Use sounds you know to read. Draw lines to match each sentence with a picture.

Jen got a cup.

Jan is on the rug.

Zip can tug a lot.

Story Structure

Who?	
Where?	
What happens?	

Name_____

Story Structure

These pictures tell a story. Look at them. Then complete the story map below.

Who and Where?	
What happens First?	
Next?	
Last?	

Double Final Consonants

Plurals with -s

**Read each sentence. Find the word with an *-s*
ending. Circle the *-s*. Write the word that is left.**

_____

1. Big Pig has three sacks. _____

_____

2. One sack has rocks in it! _____

_____

3. Can Pig lug it up the hills? _____

Topic, Main Idea, Details

Playing Outside

There are many things to play outside.

You can jump rope.

You can play ball.

You can play tag.

Topic: _____

Main Idea: _____

Detail:	Detail:	Detail:

Name_____

Topic, Main Idea, Details

Read the story and look at the chart. The topic is filled in. Add the main idea and the details.

My Dog, Tan

Tan is fun.

Tan can run.

Tan can jump.

Tan can tug.

Topic: My Dog, Tan

_____

- -

Main Idea: _____

Detail:	Detail:	Detail:

Verb Ending -*ed*

Jack packed his bags.
He filled up three bags!

Name_____

Possessives with 's

Read each sentence. Draw a line under the word that shows who owns something. Circle the word that tells what the person owns.

1. Kim's cap falls.

2. Jan's dog jumps on it.

3. Kim thanks Bill's dad.

Making Predictions

Jim is going to see Gram.

He will need warm things.

What is the weather like at Gram's?

_____

- -

_____

Making Predictions

Cut and paste the picture that shows what happens next.

  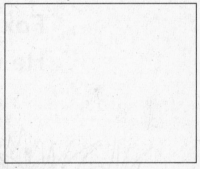

Grade 1   Theme 3: Let's Look Around!   **PMES 3–4**

Clusters with *r*

Fox hides in the grass.
He wants to trap Frog.

Frog tricks Fox.
Frog grins as Fox falls in.

Name_____

Contractions with 's

Read each sentence. Find the word that ends with 's. Circle the words below the sentence that show what the word with 's means.

"Where's my hat?" said Ben.

Where is   What is

"Here's a hat," said Fran.

He is   Here is

"But it's not my hat!" said Ben.

it is   who is

Categorize and Classify

hen   **cat**   **bird**

dog   **pig**   **duck**

Animals with 2 legs	Animals with 4 legs	Animals with wings	Animals with fur

Categorize and Classify

Read each animal name. If it names a farm animal, write it under Farm Animals.

If it names a pet, write it under Pets.

dog   cat   hen   frog   ox   pig

Farm Animals	Pets
-------------------	-------------------
_____	_____
-------------------	-------------------
_____	_____
-------------------	-------------------
_____	_____
-------------------	-------------------
_____	_____

Clusters with /

Dan plans to sled on the hill.

Tom claps and grins as Dan sleds by.

Tom and Dan are glad that they did not flip the sleds.

Blending More Short *o* Words

Draw lines to match each sentence with a picture.

1. The flock of birds is in the garden.

2. The paper is in the slot.

3. Don sees the big clock.

Drawing Conclusions

Where is Meg going?

_____

- -

_____

Why do you think so?

_____

- -

_____

- -

_____

Name_____

Drawing Conclusions

Read each story. Draw conclusions to tell how each character feels.

1. Jan ran and ran.
   Jan did win.

   _____

   _____

   Jan is _____.

2. Bill did trip and fall.
   He did miss the bus.

   _____

   _____

   Bill is _____.

Clusters with *s*

Scott slips and spills his snack.

He sees a small spot on the rug.

Scott will stop and pick it up.

Name_____

Blending More Short *e* Words

Draw lines to match each sentence with a picture.

1. Deb is on the sled.

2. Fred smells the flower.

**3. My dog sets the
ball on the steps.**

Compare and Contrast

lion

both

cat

Compare and Contrast

Read the words that go with Pat and Pam. Then write the words in the chart where they belong.

 **Pam**

has a crib
is a girl
can not run
can eat
has a cat

 **Pat**

has a big bed
is a girl
can run fast
can eat
has a cat

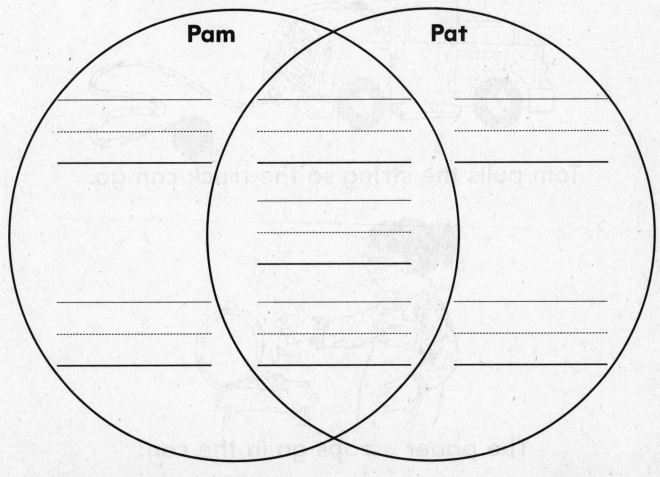

Pam   **Pat**

Triple Clusters

1.

Bud scrubs the pup.

2.

Tom pulls the string so the truck can go.

3.

The paper scraps go in the can.

Name_____

Blending More Short *u* Words

Read the story. Circle the short *u* words.

Cub and Pup get in the truck.

The truck gets stuck in the mud.

Cub and Pup jump in the mud to pull the truck.

Cub and Pup must scrub.

Sequence of Events

_____

Bake it. _____

_____

Mix it. _____

_____

Eat it. _____

Name_____

Sequence of Events

Cut out the pictures. Put them in order.

1	2	3

Jan runs fast.   **Get set!**   **Jan wins!**

Digraph *sh*

She shall mash the shed!

Digraphs *sh* and *ch*

Use sounds you know to read the story.

Finish the story with a drawing of your own!

This is Chet.

Chet is hot.

He checks the tub.

Splash!

Compare and Contrast

Meet Nat and Pat.

They both have things for playing ball.

Nat has a bat and a glove.

Pat has a glove and a ball.

Name_____

Compare and Contrast

Read to find out how Pam and Ed are alike and different. Complete the chart.

Pam is hot.   Ed is cold.

Pam likes dogs.   Ed likes cats.

Pam and Ed have hats.

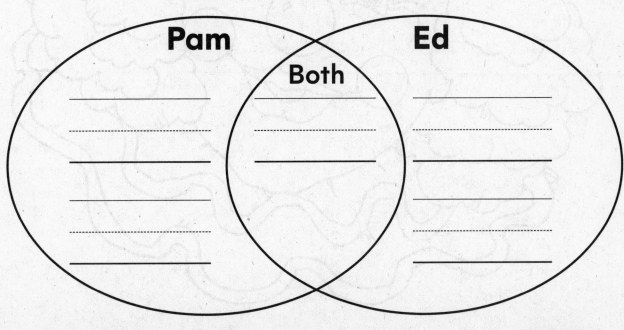

Pam   **Ed**

Both

Long *a* (CVCe)

This is a game!

Take a look.

Find and color the same shape. ▲

Name_____

Final *nk*

Use sounds you know to read the story. End the story with your own drawing.

"Thank you," said Nate.

Jane said, "I think you will like it."

"It is for my fish tank."

Grade 1   Theme 5: Home Sweet Home

PMES 5–3

Making Generalizations

Animals live
on farms.

Animals live
in houses.

Animals live
in the sea.

Animals _____ in many places.

Name_____

Making Generalizations

Use sounds you know to read the sentences.
Then circle the answer and write it in the last
sentence.

The children
sing on the bus.

The men sing in
the car.

The girls sing
outside.

_____

People _____ in many places.

sing   **sit**

Long *i* (CVCe)

Here is a line of animals.
Look for one with stripes.
The stripes are on the sides and face.

Name _____

Contractions

Use sounds you know as you read.

Circle the contractions.

It's time to dine!

We'll have lunch.

I'll make a plate of chops and rice.

You'll like it!

Cause and Effect

Why did the dog get a prize?

It can walk.   **It can do tricks.**

Name_____

Cause and Effect

Read what happens. Circle the sentence that tells why it happens.

The boy runs. Why?

He can race.   **He hit the ball.**

Long *o* (CV and CVC*e*) and Long *u* (CVC*e*)

June rode a huge mule.
She held on with a rope.

Rose broke her flute when
she fell in the hole.

Name_____

Final *nt*

Read the questions. Circle the answer.

1. Can an ant ride a bike?   Yes   No

2. Can an ant rest on a plant?   Yes   No

3. Can an ant hunt for things to eat?   Yes   No

4. Can an ant read a note you sent?   Yes   No

Story Structure

Frog can not skate.

He slips and slides on the ice.

Fox gets a sled.

He uses the sled to pull Frog.

Story Map	
Who is in the story?	
What is the problem?	
How is it solved?	

Name_____

Story Structure

Read the sentences. Circle the picture that shows Luke's problem. Then draw a picture to show how Luke could solve it.

Luke rides his bike.

A big stone is on the path.
Luke can not go.

Long *e* (CV, CVCe)

Pete will be in the play.
He will be Sox the cat.

Steve will be in the play.
He will be Chet the duck.

These two friends like to
be in the play.

Name_____

Vowel Pair *ee*

**Use sounds you know to read the story. Write the
number word that tells how many sheep you see.**

Take a peek.

How many sheep do you see?

One sheep? Two sheep? Three sheep?

Thinking of sheep makes Steve sleep.

_____

- -

How many sheep do you see? _____

Noting Details

Fox has a big hat.

Fox looks sad.

Frog has on long pants.

Frog smiles a lot.

Noting Details

Use what you know about sounds to read the story. Circle the picture that matches the story.

The cat likes the garden.

She sits by the flowers.

She looks at the bees that fly by.

Vowel Pairs *ai, ay*

First, we pay for our seats.
Then we wait for the train.
It's a long way to Gram's house.
We'll stay at her house for two
days.

Name_____

Vowel Pairs *ai*, *ay*

Use sounds you know to read the sentences.
Circle the words that have the long *a* sound.

"It is a good day to hike," said Jay.

"It will not rain."

"This is the main trail," Pat said.

"It's the best way to go."

Making Predictions

It had rained and rained.

The rain came down for days.

The street is so wet.

The van comes very fast.

The van will make a big splash.

The van will run out of gas.

Name_____

Making Predictions

Read the sentences. Circle the picture that shows what will happen next.

Ken feels sad.
His friend Jack does
not like that.
Jack tells Ken a
funny joke.

What will Ken do?

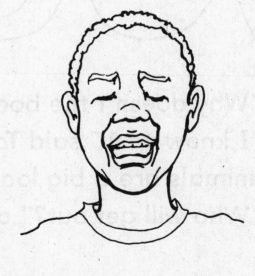

Vowel Pairs *oa*, *ow*

"Why doesn't the boat float?" asked Goat.
"I know why," said Toad. "Too many
animals are a big load for this boat."
"Who will get out?" asked Goat.

Name_____

Vowel Pairs *oa*, *ow*

Use sounds you know to read the sentences.

Draw lines to match each sentence to a picture.

1. See Goat in his coat.

2. Big flakes of snow fall.

3. Toad shows his boat to Cat.

Problem Solving

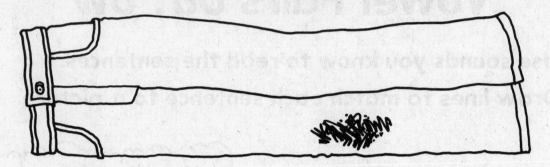

Ken eats a snack.

He spills jam on his jeans.

There is a big stain.

What can Ken do to fix his jeans?

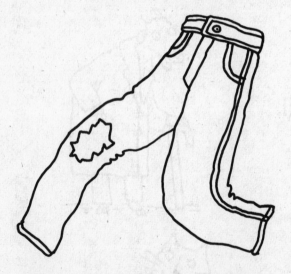 

Ken can cut out the stain.

Ken can clean his jeans.

Name_____

Problem Solving

Read the story. Circle the sentence that tells the problem.

It is lunch time.

Pam would like to sit with her friends.

She cannot.

Why?

Pam has no meal.   Pam has no seat.

Circle the picture that shows the solution.

The /o͝o/ Sound for *oo*

The cook looked in his book.

He wanted to make a cake.

He took out some eggs.

He got some milk and other things.

Mix, mix, mix.

It will be a good treat!

Name_____

Compound Words

Use sounds you know to read the sentences.
Circle each compound word you find.

The beach is fun in the daytime.

I see sailboats.

I find seashells.

I have sunglasses.

Sequence of Events

_____
- - - - - - - - - - - - - -
_____ Sox puts on his skates.
_____
- - - - - - - - - - - - - -
_____ He steps onto the ice.
_____
- - - - - - - - - - - - - -
_____ He slides and glides with
his friends.

Name_____

Sequence of Events

Read the story. Cut out the pictures.

Put the pictures in the correct order in the boxes.

Nat sees some flowers.

He smells them.

He picks one flower to take home.

1	2	3

First   **Next**   **Last**

Vowel Pairs *ew, oo,* (/o͞o/)

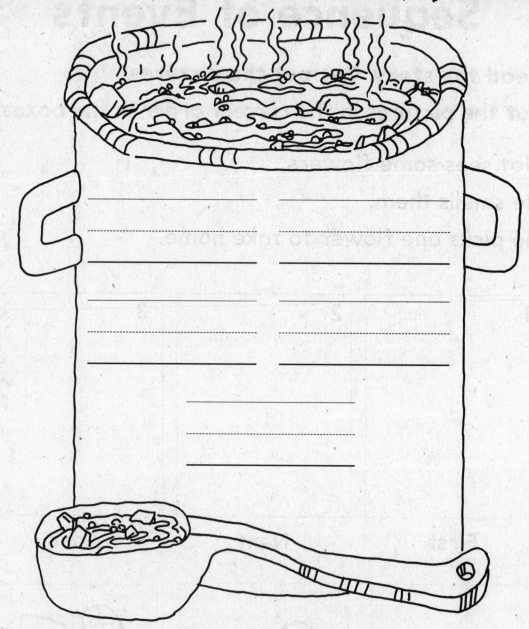

Mara dips a spoon in the pot.
She will mix the stew.
It has meat in it and beans she grew.
Soon it will be just right.
Then Mara will scoop up some to eat.

Name_____

Vowel Pairs *ew, oo,* (/o͞o/)

Use sounds you know to read each sentence.
Mark an X on the correct picture.

Which animal can hoot?

Which animal grew too big?

Which animal sees the moon?

Which animal flew to a nest?

Fantasy and Realism

Jen rides her bike.

Her pet cat rides a bike, too.

The cat sings as she rides.

Jen and the cat live in the
same house.

Real	Make-Believe

Name_____

Fantasy and Realism

Read the sentences. Circle the ones that tell about make-believe things.

1. The pig tells a joke.

_____

2. The cat takes a nap.

_____

3. She swims in the lake.

_____

4. A fish cooks a meal.

Base Words and Ending *-ing*

It is raining today.

I am walking my dog.

We are wearing our coats.

Are we staying dry?

Name_____

Base Words and
Ending *-ing*

In each sentence, find a word with *-ing*. Circle the *-ing*.
What word is left? Write it on the line.

Fox is cooking a
meal for Frog.

_____

_____

Frog is painting
a picture for
Fox.

_____

_____

Frog and Fox
are thinking of
each other.

_____

_____

Categorize and Classify

hat

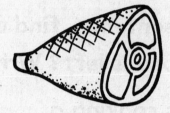

meat

shoe

coat

carrot

egg

Name_____

Categorize and Classify

Read the words.

Write each word in the place it belongs.

sink

table

tree

birds

doghouse

crib

Inside a House	**Outside a House**
_____	_____
_____	_____
_____	_____
_____	_____

Vowel Pairs ou, ow (/ou/)

My dog is a hound.
He does not growl.
But he does like to howl!

Syllabication

**Use sounds you know to read the sentences.
Draw a picture to match each sentence. Draw a
line under each word that has two syllables.**

I play outside in the summer.

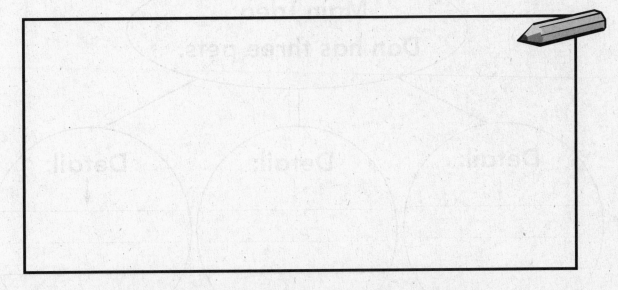

I made a snowman in the winter.

Topic, Main Idea, Details/Summarizing

Dan's Pets

Dan has three pets.
He has a big dog.
He has a black cat.
He has a hamster, too.

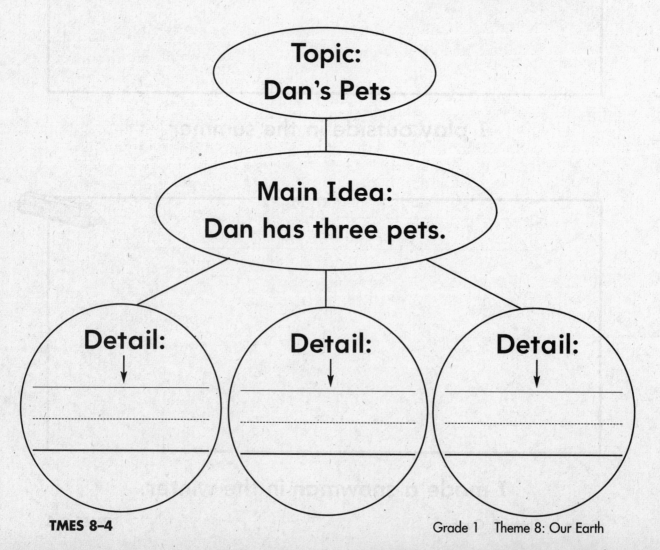

Topic:
Dan's Pets

Main Idea:
Dan has three pets.

Detail:

Detail:

Detail:

Name _____

Topic, Main Idea, Details/Summarizing

Read the story. Then complete the story web.

Our Farm

Animals live on our farm.

We have cows and horses.

We have a goat too.

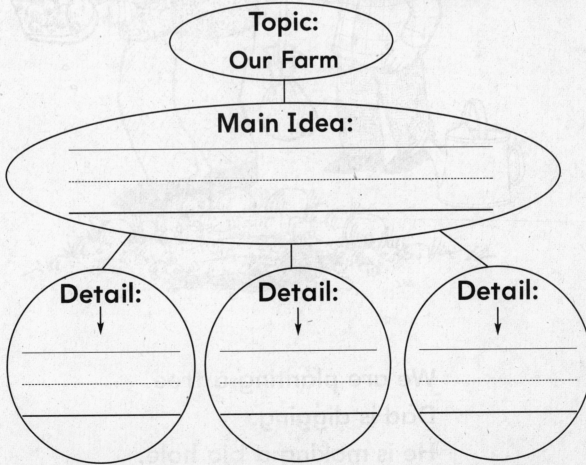

Topic:
Our Farm

Main Idea:
_____
- - - - - - - - - - - - - - -
_____

Detail:
↓
_____
- - - - - - -
_____

Detail:
↓
_____
- - - - - - -
_____

Detail:
↓
_____
- - - - - - -
_____

Base Words and
Ending *-ing*

We are planting a tree.

Dad is digging.

He is making a big hole.

Name_____

Base Words and Ending *-ing*

Use sounds you know to read the story. Finish the story with a drawing of your own.

I am making dog treats.

They're baking now.

My dogs are begging.

Now they are sharing.

Drawing Conclusions

Tuck and I like to run.

I say, "Let's go, Tuck!"

I hold onto Tuck's leash.

I give Tuck a treat when we're done.

Drawing Conclusions

Answer these riddles. Choose from the answers in the box.

cat	cook	table	teacher

I wear a white hat.
I work with food.
I bake cakes, too.
Who am I?

_____

I am a kind of pet.
I can chase a mouse.
A dog can chase me!
What am I?

_____

I like children.
I read to them.
I help them learn.
Who am I?

_____

I have four legs.
But I stand still.
You can eat on me.
What am I?

_____

Sounds for *y*

This toast with jelly
is yummy.

This dry toast is
yucky!

Sounds for *y*

**Use sounds you know to read the story. Finish
the story with a drawing of your own.**

This is my bunny. His name is Fuzzy.

He can be very shy.

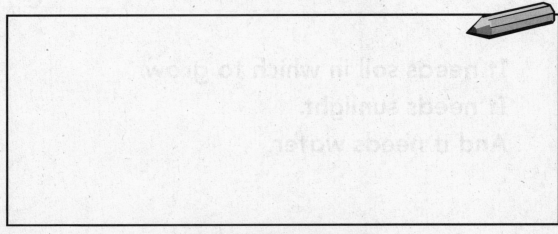

Now he is sleepy.

Noting Details

What does this plant need to grow?

It needs soil in which to grow.
It needs sunlight.
And it needs water.

Noting Details

Read the story. Draw a picture that shows the story details.

I like to go to the lake.

I see the big yellow sun in the sky.

There is a bird flying over the water.

Dad and I go for a swim.

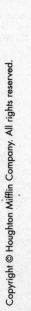

Base Words and Ending -es

Mom made two wishes.
She got two boxes.
Which box has the dresses?

Name _____

Base Words and Ending -es

Read each sentence. Circle each *-es* ending. Draw a line under the word that is left.

Jen and Pam get
new dresses.

Miss Tate puts the
dresses into boxes.

But then she mixes
up the boxes!

Story Structure

Nan is at the fair.

She gets a balloon.

Nan lets go of the balloon.

The clown gets the balloon for Nan.

Story Structure

Read the story. Then complete the story map below.

Cat is at home.
Cat bakes a cake for Pig.
Pig doesn't like cake.
Cat eats the cake.

Characters Who?	_____
Setting Where?	_____
Story Events Beginning	_____
Middle (problem)	_____
End (solution)	_____

Vowel Pairs *oi, oy, aw, au*

Too many toys may
spoil the boy.

There is a lot of noise
when Paul cuts the
lawn.

Name_____

Vowel Pairs *oi*, *oy*, *aw*, *au*

Use sounds you know to read the sentences. Draw lines to match the sentences with the pictures.

1. Paul has some coins.

2. Roy is yawning now.

3. This boy can draw.

Compare and Contrast

cat

dog

both

Name_____

Compare and Contrast

Get together with a friend. Write how you are the same. Write how you are different.

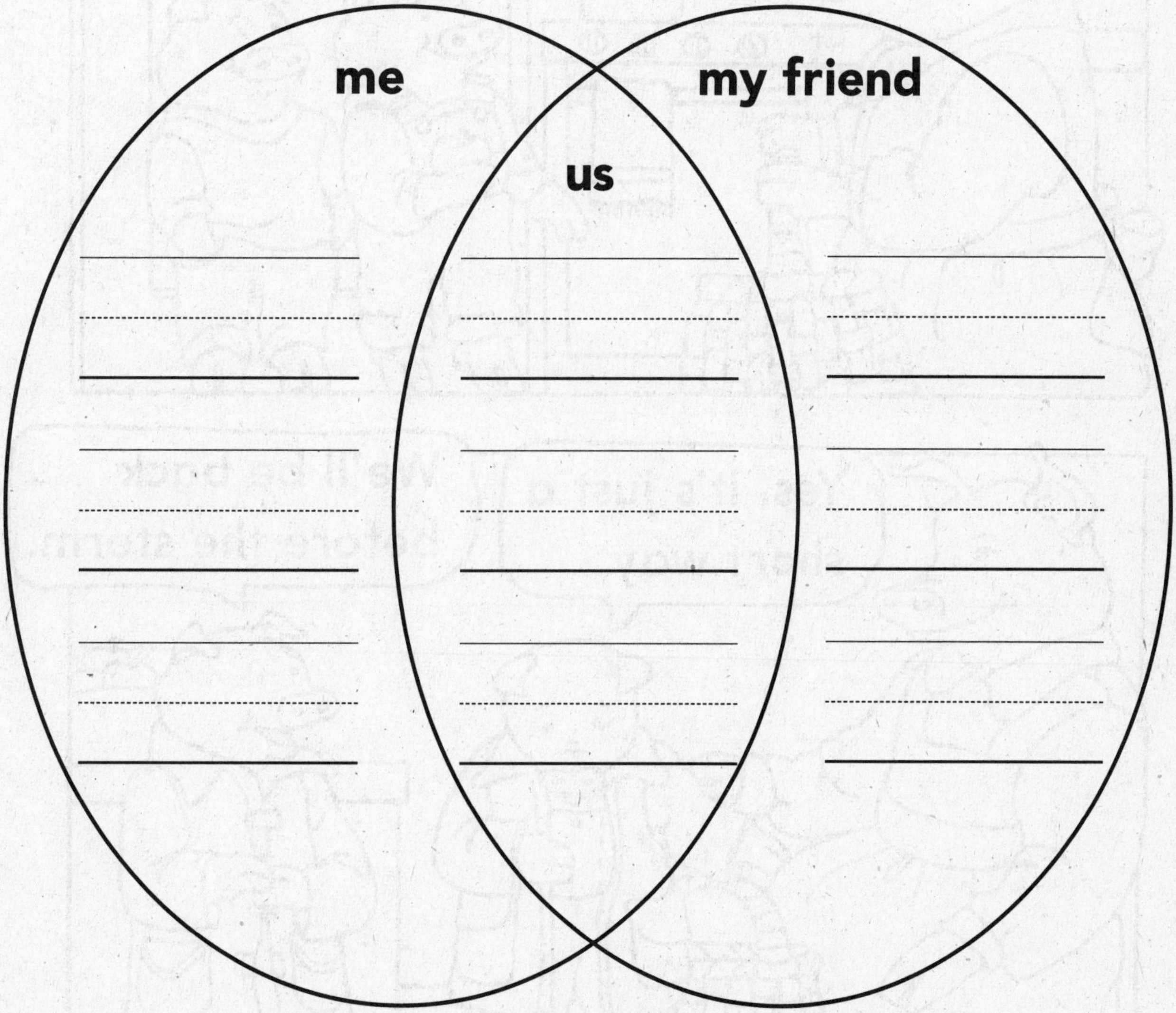

me   my friend

us

r-Controlled Vowels:
or, ore

Name_____

r-Controlled Vowels:
er, ir, ur

Use sounds you know to read the story. Draw lines to match the sentences with the pictures.

Gert fell in the dirt and hurt her leg.

Gert went to see the nurse.

The nurse fixed Gert's leg and wiped the dirt off her shirt.

Making Predictions

It is a cold, cold day.

Joy and Jan are going to the lake.

Joy and Jan like to try new sports.

They are going to _____.

Making Predictions

Read the story. Write to tell where Fred and his family went on their trip.

Fred went on a trip with his family.

Fred did a lot of things on the trip.

He went swimming.

He walked in the sand.

He found shells and put them in his pail.

Where do you think Fred and his family went?

_____

_____

They went to _____.

r-Controlled Vowels: *ar*

The car won't start.
But I can see a barn.
Let's walk to the farm.
It's not too far!

Name_____

r-Controlled Vowels: *ar*

Use sounds you know to read the sentences.

Draw lines to match each sentence with a picture.

Mark made a card for
me.

They'll start to march
soon.

Art's scarf has stars
on it.

Sequence of Events

First, we put on our skis.

Next, we ride to the top of the hill.

Last, we ski down the hill!

Name_____

Sequence of Events

Cut out the pictures at the bottom of the page. Then read the story. Paste the pictures in order to match the story.

> First, Jed climbs to the top.
> Next, Jed goes down the slide.
> Last, Jed lands in the water.

1   **2**   **3**

First   **Next**   **Last**

Base Words and Endings
-er, -est

The vest is warm.

The jacket is warmer than the vest.

The coat is the warmest of all.

Base Words and Endings
-er, -est

Read each sentence. Circle something in the picture that answers the question.

Is the bag or the box lighter?

Which flower is the longest?

Which bug is smaller?

Cause and Effect

Pam wants a pet kitten because she thinks kittens are fun to play with.

Ed puts on his hat and coat because he wants to play outside.

Grade 1 Theme 10: We Can Do It!

Cause and Effect

Read the story. Circle the correct ending for each sentence below.

Ruff dug up Miss Brown's roses.
Miss Brown was mad.
Ruff was mad too.
Some sharp thorns got stuck
in his paws.
He won't dig up the roses again.

1. Miss Brown was mad because _____.

    Ruff chased her cat up a tree

    Ruff dug up her roses

2. Ruff won't dig up roses again because _____.

    the thorns hurt his paws

    he found a friend to play with

V	R	M	I	E	A
W	R	N	I	E	A
W	S	N	J	E	A
X	S	O	J	F	B
X	T	O	K	F	B
Y	T	P	K	G	C
Y	U	P	L	G	C
Z	U	Q	L	H	D
Z	V	Q	M	H	D

Grade 1

a	e	i	m	r	v
a	e	i	n	r	w
a	e	j	n	s	w
b	f	j	o	s	x
b	f	k	o	t	x
c	g	k	p	t	y
c	g	l	p	u	y
d	h	l	q	u	z
d	h	m	q	v	z

Grade 1

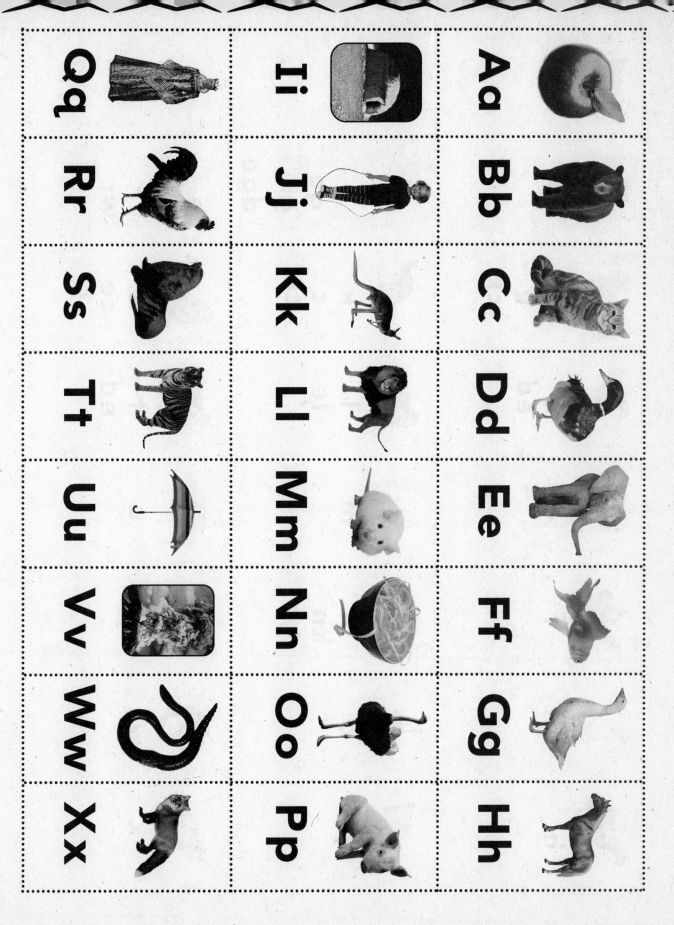

Aa	Ii	Qq
Bb	Jj	Rr
Cc	Kk	Ss
Dd	Ll	Tt
Ee	Mm	Uu
Ff	Nn	Vv
Gg	Oo	Ww
Hh	Pp	Xx

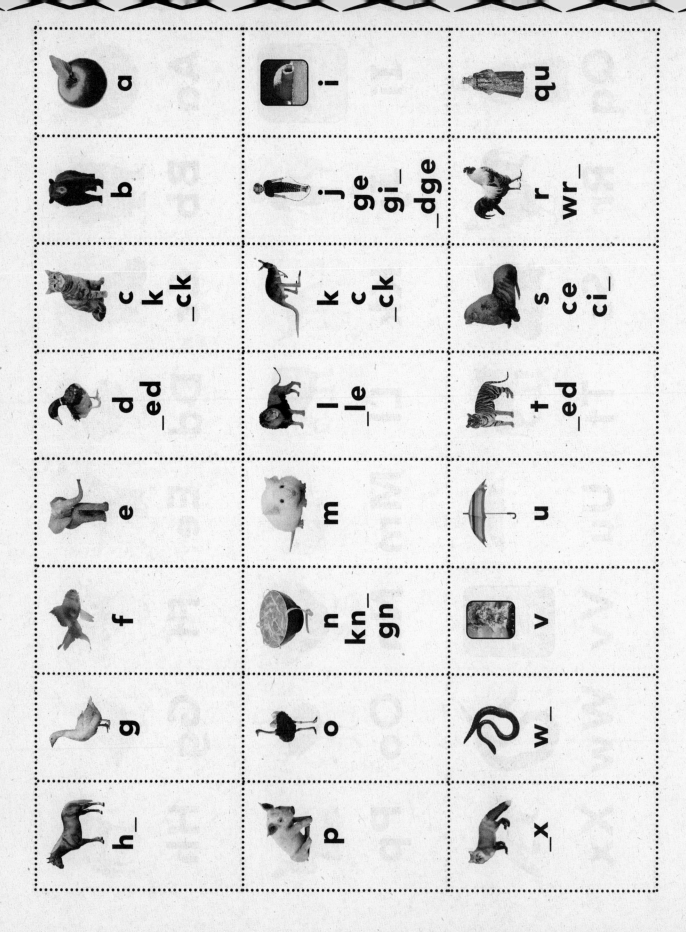

a	i	qu
b	j ge gi_ _dge	r wr_
c k _ck	k c _ck	s ce ci_
d _ed	l _le	t _ed
e	m	u
f	n kn_ _gn	v
g	o	w_
h_	p	_x

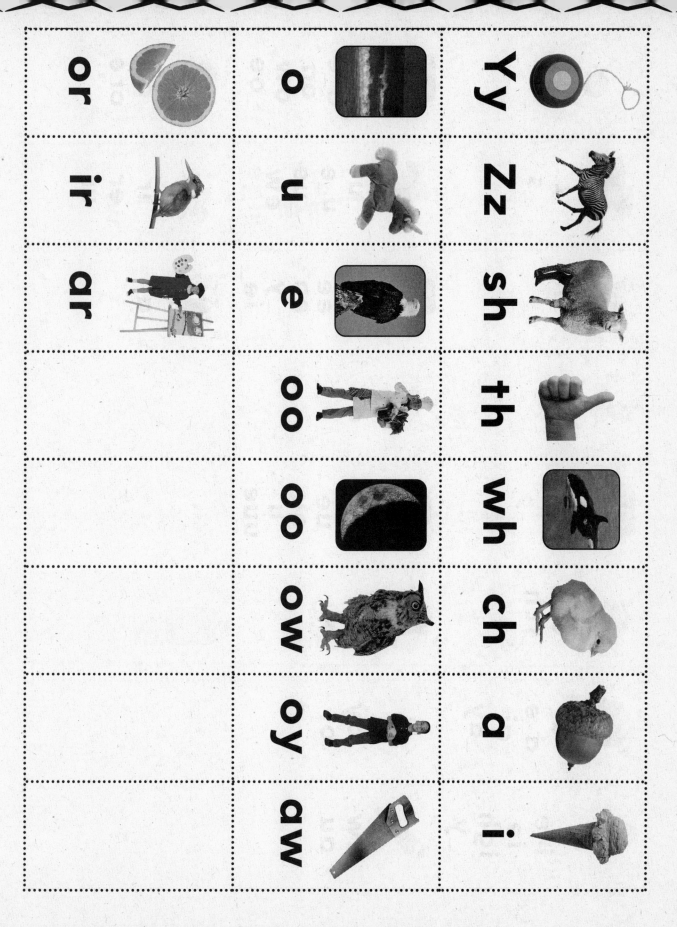

or

ir

ar

o

u

e

oo

oo

ow

oy

aw

Yy

Zz

sh

th

wh

ch

a

i

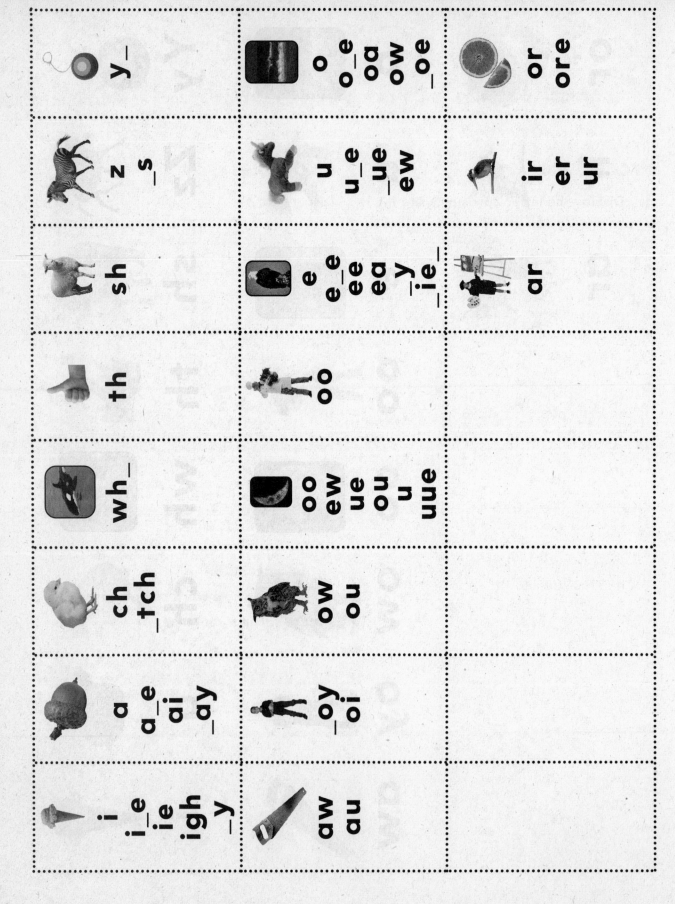

Blending Routine 1
Continuous Blending

Procedure

1. Display the letter cards or write the letters for the word.

2. Have children listen as you blend the sounds of the word, "stretching out" the word while pointing to each letter in a sweeping motion. Then say the whole word naturally.

3. Repeat step 2, this time having children blend the word with you.

4. Have children blend the sounds on their own and then say the whole word naturally.

5. Now have children blend the word silently, in their heads. After they say the whole word aloud, have them use it in a sentence.

Example: *sat*

Display *sat*.

| s | a | t |

Point to *sat* and say *sssăăăt, sat.*

| s | a | t |

Children blend *sat* with you, saying *sssăăăt, sat.*

Children blend *sat* on their own, saying *sssăăăt, sat.*

Children look at the letters and then:

- blend the sounds in their heads, saying *sssăăăt*
- say the whole word *sat* aloud
- use *sat* in a sentence

Blending Routine 2
Sound-by-Sound Blending

Procedure

1. Display or write the letter or letters that stand for the first sound in the word. Point to the letter as you say the sound.

2. Have children say the sound as you repeat it.

3. Display the letter or letters for the next sound and say the sound. Then have children say it with you.

4. Model blending the displayed letters, pointing to the letters in a sweeping motion as you say the sounds. Then have children repeat this with you.

5. Display the letter or letters for the third sound and say the sound. Children say it with you. Have children listen as you blend the sounds so far; then blend together. Add any remaining letters, one by one, and continue this procedure.

6. Model blending the whole word, pointing to the letters in a sweeping motion as you blend the sounds. Then have children blend the word silently in their heads. Finally, have children say the whole word naturally and use it in a sentence.

Example: *mask*

Display *m* and say /m/.

m

Children say /m/.

m

Add *a* to display *ma*. Point to *a* and say /ă/. Children say /ă/ with you.

m a

Model blending *ma*, saying *mmmăăă*. Repeat. Children blend *ma* with you.

m a →

Add *s* to display *mas*. Point to *s* and say /s/. Children say /s/ with you. Model blending *ma* and *s*: *mmmăăăsss*. Children repeat. Now add *k* and say /k/. Children repeat.

m a s →

m a s k →

Model blending *mask*, saying *mmmăăăsssk*. Children blend *mask* silently in their heads. Children say the whole word *mask* and then use it in a sentence.

m a s k →

Blending Routine 3

Vowel-First Blending

Procedure

Example: *sat*

1. Display or write the letter that stands for the vowel sound in the word. Point to the letter as you say the sound.

Display *a* and say /ă/.

a

2. Have children say the sound as you point to the letter and say the sound again. Explain that when you come to this letter as you blend the word, you will remember to say that sound.

Children say /ă/ as you point to the letter *a* and say /ă/. Say: *When we come to this letter in the word, we will say /ă/.*

a

3. Display the letter for the first sound in the word and say the sound. Then have children say it with you.

Display *s* and *a*. Point to *s* and say /s/. Have children say /s/ with you.

s   a

4. Model blending the word through the vowel, pointing to the letters in a sweeping motion as you say the sounds. Then have children repeat this with you.

Model blending *sa*, saying *sssăăă*. Repeat, having children blend *sa* with you.

s a →

5. Display the letter for the final sound and say the sound. Then have children say it with you.

Add *t* to display *sat*. Point to *t* and say /t/. Then have children say /t/ with you.

s a   t

6. Model blending the whole word, pointing to the letters in a sweeping motion as you blend the sounds. Have children blend the word with you and then silently in their heads. Have children say the whole word and use it in a sentence.

Model blending *sat*, saying *sssăăăt*. Repeat, having children blend *sat* with you. Children blend *sat* silently in their heads, then say the whole word. Have a volunteer use *sat* in a sentence.